55916

JK 311 .G84 1983

The Growth of federal power
in American history

|  |  |  |  |
|--|--|--|--|
|  |  |  |  |
|  |  |  |  |
|  |  |  |  |
|  |  |  |  |
|  |  |  |  |
|  |  |  |  |
|  |  |  |  |
|  |  |  |  |
|  |  |  |  |
|  |  |  |  |
|  |  |  |  |

**COMMUNITY COLLEGE
OF DENVER
RED ROCKS CAMPUS**

# The Growth of Federal Power
# in American History

*This Volume of Essays is Dedicated to*
*William R. Brock*

# The Growth of Federal Power
# in American History

edited by

## RHODRI JEFFREYS-JONES
University of Edinburgh

and

## BRUCE COLLINS
University of Glasgow

NORTHERN ILLINOIS UNIVERSITY PRESS
DEKALB

RED ROCKS
COMMUNITY COLLEGE

55916　#9731952

JK
311
G84
1983

First published in the United States of America by
Northern Illinois University Press,
DeKalb, Illinois 60115

First published in Great Britain by
Scottish Academic Press Ltd.
33 Montgomery Street, Edinburgh EH7 5JX

**Library of Congress Cataloging in Publication Data**
Main entry under title:

The Growth of federal power in American history.

  Bibliography: p. 193
  Includes index.
  1. Federal government—United States—History.
I. Jeffreys–Jones, Rhodri, II. Collins, Bruce.
JK311.G84 1983        353'.0009        83-13177
ISBN 0-87580-099-8

© 1983 Scottish Academic Press

All rights reserved. No part of this publication may be reproduced,
stored in a retrieval system, or transmitted, in any form, or by any
means, electronic, mechanical, photocopying, recording or otherwise,
without the prior permission of the Scottish Academic Press Ltd.,
33 Montgomery Street, Edinburgh EH7 5JX

Printed in Northern Ireland by
The Universities Press (Belfast) Ltd.

# Contents

RED ROCKS
COMMUNITY COLLEGE

# Editors' Preface

The growth of federal power in American history is a subject of perennial interest and controversy. It could be argued that many of the great clashes in American politics have centred upon the extension or contraction of federal power. Such was indeed the case in Jefferson's break with Hamilton, in the Jacksonians' battle against 'monopoly' powers both imagined and real, in the sectional crisis leading to Civil War, in the conflicts over Reconstruction, in the Progressive era, during the New Deal, and in the formulation of, and subsequent attack upon, the 'Great Society' legislation of the mid 1960s. Moreover, lawyers and judges have long, and inconclusively, debated the nature and reach of federal judicial power. Whether the Constitution itself should serve as a loose guide-line or as a constraining decree, in relation to federal executive and legislative power, was already a question hanging over that document as it was being drafted. Finally, economists and historians have variously analysed and interpreted the federal government's role in promoting or delaying, or having little to do with, economic development and growth. Some – notably Morton Keller, Douglass North, and Jonathan Hughes – have challenged the frequently expressed contemporary view of a recent crisis in the growth of federal power, itself following on from the New Deal, by locating the important changes in federal economic policy in the two or three decades before World War I.

The present volume provides a variety of discussions of the ways in which federal power has been established and expanded in the last two hundred years. In doing this, it attempts to show the extraordinary range of ways in which federal power has been, and may be, described, invoked, or decried. By illuminating the different periods, the volume does have some contemporary relevance.

An initial essay introduces some of our subject's recurrent problems; two concluding contributions supply an interdisciplinary-historiographical over-view and a summing up, respectively; Chapters 1, 6 and 10 supply overviews of separate periods and will help readers who are comparatively new to the history of American government. Other chapters are more in the nature of learned essays. Each chapter, however, illuminates certain specified common themes, and the chapters together supply a chronological coverage. This enables us to reflect on the question: is the recent growth in federal power a radical departure from American tradition? Collectively, the authors of this volume help to answer the questions 'when', 'how', and 'why?'. They also variously discuss the idea of the Union's being practical or ideological, the relationship between war, Union, and the growth in the scope of federal government, and recurrent myths and expectations concerning federal power.

This volume is in honour of William R. Brock, pioneer of U.S. history teaching at Cambridge University, Professor of Modern History at Glasgow University, and author of several distinguished books on the American past. It is not a *festschrift* in the sense of being a representative collection of the best work of his closest colleagues and numerous research students. Instead, it is an exploration of a problem of interest to William Brock by some of his former colleagues, former research students, and friends within the historical profession. All the contributors have exchanged ideas with him and many of them have been very much aided in their careers by his advice, encouragement and help.

# Introductory: Federal Power as a Contemporary American Dilemma

## by Bruce Collins*

### I

The extent and proper limits of federal power have always been subjects of lively political debate in America, even if that debate varies in intensity and in the direction that it takes. By most historical standards, the 1970s and early 1980s witnessed both a much accentuated debate over the excesses of federal power, and an effort to halt and even reverse the steady accretion of federal duties. All this stemmed both from the contingent happenings of politics and from a longer-term flowering of conservative thought. Among the events that aroused suspicions of federal power were, notably, the Cambodian invasion of 1970 and the Watergate escapade of 1972 and its subsequent exposure. At the same time, and as the 1970s moved on, there was a growing sense of disillusion with some of the bolder social policies of the 1960s. While liberals criticised President Nixon's 'abuse' of federal power in overseas adventurism and in domestic party politics, conservatives, including so-called 'neo-conservatives' such as Irving Kristol and Senator Patrick D. Moynihan, who had moved away from their own earlier reformist beliefs, asserted that federal power could never be applied effectively or efficiently, or with sufficient fairness to taxpayers, to 'solve' the social problems attendant upon, if not necessarily created by, differences in wealth, income, colour, and educational attainment. The one side called for congressional limitations upon presidential war-making powers, since the presidency was typically regarded as the most dangerous branch in the forceful conduct of foreign relations. And the other called for various trimming measures, including, for example, 'sunset' laws by which federal agencies' lives would be automatically curtailed by legislation: the burden would be on the government agencies themselves to prove their value or necessity, and hence to establish a good cause for their continued existence.[1] Such bureaucratic mechanisms were rooted partly at least in ideas of straightforward utility; the federal government was overburdened and lacked the capacity to deal with all its responsibilities. But conservative thought also flourished in the 1970s because economic performance, especially after the oil price increases of 1973, did not match customary expectations, and because economic shortcomings were attributed to federal mismanagement and its effects upon social values.[2]

* Lecturer in Modern History, University of Glasgow.

Conservative attacks upon expanded federal power arose from several sources. One was libertarianism. In a philosophical treatise which commanded greater respect for its technical daring and ingenuity than for its acceptability to most professional philosophers, Robert Nozick of Harvard University proposed in 1974 the most sophisticated modern argument for a truly minimal state.[3] His libertarian conclusions – running against government interference with individual conduct unless that conduct posed a threat, and an unacceptable threat, to others – did not, however, square readily with the demands of increasingly vociferous moralists that personal behaviour be strictly regulated by government, be it state or federal. The demand for the suppression of abortion and pornography, the demand for the teaching of a Biblical as well as a Darwinian theory of evolution in Arkansas, the wider urging that law and order be more strenuously maintained, all point to the anti-libertarian strain in much thought that would customarily be regarded as conservative. Modern critiques of federal power are thus confusingly various. If one strand of opposition to such power is the belief that all but the most minimal forms of government interference with individual rights are intolerable, another species of opposition is far more pragmatic; that the application of federal power does not remove the problems it is supposed to. And the New Right would, apparently, extend federal power in order to regulate personal morality.[4]

If the New Right would regulate personal morality, American liberals of the last twenty years or so have asserted that a just society cannot be founded simply upon a broad equality of civil rights and civil liberties, but must, inevitably in contemporary conditions, be buttressed by some measure of economic redistribution to ensure an adequate material provision for the poor and the disadvantaged. The concept of relative deprivation supports the argument that 'poverty' – and what constitutes a basic minimum income or access to health care and educational opportunities – is a fluid notion, constantly adjusted to what the level of social expectations are and what the majority feel may be legitimately accorded the most deprived groups.[5] This argument gained considerable currency during the economic boom of the 1960s when a collective conscience cost comparatively little; the federal government for the first time then engaged in schemes which were deliberatley redistributive in intention and effect.[6]

Deliberately redistributionist enactments, however, swiftly provoked a spirited reaction. If interventionists claimed that modern notions of equality included some basic element of economic entitlement – and the emphasis was on basic as well as entitlement – their opponents quickly rejected such contentions as running counter to the American tradition of entre-preneurship, individualism, and equality of opportunity not subjected to, or falsely constrained by, considerations as to equality of outcome. Straitened economic circumstances after 1973 probably strengthened the appeal of this counter case. Since the age of individualism and of apparent *laissez-faire* had also been the age of fast economic growth, it became plausible, at an exceedingly broad level of generalisation and aggregation, to assert that *laissez-faire* values and rapid economic growth were causally inter-related. Moreover, Milton Friedman and his numerous followers among economists argued that the federal government's salving of the liberal conscience on the cheap, or on credit, during the 1960s actually helped bring an end to the very economic boom upon which social welfare programmes were founded. For these programmes in turn created inflationary pressures which disrupted monetary arrangements, credit systems and investments, and thereby, ultimately, halted economic growth. The best way of stopping inflation and reviving economic growth was, according to Friedman, to curtail the money supply and to transfer resources away from the public sector to growth-generating private investment.[7] While Friedman's proposals were highly technical in detail, they were also fervently moralistic in their assumptions and character. For behind them lay an intensely moral image of what a just society was: a society of the sort Samuel Smiles so graphically described in 1859 in *Self-Help*, one in which men rise to riches and fame unaided by a paternalistic government and unhampered by an over-taxing authority.[8] This powerful sense of what a moral economy should be led Friedman into a double-barrelled onslaught against excessive government economic regulation and against heavy taxes. His ideal of the late nineteenth-century golden age was graphically described in *Free to Choose* (1980):

> The catchwords were free enterprise, competition, laissez-faire. Everyone was to be free to go into any business, follow any occupation, buy any property, subject only to the agreement of the other parties to the transaction. Each was to have the opportunity to reap the benefits if he succeeded, to suffer the costs if he failed. There were to be no arbitrary obstacles. Performance, not birth, religion, or nationality, was the touchstone.[9]

This somewhat partial view of late nineteenth-century America inspired the dubious contention that expanded federal power eroded entrepreneurial values.

The belief that fundamental values are at stake galvanises the political movement to balance the federal budget and to lift federal regulations on industry and commerce. But, in vital aspects, that belief merely reflects a stock rhetorical device employed by polemicists throughout American history. Extensions of central government power – as, for instance, in the 1760s and 1770s (when the expanding power lay on the Thames rather than on the Potomac); in the 1850s when the arguments for and against slavery's extension were suffused with fears and doubts about augmented federal power or in the 1930s when the New Deal was commonly equated by friend and foe alike with revolution – typically elicit rhetoric of the sort used by Friedman and other modern anti-federalists in associating growing government with moral decline.[10] To say that the rhetorical technique is commonplace does not mean, of course, that the upsurge of conservative thought and argument in the 1970s and early 1980s is not historically important and distinctive. It clearly is; and in four respects.

First, the debate over declining moral values is more pointed than it was in the 1950s and 1960s. If American conservative thought in those decades gave great prominence to religious and spiritual aspirations, the Moral Majority of the late 1970s and early 1980s is far more militant and explicit in its introduction of moral concerns into politics than conservatives of the 1950s and 1960s were. More generally, even sociologists who do not share traditional conservatives' religious preoccupations – notably Daniel Bell and, in the *Last Half-Century* (1978), Morris Janowitz – argue that, despite all the advances of what J. K. Galbraith called the techno-structure, despite all the centralisation and standardisation of contemporary post-industrial or advanced industrial society, Americans are losing an earlier coherence of belief and objective.[11] In other words, those who believe that America is increasingly regimented by the federal government preach the necessity of resuscitating individualism; others share this sense of moral crisis, but attribute it to a process of social fragmentation (or 'dysfunctionalism') which has burgeoned despite the growth of federal power and federal regulation in economic policy, education, social welfare provision, transport, trade, and all manner of daily traffic. If the origins of the alleged moral crisis are variously explained, the existence of such a crisis is widely believed in. This belief contributes significantly to the conservative pressure for reduced federal economic and social intervention.[12]

The second change is that the 1950s and 1960s witnessed a consensus over macro-economic policy which, if exaggerated, largely cut across party divisions. The theoretical writings and the public rhetoric of the Chicago School led by Milton Friedman at last succeeded – and the publicists' effort was indeed lengthy – in providing an intellectually respectable alternative to Keynesian doctrine. Sea-changes in the flow of ideas are often difficult to detect or to pin-point accurately; but the whole debate over economic policy became more fluid, and hotter, in the 1970s than it had earlier been.[13] So, too, Nozick's philosophical writings brought a new level of intellectual sophistication to a conservative creed which too often in the 1950s and 1960s consisted in mere jeering at the pretensions of the potentates of liberalism, mere whinings at the passage of a romantic, and romantically distorted, past, and a frustrated Burkean hankering for organic (by which was meant, exceedingly slow) change in a society deeply enamoured of, at least superficial, novelty.[14]

These changes in thought were matched by shifts in power, the most notable being the realignment of the Supreme Court in the years 1969–75. Although Supreme Court justices are neither stooges nor partisans, they do act in broadly ideological ways. The fact that five justices were appointed by Presidents Nixon and Ford, and that three of them act in a conservative fashion, while two of them lean towards conservatism, produced a real shift from the liberal Warren Court of 1953–69 to the far from liberal Burger Court of the 1970s. The conservatism of the Burger Court gained clarity, cohesion and forensic purpose particularly from the opinions written by Justice William Rehnquist, appointed in 1971. Rehnquist's general aim is to reduce the active intervention of the federal courts and congress in state affairs; to revive, in brief, a form of dual federalism wherein a critical role in constitutional interpretation is given to assigning power as between state and federal courts and state and federal governments. This assiduous respect for constitutional federalism was last displayed in the 1930s before the Court finally, and under fierce political pressure, approved the New Deal. In *Rizzo* v. *Goode* (1976) a suit was rejected on the grounds that federal institutions should not properly oversee state agencies. Such reasoning returned to the states the supervision of federally-guaranteed constitutional rights that *Brown* v. *Board of Education* (1954) and decisions in the 1960s placed upon the federal courts. Constraining the federal judiciary was parallelled by efforts to constrict the federal congress. In *Pennhurst State School* v. *Halderman* (1981) federal efforts to spell out a bill of rights for the mentally retarded (in an act of 1975) was invalidated on the strict constructionist grounds that Congress must specifically invoke constitution- al powers whenever it legislates in such manner as may impair the rights and responsibilities of the states. While these decisions – and others like them emphasising once more the rights of states – may not amount to a constitutional revolution, they mark a real change in judicial attitudes (the result of changes in the Supreme Court's personnel) and form a road-block to the easy and steady advance of federal power.[15]

The fourth change affected congressional politics. In 1980, the Republi- cans gained control of the Senate, the first time they controlled either house on Capitol Hill since 1954. They achieved this victory through the biggest turn-over of Senate seats since 1958, through their superior organisation and resources, through the timeliness of their attacks upon bloated federal power and crumbling moral values, and through their demands for higher defence spending and a more assertive foreign policy.[16] Their surprising success in winning the Senate meant that, for the first time since 1946 (under Senator Robert A. Taft's leadership), Republicans felt confident enough, and powerful enough, to try to roll back the encroachments of federal bureaucracy and federal power. Whether they would be able to translate the radical ideas of the alarmist New Right and the Moral Majority into effective policy depended, of course, partly on political luck and political leadership, given the absence of a firm conservative majority in the House. But it also depended on the historical traditions that gave birth to and sustained and justified expanded federal power.

In short, American conservatives' fortunate moment – to use Burke's phrase – appeared to have arrived with President Reagan's accession to office in 1981. Conservatives possessed more intellectual, judicial and

political power than they had enjoyed since the 1920s. Why, then, did the
conservative case against federal power strike liberals as so historically
fallible, and so unlikely to be vindicated by subsequent events?

## II

The case for devolving greater powers to the states, and for leaving the
states to initiate reforms and to take on additional responsibilities, is a
difficult one to make. Historically, federal power expanded to fill vacuums
left by state incompetence, failure, or lack of interest. During the 1930s the
New Deal's social welfare programme was enacted because the states
individually failed to afford basic relief to the unemployed and the destitute.
Even in the nineteenth century, the classical age of state power, the states
often looked to Washington for aid. The most notable example of state
relative helplessness in the ante-bellum period was the slave states'
determination to use federal power to protect slavery; by getting the federal
government to expedite the return of fugitive slaves and by pushing the
federal government into defending slavery in the territories. The states in
the 1850s also reached out for federal grants of land to help them foster
railroad building. And when railroads changed from a boon to be boosted
to a burden to be eased, the states, after initiating railroad regulation,
pressed for federal supervision, provided eventually in the shape of the
Interstate Commerce Commission (1887). On important occasions, therefore, the states themselves fostered the extension of federal government; for
when political opinion runs against congressional action on certain issues, it
may also be mobilised against state action on those same issues. The classic
instance of this was in the early twentieth century when some states were
prevented by federal courts from laying down maximum hours of work, or
restricting child labour.[17]

Secondly, and, in broad outline, the extension of federal power has
historically occurred through the expansion of functions specifically
confined to the federal government. Before the 1930s, only in wartime and
in the immediate aftermath of wars did the federal government's spending
account for more than three per cent of G.N.P. During peacetime, the
nineteenth-century federal government was the protector and messenger-
boy of the republic. In 1821, of 6,914 civilians employed by the federal
government, 4,766 worked in the post-office; by 1861 the totals were 36,672
and 30,269 respectively. By 1901, admittedly, the post-office contingent
loomed less large; 136,192 or 239,476 federal civilian employees were so
absorbed in stamps and deliveries. But, of the remainder, no fewer than
44,524 were mechanics, workmen, and officials in the War and Navy
Departments. The 77 million Americans of 1901 were neither overburdened
by their federal bureaucracy, nor much governed by gods other than Mars
and Mercury. If the New Deal altered this pattern of federal civilian
employment by multiplying the number of short-term and relief jobs

available, it did not destroy past habits; in 1936, forty-nine per cent of federal civilian employees were still engaged by defence departments and by the post-office. Moreover, the greatest expansion in federal work flowed from World War II, not from the depression preceding it. The federal civilian work-force rose from just over 600,000 in the early 1930s to one million in 1940 and then settled at around 2,500,000 in the mid 1950s. Yet of this *civilian* labour-force in 1956, no less than seventy per cent were employed in defence and in the post-office.[18] These functions were hardly the sort that could practicably be fobbed off upon the states.

What subsequently altered the character of federal action and, to a milder degree, federal employment was the Social Security Act of 1935, its extension in 1939 and 1956, and its supplementation by Medicaid and Medicare in 1965. In 1960 nearly eight per cent of G.N.P. was absorbed by all public spending on social welfare; by 1974 the proportion had doubled to sixteen per cent.[19] The American welfare state was created by the legislation of 1935 and 1965.

The welfare state was essentially federal in origin, and federal in character. The states severally failed to cope with the social consequences of the great depression. A generation later, poverty as most Americans conceived it far outran state or municipal cures. In setting up and in extending the welfare state, the federal government did not dislodge the states from their rightful duties or strip the states of well-entrenched and much-used powers. Rather, the politicians of 1935 and 1965 acted under public pressure to tackle problems which local and state authorities ignored, declined to meet or tackled in piecemeal, fragmentary fashion. Yet in seeking national solutions to national problems, the federal government carefully made the provision of much welfare dependent upon state initiatives. For instance, social security as provided in 1935 and Medicaid as devised in 1965 were joint federal–state programmes. Some of the abuses, and much of the bureaucratic waste, associated with the American welfare state result not simply from official high-handedness, or from the distance between officials and welfare clients, but also – and very importantly – from the structural complexity of all administrative programmes that attempt to blend federal and state interests, requirements and perspectives together. It is the federal government's care in respecting the states' rights and needs that helps make federal bureaucracy so cumbersome, so much more expensive than it might be, and so apparently unresponsive to swift reform.[20]

The fact that federal power was required to provide national unemployment and old age insurance cover is scarcely surprising. To argue, as Milton Friedman does, that some private sector alternative to comprehensive social security could be found, is to miss the very basic point that none exists and that none has existed. Government – even in nineteenth-century America – has customarily stepped in to fund programmes that require bulky long-term financing and that fail to attract sufficiently plentiful private capital. The story of nineteenth-century state (and federal) support for canals and railroads was the story of inadequate private responses to very widely perceived public needs.[21] And so the sheer financial size and complexity of all-inclusive insurance and pension arrangements have induced federal action. That action was, and is, related to social needs and social developments. When old age pensions under the act of 1935 began to take effect, only twenty per cent of workers qualified. By the late 1970s, over ninety-five per cent of all Americans aged over sixty-five benefited from social security. Such ample provision of assistance corresponded with – and probably encouraged – a dramatic increase in retirement among those over sixty-five years old. In 1947 forty-eight per cent of Americans over sixty-five years worked; thirty years later, twenty-one per cent did so, This drop-off in working among the old occurred at a time when life expectancy lengthened markedly (from forty-seven in 1900 to seventy by 1960) and when those over sixty-five years increased from three per cent in 1900 to eleven per cent of the total population by 1980.[22] Social misery in the 1930s, long-term shifts in habits of retirement and in the age-structure of the population, and the fact that the relative deprivation of about twenty per cent of Americans alarmed or disturbed liberal publicists and politicians, together produced the federal welfare state.[23]

Yet the use of federal power to erect a welfare state was much qualified by administrative and social restraints. First, the bald figures for government spending are somewhat misleading. In 1940 the federal government's self-financed expenditure accounted for 10 per cent of G.N.P., while state and local governments' self-financed expenditures amounted to 8.5 per cent of G.N.P., a grand total of 18.5 per cent. By 1978 the proportions were 21.6 per cent and 10.6 per cent respectively. These figures suggest why outraged cries have been raised against federal power expanding vastly, and at the states' and localities' expense. But a number of complicating facts contribute to these startling aggregates. Over 11 per cent of G.N.P. accounted for by the federal government in 1978 was in the shape of direct lending and loan guarantees. Another 2.7 per cent of G.N.P. took the form of federal grants to states and localities. Allowing for these facts meant that *purchases* of goods and services by all levels of government totalled 20.5 per cent of G.N.P.; the federal government spent 7.2 per cent and the states and localities, their direct spending power augmented by federal grants, spent 13.3 per cent. The welfare state expanded through a complex series of inter-governmental transactions between a federal tax-gatherer and broad planner and the state and local distributors.[24] It is difficult to see how any other system could work, given the national need for uniformity in pension and social insurance payments which was in turn created by the extraordinary level of geographical mobility displayed by the American population, and given also the national complexion of such social problems as continuing poverty. Moreover, the overwhelming bulk of welfare spending takes the form of transfer payments which leave actual spending in the hands of recipients, not of government itself. Finally, it is worth noting that the professionalisation of knowledge, and the increased complexity of making choices in social policy, naturally lead to a certain amount of inefficiency, duplication of effort, and bureaucratic waste, as the number of decision-makers increases with the proliferation of areas of expertise.[25] Even so, the most controversial welfare schemes, and the programmes which most commonly attract criticism for their failures and their cost, absorb but a small fraction (one economist estimated 1.7 per cent in 1976) of G.N.P.[26]

Secondly, the social context in which federal domestic spending has expanded must not be ignored. Critics of this form of federal power often ascribe social problems' origins to the very measures devised to cure them. Thus Milton Friedman dismissed federal domestic legislation of the 1960s and 1970s: 'Their major evil is their effect on the fabric of our society. They weaken the family; reduce the incentive to work, save, and innovate; reduce the accumulation of capital; and limit our freedom. These are the fundamental standards by which they should be judged'.[27] Yet it is difficult to see how freedom is limited or incentives are destroyed by elaborate provisions to maintain the income and health of the old and the indigent, or to improve the position of American blacks. Nor, if politicians choose, under pressure, to funnel revenues into social security, can the relative decline in capital accumulation be regarded as anything but a public good. Moreover, the period 1964–74 was one in which the American labour force rose by 1,740,000 a year, virtually double the rate during the years 1953–63, and hardly evidence of a rampant disinclination to toil. Only from the mid 1970s, when the international economy spluttered, did unemployment rise appreciably; and this rise in turn increased welfare spending and so padded out the share of G.N.P. accounted for by the federal government. (To overcome this distorting effect economists sometimes use a measure of non-recession G.N.P.)[28]

Finally, much structural unemployment, as distinct from short-term unemployment, results from the speed of technological innovation, and the displacement of unskilled, unadaptable or poorly educated workers. Friedman's comparisons between late nineteenth century and late twentieth-century work ethics are shaky because working conditions have so profoundly altered in the last century. Late nineteenth-century workers required little schooling beyond the age of fourteen or fifteen years. 41.7 per cent of the male workers in 1900 were engaged in agriculture, often in jobs demanding merely basic skills. Although farm life was hard, and hardly immune to the vicissitudes of the trade cycle, at least these bread-winners were involved in the most direct means of winning bread. By 1975, only 4.8 per cent of the male work force was so employed.[29]

Liberals' scepticism towards conservative claims, therefore, flows largely from different historical perspectives, as well as from different ideas of social justice. If, in Friedmanite eyes, the late nineteenth century was an epoch of dynamism whose individualism, enterprise, and adventurousness need to be revived, its values of self-help, arising from a relatively unskilled, predominantly youthful, rural and small-town society, do not strike liberals as being very relevant to the dilemmas of a highly interdependent, technologically advanced state.

## III

In 1888, James Bryce described the essence of dual federalism:

> The characteristic feature and special interest of the American Union is that it shows us two governments covering the same ground yet distinct and separate in their action. It is like a great factory wherein two sets of machinery are at work, their revolving wheels apparently intermixed, their bands crossing one another, yet each set doing its own work without touching or hampering the other.[30]

This tidy separation of spheres – perhaps never as pleasingly complete as Bryce described it – ended in the legislative spasm of the New Deal. Since the 1930s the federal government has been the planner, provisioner and primary entrepreneur in domestic policy, even though much scope has been left for state and local variation on grand federal themes.[31] Yet it would be wrong to suggest that the gradual subordination of the states to the federal government has been a systematic and steadily progressive process. Accretions of federal power have been piecemeal, much contested, often much agonised over and legislatively qualified, and normally the outcome of emergency, or of powerful public pressure to stave off international or domestic disasters. Moreover, just as extensions of federal power (as here, a far too frequently homogenised commodity) are typically accompanied by disagreements over the *distribution* of powers within the federal government, so extensions of federal domestic activity during and since the New Deal have been remarkable for their assiduous respect for federalism. If the federal and state machines of government are not as distinctively separate as Bryce observed them to be, at least the state machinery continues to function, and indeed is encouraged to function, by the federal juggernaut.

# Chapter 1

## *Preconditions of American Unity*

### by J. R. Pole*

The United States is a federal republic. No one doubts that the republic's character is federal; no one doubts that the federation collectively constitutes a republic. But the two elements are held together in an ironic tension; the concept of 'federation' has been as profoundly modified by the nature of the Union as the republic, in its unity, has been affected by its essential federalism.

Such tension can never be entirely ruled out in federal systems, where two or more authorities periodically probe the frontiers that lie between them. But in American history the problem has been inherent in the system from its first beginnings, has caused the greatest convulsion in the nation's history, and has never been wholly eliminated. If the responsibility for adjudication has passed from the armies of the Union and the Confederacy to the political parties, the Congress and the Supreme Court, the issues have nonetheless arisen in a context directly related to the origins of the Republic.

Without a previous unity of laws, customs and sentiment, the peoples of the several and widely separated colonies could never have worked together in the measure of unison that was the minimum required to oppose British power and establish American independence. But this considerable residue of common ground, these shared ideals and principles, did not in themselves dictate any specific consequences for the collective government of the colonies. American union at every phase of its development was an artifact, wrought by the concentrated endeavours of men. There was nothing inevitable about the United States Constitution; there was indeed nothing inevitable about the Union, as the southern states attempted to prove more than seventy years after the original states had joined together with the express intention of making it 'more perfect'. An attempt to understand the character of the Union that was founded in so many ambiguities must begin with some analysis of the conditions that preceded independence and made it possible.

The American colonies were always parts of a larger unity. In many respects they were far more distant from one another than from London, where the Board of Trade and the Privy Council deliberated over the

* Rhodes Professor of American History and Institutions, Oxford University.

strategies and policies that occasionally, episodically and without conveying to the colonists themselves much sense of sustained purpose, co-ordinated the energies or aims of the British Empire. All the colonies owed a common allegiance to the Crown. But they owed much more than this – more, one suspects, than they themselves were fully aware of – to their British heritage. The colonial legislatures were free to develop their own laws according to their sense of local needs, and for the most part they did so with a mixture of practical common sense and occasional partisan interest; but they were not allowed to pass laws repugnant to the laws of England. This meant that their acts were subject to review and in some cases to disallowance by the Privy Council in London.

Except for the navigation acts, and for certain measures designed to protect – or enlarge – the interests of the Empire, Parliament interfered very little in colonial affairs. Until the 1750s it had shown no disposition for the development of a comprehensive colonial policy. But the navigation system did represent an important exception. As Parliament extended the operation of new laws through increasingly detailed measures of control and enumeration the colonies could not but be aware of themselves, not merely as independent political entities with ties to the source of authority in London, but as elements in a much larger whole. This sense inevitably grew by immense bounds during the long mid-century wars, which L. H. Gipson aptly called the Great War for the Empire.[1] In particular, this was because some of the colonials – notably those of Massachusetts – contributed materially to successes against the French to the north of them. They also suffered very substantial losses in men, which denuded the population of part of its labour force, deprived women of husbands and threw more families onto the inadequate systems of poor relief.[2]

The wars, first against Spain and then against France, naturally served to enhance the colonial sense of British identity. But they also accentuated the internal conflicts of authority which sharply reminded colonial politicians of the restraints that British authority placed on their domestic powers. Colonial governors gained increased patronage through military appointments; in New England, the Earl of Loudoun, commander-in-chief of the British forces, clashed angrily and often with local authorities over such abrasive issues as the billeting of British troops.[3] The consequences were paradoxical. The victories which made the colonies more secure than ever before, and to which their own contributions gave them a just sense of achievement and control over their own environments, helped them to identify with British nationhood and to establish their place in the greatest overseas Empire since Rome. And yet at the same time and through much the same processes, they learnt also to appreciate their separateness from their British rulers. Separateness was a precondition of any form of colonial political consciousness, but did not imply unity; there existed no colonial authority that could give laws or even suggest general policies to the British for the continent as a whole; and there existed no colonial legislature that had the power to oppose collective colonial interests to those which Britain might wish to promote. The idea of such an assembly when proposed in the Albany Plan of 1754 proved as unattractive to the colonial legislatures as to the British government.

It is a familiar theme that the colonies had to learn to think of themselves as British in order to think of themselves as American. Our concern here is with the growing, if vaguely realised, apprehension of *unity* – and, from unity, eventual union. If one of the sources of this powerful though very unspecific apprehension was the fact that all the colonies were ultimately subject to British law and British law-givers, it is also true that all this authority was conveyed in the English language. A common language is certainly not an invariable key to agreement. But it did have the important incidental effect that the colonists could easily communicate with *each other* in the same language. When the itinerant ministers who pursued their missions from town to town and settlement to settlement passed, as they often did, from one colony to another – the Massachusetts Baptist John Leland, for example, spending much of his missionary life in Virginia – they had no language barrier to cross; George Whitefield could preach in New England and in Georgia using an English that was instantly understood wherever he went. Alan Heimert has argued that the Great Awakening sowed the seeds of a religious unity which in turn made other, more political unities, seem much more easily within the grasp of widely separated people.[4] Claims of this sort are impossible to reduce to quantities and measurements; and it is always wise to remember that the convulsions of the Awakening produced great divisions within colonial society as well as a new form of unity. But the central point remains: colonists, many of them the ones who suffered from loneliness, began to see each other as neighbours with common interests – and these could easily pass beyond the questions of personal salvation.

The Great Awakening profoundly changed many communities and many lives. But as an event, or series of events, it died away, to be followed by renewed stirrings at intervals over the whole period leading to and beyond the American Revolution. It is difficult to relate these religious movements, whose content was not political and whose aims were pitched at higher things, to the character of colonial political consciousness. It is also difficult to assess the relative contribution of these spiritual phenomena to the kind of political consciousness evoked by the mid-century wars. What is clear, however, is that the British policies which aroused such unexpected resistance in the years that closely followed the end of the Seven Years War, fell on a populace which was far more responsive, more rapidly alerted to dangers to its own interests and sense of identity, than at any previous period of conflict with British authorities since the overthrow of Andros in 1689. And far more than was the case in America's model of the Glorious Revolution, the consciousness was now American as well as being British, American as well as being simply colonial.

The rise of the newspaper press in the colonies was a scattered series of local events, gathering considerable pace and concentration in Boston, New York and Philadelphia in the mid-century. But in a very strong if perhaps little noticed way, the newspapers made their own contribution to the unity of colonial thought, and this was through the similarity of so much of the more important information they conveyed to their readers. The reasons for this lay in the character of the colonial press. There was no independent news-gathering service and the printers, who were also editors and frequently writers of their own papers, depended on whatever information they heard of, received from volunteer contributors, or copied from other newspapers. The most consistently important source of news from every point of view throughout the colonies as a whole, however, was not American but British; the arrival of the packet from England, the unwrapping of *The Gentleman's Magazine, The London Magazine, The Annual Register* and the numerous English newspapers was always quickly followed by the copying of significant items of British news into the colonial papers. In this way the reading public, which was large in New England, New York and Pennsylvania, but which tapered away in the southern colonies, absorbed a remarkable amount of information about distant eminences and institutions – which for the most part remained totally divorced from their course of daily life.

The time came, however, when British events did begin to affect American life. Reports of debates or individual speeches in either house of Parliament, reports from the law courts, and especially any involving John Wilkes, and numerous other items from court to town and town to country, informed the colonists of British policies and commerce far more intimately than they were ever informed of each others'. One lesson they learnt from this flow of information was that they had friends in Britain. As Paul Langford has recently shown, the British correspondents of American newspapers confined themselves almost exclusively to giving pleasing or flattering reports.[5] The truth, however, was far otherwise; only a small minority in Britain took any consistent interest in the colonies, and of those still fewer did so from a sympathetic interest in colonial points of view. Even Britain's radicals generally regarded the colonial issue as peripheral. But the few reports to American newspapers which gave accurate accounts of the general state of British opinion tended to be dismissed as falsehoods. The resulting misconception of prevailing British sympathies had significant political implications. American whigs read reports of such events as public demonstrations for Wilkes as emanating from sentiments that were not only radical but, almost by definition, pro-American. And the strength of this feeling was grossly over-estimated. It was not really until the general election of November, 1774, which returned for George III just the kind of Parliament he wanted for the coming struggle, that Americans discovered how frail was the political influence of their British friends – and how few those friends were.[6]

This observation may appear to digress from the central issue of the unity – or unification – of American thought around a corps of unified information. But to pursue the point is, I think, to suggest a deeper significance. Americans formed a sort of collective consciousness of the prevalent state of British opinion, and this information, often copied verbatim from one paper to another until it reached from Boston to Charles Town in identical language, at least encouraged them to believe that defiance of British impositions would encourage support from the British opposition. When they came to discover the unpleasant truth that they had fewer friends than they imagined, and that although these friends were sometimes eminent and often eloquent, they carried few votes and still fewer parliamentary seats, that too was a *collective* discovery. The unity of American disillusionment is a factor to be weighed in considering the formation of the public opinion that converted independence from a distant and desperate remedy to a practical programme during the winter of 1775 and the spring of 1776.

John Adams observed late in life that the revolution occurred before the war began. 'The revolution was in the minds and hearts of the people.'[7] This oft-quoted reflection is of the rhetorical kind that does not seem to call for concentrated analysis: it exonerated a highly conservative elderly Adams from the associations of a revolutionary youth. Since he also said that one third of the colonists were against the revolution, accuracy would have required him to amend his comment to the effect that the revolution was in the minds and hearts of not more than two thirds of the American people.[8] The point to retain, however, is that Adams was talking about the growth of a substantial body of similarly informed and like-minded opinion. Without this formation, co-ordinated action would have been impossible and the congresses and conventions would have been without authority.

Another experience contributed to this effect. Americans had accumulated a long experience of self-government. If each colony is considered to have incorporated a quasi-sovereign identity, it may be argued that most of them had a longer experience of self-government than the common people of Britain. Parliament was less representative in every way than were the colonial assemblies, which had comparatively larger electorates, a wider franchise and far more frequent elections. More than this: parliaments were summoned by English sovereigns when they needed money or for other important causes. William III told the Marquis of Halifax in 1689 that he supposed he would need a parliament so long as he was at war.[9] It was only gradually, through the political struggles of the reigns of William and Anne, that Parliament came to be required continuously for the legitimation of royal policy and actual conduct of government.[10] During the eighteenth century, as an increasingly large amount of public as well as private business took the form of legislation, the statute books grew steadily in size. Parliament was coming to be involved in the running of the country. By about the middle of the century this process had become definitive and irreversible. This was a profound change in the constitution and government of Britain – and no less, in Britain's Empire, as the colonies were to find. For certain high purposes, a parliament had always been necessary to the monarch's authority and to the lawfulness of the law; but it is not perhaps generally appreciated that England had no history of *continuous* parliamentary connection with the *process* of government, and still less of what we would now call 'parliamentary government'. Compare this situation to that of the colonies. They had experienced neither complete interruptions of the legislative process as in England from 1629 to 1640 (except for the isolated instance of the Andros regime in New England, and a period of four years, 1706–1710, when the council ruled Virginia), nor any 'long parliaments'. Their administrative and political history was not uneventful; but it was strikingly smooth in formal continuity.[11] Colonial assemblies managed their affairs through regular committees and acquired a knowledge of parliamentary procedure and a common language of political conduct in the course of their ordinary business lives. It is well known that they became extremely conscious of their parliamentary character and modelled themselves on the House of Commons, a process which has been described as a form of 'political mimesis'.[12] But it should be noted that this imitation concerned itself with two different though closely connected principles. The most important, for the assemblies, was the assertion of political and financial power; and this was accompanied by the second, an assertion of parliamentary privilege.[13] A development that was less noticed because it was more mundane was the acquisition of ordinary, day-to-day and session-to-session procedure.

The significance of this appeared silently when the Continental Congress convened in Philadelphia in September, 1774. Few of the members had ever met; probably none had ever had to collaborate outside their own provinces except by correspondence. In spite of this, the Congress got down to business with remarkably little difficulty. Certain matters of substance had indeed to be decided, notably the question of whether votes were to be taken by colonies or by individuals. But this very contentious question was easily settled.[14] The point under observation here is not *what* the Congress decided to do, but *how* its twelve delegations managed to work together with such remarkable facility. They had no guide to parliamentary procedure to hand. (It is not at all certain that any of the colonial assemblies used such a guide.) The explanation lies in the fact we have just mentioned. They relied on their knowledge, acquired from many years' experience in the forms and practices of parliamentary procedure. Unity of this sort does not spring easily to sight and is not commonly noticed by historians. It has to be inferred from the interstices of formal records such as assembly journals and in turn those of the Congress itself. But when one is considering how a collection of settlements scattered along some thousand miles came to be able to act in unison, how 'thirteen clocks were made to strike as one', such procedural similarities come to be more than matters of procedure; they provide the effective working conditions for unity of action.

These unifying preconditions applied particularly to the leaders. The men who convened at Philadelphia, chosen by their provincial conventions for their prominence and integrity in public life, were drawn from the class who had been schooled most intensively in the ways of parliamentary procedure and who for the most part had taken some of the burden of promoting American protests against earlier parliamentary and royal policies. As men of education they had also been schooled in English history, with its intense emphasis on liberty as a manifestation of the rights of property. At Harvard, Yale, King's College, Princeton, the College of Philadelphia and William and Mary College as well as at other academies, they had been instructed in the teachings of ancient history and philosophy and they shared the contemporary British adulation for the republican and libertarian writings of Cicero.

All this makes it easier to understand the reception of the 'Commonwealth' tradition which Bernard Bailyn has made the principal theme of eighteenth century American political ideology.[15] There is no need now to enlarge on this illuminating conceptual formulation. But there has always been some need to explain why a tradition of political thought that always seemed peripheral to the main considerations of British politics came to occupy so central a position in the American colonies. And although the colonies varied so widely from one another, the dominating powers in each colony could read the doctrines of the English Old Whigs as being true to their own situation. There existed no body of countervailing Tory history, doctrine, or prevalent institutions to take the place in colonial minds or the colonial life-style which was occupied by Britain by the court, the aristocracy or the Church of England – not to mention the ancient universities. Where such institutions did exist in the colonies, it might be said that the scale of their relationship to the rest of the colonial life was the reverse of their position in Britain.

A handful of British politicians and officials were aware of the potentialities of the American situation. Burke, Camden, Barré and occasionally others spoke forcibly but with remarkably little effect in Parliament; administrators such as James Abercromby and William Knox tried at widely different times to instruct their political masters of the dangers;[16] but for the most part, the British political patriciate did not merely under-estimate the implicit unities of the Americans, they ignored them completely. On the other side of the Atlantic, the Americans took them for granted. The silence of American sources on the question of their underlying unities is itself evidence for their existence. Where a common fund of political discourse was already in current use, there was no need to discuss the question of how to bring it into being.

For these reasons it is worth reminding ourselves that these preconditions of unity were nothing more than that. Americans speaking the same language had often disagreed with each other. Recently they had experienced acute difficulties in reaching a common policy of non-importation in reply to the Townshend tariffs. The more extensive restrictions debated by the Continental Congress in 1774 aroused serious divergences between colonies. Non-exportation was much more difficult than non-importation.[17] And far deeper divisions lay in the future.

American unity was not the enactment of a plan. Some thinking about the terms of association went on amid the turmoil of events; in July 1775 Benjamin Franklin presented Congress with a provisional plan of association, to last only until a reconciliation with Britain, but capable of becoming more permanent;[18] Thomas Paine included a plan of union in *Common Sense,* published in January 1776.[19] Proposals for some form of colonial union could be traced to the Albany Plan of 1754, which Franklin had helped Governor William Shirley of Massachusetts to draft. But even in the stress of the crisis facing the Second Continental Congress, unity was more an instrument of effective action than an end in itself.

The Second Continental Congress bears the historic responsibility not only for American Independence but for the first enduring form of American unity. But to sustain this claim, and to understand its historical significance, one has to look, not only at the Declaration of Independence and the Articles of Confederation, but at the working problems which the Congress faced. The fact is that from 26 May 1775, when the Congress resolved to place the colonies in a state of defence, it found itself inescapably acting as a *government.*[20] As the sole collective agency of colonial action, the Congress had to raise an army, which it did in June; to pay for the army and provide for its other agencies, the Congress had to raise money – first by attempting, not very successfully, to raise loans, then by requisitions; having no direct power over individuals, it laid its requisition demands on the colonies, later the states. The exercise of this power was crucial to its other claims to authority; its continued exercise gave the Congress increasingly the character of a government. When in the 1780s some of the states became delinquent, and some even assumed their citizens' share of the Congressional debt, Congress visibly faced its most serious crisis.

The Congress had also to assume responsibility for foreign affairs. Its credit depended on being able to speak for the colonies collectively. In September 1775, it established the first of its standing committees, for the purchase of military supplies; in November a Secret Committee of Correspondence was set up to deal with external relations.[21] These were the duties that Congress assumed in order to discharge its minimal purposes – to make independence a reality in face of British arms and through the assistance of France. The complicated story of the Articles of Confederation does not need to be rehearsed here; the point is rather that the effective exercise of the powers of government *preceded* the drafting of the conditions of a permanent association. And even then, union was far from certain, far from permanent.

Although the Articles formally looked to a perpetual union, the declining authority and impaired finances of Congress in the early 1780s opened the most fundamental question as to whether even the limited union that already existed could be kept in being. These doubts were settled by the Constitutional Convention and the ratification of the Constitution; which meant, in effect, that whether the old Confederation could have survived in toughened form was never put to the test. But it was no mere alarmist rhetoric that led Hamilton and Jay to direct the opening numbers of *The Federalist* to the dangers of disintegration;[22] the dangers were real and were under discussion, and in all probability the alternative would have been a splitting up into at least three new confederated groups of states. The fierce ambitions loosed by westward expansion could easily have led to internal wars.

An influential school of modern historians, on the other hand, has held that an enduring union could have been formed on the basis of a strengthened form of the Articles. The Constitution was unnecessary. The real motive behind it was a counter-revolution directed against the legitimate aspirations of American democracy as expressed in the Declaration of Independence. The sources of this interpretation can be found, not in the records of the eighteenth century, but in a mood of profound disenchantment with the character of America more than a century later.[23] But this is not the only form of 'alternative union' available to historical memory.

The idea of an 'alternative union' has also been the refuge of the cause of states' rights, which has always needed a historical basis. That cause, associated with the special position of the South, had not begun to take its later shape at the time of the Convention. It was William Patterson of New Jersey who propounded the case for a strengthened Confederation; and after him, Luther Martin of Maryland and Gunning Bedford of Delaware made the strongest pleas for what, historically, becomes an alternative vision of the union.

Bedford 'contended at great length and with great eagerness that the General Government was meant merely to preserve the State Government: not to govern individuals: that its powers ought to be kept within narrow limits; that if too little power was given to it, more might be added; but if too much, it could never be resumed: that individuals as such have little to do but with their own States'.[24] This speech, which lasted the better part of two days, took off from an entirely different point of departure from that of his nationalist opponents. Martin's view was based on a respectable political theory. The overthrow of the Crown threw the states back into a 'state of nature' in their relations with each other and it was in this condition that they had come together to form the Confederation for their mutual protection. If the Confederation were dissolved it would simply mean that the natural powers of self-government reverted to the states. No basis existed for any concept of a unified American people. Gunning Bedford in turn observed that if the Confederation were dissolved, some of the small states would doubtless associate themselves with other powers – a remark which was interpreted as a threat to the nationalists that unless they made concessions, the powers of Europe would be brought back into the American continent. Rebuked for this gesture, Bedford later tried to modify it into a prophecy rather than a threat; but he did not eradicate the impression that Delaware – not one of the more imposing powers on the face of the earth – took its sovereignty so seriously that it could envisage a European alliance against, say Pennsylvania.[25] The threat would have been far more serious if it had come from South Carolina or Georgia, both of which held keys to the Southwest. These were the states which insisted most intransigently on protecting slavery; and although the concessions by which they were mollified did not arise from threats of foreign alliances, it is significant that the non-slave states thought the concessions worth making. A union could geographically have been formed without South Carolina and Georgia more easily than without almost any other pair of states; but no one seems to have thought the risk worth taking.

The small state representatives knew their enemies. Rufus King had perceived 'a national character' resulting from the union of states; James Wilson and James Madison opposed equality among the states because, once the union was fully formed, it would supersede the states.[26] Madison at one point hinted that states could be reduced to the status of counties.[27] The fundamental issue here was concealed behind the distinction between great and small states; it was in truth whether the United States was to have a national government or whether it was to survive as an association of state governments. In *The Federalist* Madison sought support from the doubtful by arguing that the new Constitution would be 'neither wholly national, nor wholly federal'.[28] From one of the Convention's strongest nationalists, this was probably an unwilling concession; but in the views that Madison then held, the 'national' element was essential to the survival of the 'federal' (i.e., *con*federal); the 'federal' element was inessential except as a politically unavoidable concession.

George Washington deplored the formation of political parties under his presidency. He regarded them as constitutionally extraneous and as a threat to the growth of what we might now call the 'organic' unity of the new nation. It would have been difficult for a public man of his generation, especially one so deeply involved as Washington had been in recent controversy, to have stood back far enough to observe that in fact two *types* of political conflict were at work. The political struggle between the Federalists and the newly forming Jeffersonian Republicans turned on matters of high policy and involved the question of what kind of nation the United States was to become: this was no affair of shadow-boxing, nor was it limited to the politics of personal rivalries. But in certain respects it was, curiously enough, a unifying rather than a dividing contest. The Jeffersonian Republican axis from Virginia to New York held together some of the dominant elements in a union that also had undercurrents of a more dangerous form of division. And that, of course, was the ominous, if only incipient conflict of interest and sentiment between the slaveholding and the free states. Madison and King had already warned the Constitutional Convention that this was the great danger to future harmony, Madison pointing out that it was a more serious matter than the controversy between the so-called great and small states.[29] The bitter controversy in the old Constitutional Congress over the terms of the draft treaty drawn up by John Jay and the Spanish minister Gardoqui – terms which offered to trade the closure of the Mississippi for thirty years in return for access to mainland Spanish ports for the merchant shipping of the Eastern ports – had earlier indicated conflicts of economic interest between the great geographical sections. These sections would grow in area and population as the peoples moved westward: would the divisions between them also grow deeper, and would the formal structures that had been so painfully wrought be able to hold them together?

The deeper threat lay there. Washington, who had given so much for the preservation of America's self-declared independence, and who had sacrificed his hoped-for retirement to take up the presidency, gave his last political breath to warning his countrymen. Better than many of his compatriots even as late as 1797, Washington knew when he drew up his Farewell Address that unity had been the indispensible precondition of American success in resistance to Britain and was equally indispensible for the future.

The second section of the Address, in which Washington passed from personal expressions of leave-taking to broader considerations of policy, was drafted by Alexander Hamilton. When Hamilton urged the theme of union he came close to Washington's own central concern. The theme of the union embraced that of liberty, which for these makers of the American nation were as inseparable as they later were to Daniel Webster. Washington came to the point in plain language: 'The unity of government, which constitutes you one people is also now dear to you. It is justly so; for it is a main pillar in the edifice of your real independence; the support of your tranquillity at home; your peace abroad; of your safety, of your prosperity, of that very liberty which you so highly prize'. And he then invoked national pride in 'the name AMERICAN, which belongs to you in your national capacity' – which he significantly placed above 'any appellation derived from local discriminations'.[30]

The argument was carefully constructed. Independence had to be maintained in order to defend all the values that followed: tranquillity, peace, safety and prosperity, which in turn were the objects of liberty; disunity would threaten to ruin all these aims. Washington mounted his attack on 'all combinations and associations, under whatever plausible character' that aimed to obstruct the execution of the laws; he then passed from the dangers of parties based on geography to the 'baneful effects of the spirit of party, generally'. He and Hamilton clearly felt that party conflict could too easily turn on sectional conflict; they could therefore take no comfort in the fact that both parties had trans-sectional support. A quarter of a century later the aged Jefferson and Adams were to see the peril of political divisions formed along geographical lines after the fateful Missouri Crisis and Compromise.

Washington's Farewell Address is remarkable, among other things, for its awareness of the artificial character of the union so far created. 'We are authorized to hope', he said 'that a proper organization of the whole, with the auxiliary agency of governments for the respective sub-divisions, will afford a happy issue to the experiment. It is worth full and fair experiment'. The word 'experiment', thus used twice in two lines, did not seem to resound with ancestral patriotism; yet it was carefully chosen. To experiment was to prove a proposition by the experience of facts. Washington appealed to Americans to put the values he had listed to the test of experience. Patriotism itself would arise from the trial of that experience, and would adhere to the symbols of the new nation – its carefully constructed emblems – to its lands and people. Patriotism would also attach to its formal agencies of government. The underlying unities that had preceded independence had been transformed into the most carefully wrought of political systems. The preservation of unity for the future would be inseparable from the Constitution. To Washington's ageing but clear eyes the outcome was not yet certain. It was to remain doubtful for nearly a lifetime after his death.

# Chapter 2

## The Triple Crisis

### by Duncan Macleod*

In an open letter to the agricultural societies of Virginia, John Taylor of Caroline asserted in 1821 that the United States faced a triple crisis, 'the fanatical crisis, the avaricious crisis, and the geographical crisis'. 'The fanatical crisis', he wrote, 'exhibits the curious phenomenon of an enthusiasm against negro slavery, and in favor of the slavery inflicted by monopoly' – curious, because black slavery provided homes, food, clothing and happiness for its slaves whilst monopoly bred poverty, death and misery.[1] The engines of fanaticism were ambition and avarice which also combined to create the 'geographical crisis' stemming from the sectional patterns of slavery and anti-slavery. Ambition and avarice 'both infringe the rights of the states, and the rights of industry and property', Taylor continued, 'and they must therefore meet, if successful, in an arbitrary form of government'.[2] Taylor's proposed solution to the triple crisis, namely the establishment in the legislatures of the hegemony of the agricultural interest, may have been excessively naive, but the fears he expressed were real enough and they were shared by more hard-harded and practical politicians than himself.[3] He was not alone, moreover, in thinking he detected a fusion of many different social trends: economic, moral and political. Antagonisms over slavery and other sectional differences, over tariffs, banks and internal improvements, all appeared to Old Republicans like Taylor to be parts of a single pattern. The events of 1819 and after highlighted that pattern for them more clearly than ever before and enabled them to develop a powerful and coherent critique of many of the trends of their day. In particular, they permitted the opponents of anti-slavery, of capitalism and of political centralisation to articulate that opposition within the framework of a thoroughgoing provincial philosophy.

The events of 1819 did not arrive unheralded: they constituted a culmination and convergence of trends long evident. It was the Missouri crisis, sparked off by attempts to require Missouri to enter the Union with an anti-slavery constitution, which finally gave full scope for the elaboration of a provincial ideology, but it might be more useful to begin by looking at controversies over economic matters. It should be stressed at the outset that economic controversies revolved less around different types of economic

* University Lecturer in American History, Oxford University.

activity than around the organisation of that activity and its relationship to political agencies. There *were* deep differences of opinion concerning different types of activity: agrarians were convinced of the moral and social superiority of agriculture to industry and to many forms of commerce; but whilst such differences were obviously significant in the creation of different ideologies they did not normally provide the specific content of political controversy. That was provided by the forms of capitalist organisation then mushrooming everywhere in the United States and by the role of government, especially the federal government, in fostering and protecting those forms.

It has been suggested that the Jeffersonian Republican party, including its old Republican members, were not anti-capitalist. On the contrary, they were the main beneficiaries of an expansion of commercial farming incident upon the opportunities presented by the Napoleonic wars: an increasing proportion of the farm population was thus brought into a direct involvement in the world market.[4] That is true, but some features of that 'agrarian capitalism' should be noted. Its organisation still derived from the farm or plantation with its family orientation, and in so far as it made possible capital accumulation, that accumulation was not commonly conceived of as providing an extra gearing for economic activity. It might produce a more *extensive* economic activity but not a more *intensive* one, and not one newly characterised by such considerations as increasing productivity or increasing returns to scale. Farmers were becoming ever more prosperous and market oriented without at the same time developing a wholehearted commitment to a capitalist ethos. Yet their market orientation generated additional demands for transportation and banking developments that could not be so easily accommodated within existing social institutions and values. From the 1790s onwards turnpike, bridge and canal companies began to proliferate along with banking and shipping concerns. The principal form of organisation adopted by those engaged in these operations was the corporation. Corporations were established by the grant of legislative charters, which frequently provided as inducements monopoly or near-monopoly privileges. At a time of great capital shortage it must have appeared to be a simple and efficient means of encouraging the development of an extensive transportation and financial infrastructure. Even these measures appeared to many to be insufficient and governmental funds were often poured into such activity or solicited for it. The growing commercialisation of agriculture had fostered an increasing ideological latitudinarianism within the Republican party, which spilled over in the immediate post-war years into such measures as the chartering of the Second Bank of the United States, the enactment of a protective tariff (both in 1816) and the passage through Congress the following year of a wide-ranging package of internal improvement measures. From 1817, however, these trends began to run into stiffer resistance. President Madison vetoed the internal improvements bill on the grounds that

Congress lacked the constitutional authority to enact it; and, despite all the efforts of Henry Clay, it proved impossible the following year to generate a majority in the House of Representatives to pass anything similar.

There were many, however, who had found these developments alarming and who remained unconvinced by the recent reverses they had suffered. Defining aristocracy as the possession of privileges granted by law, they characterised the corporations as aristocrats, a characterisation which seemed the more cogent when those privileges were granted in perpetuity. 'All corporate bodies', wrote Thomas Ritchie, editor of the *Richmond Enquirer*, 'and particularly those which are licensed to exact contributions from the public, are not only objectionable in themselves on account of the temptations which they constantly hold out to go beyond the object of their original creation, but because the exclusive privileges with which they are clothed are encroachments upon the common rights of the people and contrary to the avowed principles of republican government'.[5] The dependence of capitalists upon legislation for the grant of charters made it easier to conceive of capitalism as a consolidating force in American society, and that tendency was greatly enhanced by the intervention of the federal government. In *Fletcher* v *Peck* in 1810 the United States Supreme Court ruled that a legislative grant of property constituted a contract within the meaning of the contract clause of the United States Constitution; in 1819, in *Dartmouth College* v *Woodward*, it defined a charter in similar terms and so extended federal protection to corporations; and in *Sturges* v *Crowninshield*, also in 1819, the court applied the contract clause to a state bankruptcy law.[6] These rulings constituted a serious limitation upon the powers of state legislatures. The latter could legislate corporations into existence, for example, but were apparently unable to reverse the procedure. As a result state governments lost considerable discretion in the regulation of economic affairs in their own states. The attempts of the United States Supreme Court to establish its supremacy in this and other fields did not go uncontested. Speaking from the bench of the Virginia Court of Appeals, Judge Spencer Roane in *Hunter* v *Martin* (1814 – the decision was not reported until 1815) rejected the claim of the federal court to overrule state courts, a position firmly squashed in 1816 by the federal court's riposte in *Martin* v *Hunter's Lessee* (1816).[7] Over the next few years the two courts were to engage in similar battles, which always had the same outcome.

While most corporations were the creatures of state governments, it was the one chartered by Congress upon which most attention was focused. From the moment when Alexander Hamilton first proposed in 1791 to create a national bank the subject had stirred almost continuous controversy. In 1810/11 attempts to re-charter the Bank at the end of its allotted twenty year life had failed. However, the sorry state of the nation's finances as it emerged from the war with Great Britain persuaded both Congress and President Madison to charter the Second Bank of the United States in 1816. In the first years of its existence the new Bank was neither efficient nor wise in its operations and it was widely held to be at least partly responsible for the financial failures of 1819. Indeed, attempts in Congress to withdraw the charter ended in failure only days before Marshall handed down his epic decision in *McCulloch* v *Maryland* on 6 March 1819.[8] By then, many who opposed the Bank, whether on constitutional or other grounds, had reconciled themselves to its existence. It was not the Court's finding that the Bank was constitutional, nor even its denial of the right of a state to tax it, which generated controversy; it was the reasoning upon which Chief Justice Marshall rested those opinions which proved so alarming. He appeared to be arguing for an almost unlimited discretion for Congress to legislate, leaving it to that body to determine the boundaries of its own constitutional authority. In an anonymous newspaper defence of his reasoning, Marshall denied that the grant of discretion was unlimited, but the language of the decision itself was certainly far-reaching.[9] Thus the Supreme Court, having acted seriously to limit state legislative discretion, now appeared to be offering Congress a free hand. It is not surprising to find, perhaps, that the most bitter, extended, yet thoughtful criticism of the Court's opinion should have been penned by Judge Roane, writing over the pseudonym, *Hampden*. Roane interpreted the decision, with its advocacy of a liberal reading of the Constitution, as tending towards consolidation and the erosion of states rights, with the inevitable consequence that it would prove the forerunner of attacks upon individual liberties. 'The crisis', he wrote, 'is one which portends destruction to the liberties of the American people'.[10]

The attack upon *McCulloch* v *Maryland* came mainly from Virginia and was, of necessity – since it concentrated not upon the verdict but upon the reasoning of the Court – cast in sufficiently abstract terms that it could hardly become the base from which to launch a wholesale onslaught upon the centralising tendencies of the day. The opportunity for that was provided by the Missouri Crisis, but during the debates over Missouri's admission, both in and out of Congress, the Bank decision was constantly cited as evidence of a determined conspiracy to create a consolidated government and nation, a movement of which the attempt to restrict the spread of slavery was but another feature. Many, indeed, saw the issue of anti-slavery and the admission of Missouri simply as a Trojan horse concealing the shock troops of capitalism and Federalism. During the congressional session of 1817/18 there was a prolonged and bitter debate over the operation of the fugitive slave law and its possible reform. Freshman Senator William Smith, an Old Republican from South Carolina, had no doubts but that anti-slavery and banking activities had much in common. He insisted that the growth of banking was closely associated with the growth of anti-slavery: 'The States which have taken measures to abolish slavery, have become perfectly bank mad. New York has abolished slavery after ten years, and she is convulsed with banks, and not yet satisfied'.[11] After a more extended criticism of banking mania he went on to argue that the American commissioners who negotiated the Treaty of Ghent only agreed to cooperate with England to eradicate the international slave trade because of their friendliness to banks. The same association was made during the Missouri debates, most notably by Virginians who saw it as an explanation for the fragmentation of the Republican party and the decay of their authority within it. Writing to President Monroe, a sympathetic listener, Judge Spencer Roane insisted that the ambition of Federalists, not slavery, was the real issue at stake. 'It finds a Clue, however, in their lust of dominion and power... This is the only string which they could touch to detach the great State of Pennsylvania from the folds of republicanism; and these master spirits have touched it truly. I hope, therefore, that she will see and detect the plott which has been laid to Ensnare her.'[12] Jefferson made the same point. He also referred to the proponents of slavery restriction in the West as the Holy Alliance. The analogy with events in Europe implied that it was the South which stood for freedom and republicanism and the North and East which stood for tyranny, in this case the tyranny of money, numbers and moral arrogance. While they have normally rejected the specifics of these charges, historians have tended to interpret the crisis over Missouri's admission to the union in terms of sectional antipathies rather than as resulting from an outburst of genuine anti-slavery feeling. To the extent, moreover, that they have inclined towards acceptance of the view that slavery was being used as a stalking horse, they have tended to accept the thrust of the Virginian/southern argument. What they seem not to have considered is the alternative: that it was the Old Republicans who were using slavery as a stalking horse in the pursuit of *their* objectives, that *they* exploited southern fears to generate a general resistance to the advances of a centralising, capitalist movement.

The Missouri Crisis was precipitated when, on 13 February 1819, James Tallmadge of New York introduced in the House of Representatives an anti-slavery amendment to the Missouri statehood bill:

> that the further introduction of slavery ... be prohibited ... and that all children of slaves, born within the said state after the admission thereof into the union, shall be free, but may be in service until the age of twenty-five years.

The measure passed the House four days later. Voting on the amendment was in two parts: 87–76 to prohibit further slave importations into Missouri; and 82–78 to liberate slaves born in the state after its admission. Voting was strictly along sectional lines with scarcely half a score of northerners defecting to the southern cause. On the day the amended Missouri bill passed, 17 February, the House took up the bill for organising the Arkansas Territory. John W. Taylor of New York introduced amendments identical in effect to those suggested by Tallmadge for Missouri. In this case the amendments, also voted upon in two parts, were rejected – 71–70 with respect to slave importations, and 75–73 (89–87, on a reconsideration) on the issue of manumitting those born in the Territory after its organisation.[13] Why the outcome should have differed from that obtaining on the Missouri bill is not clear. After all, Congress was on firmer constitutional ground in attempting to apply a restriction to a territory rather than to a state. Perhaps the ferocity of southern opposition on the Missouri question had alarmed some northerners; perhaps it was a straightforward calculation about political power (the West should continue to be divided equally between North and South as had been the custom since the formation of the union); perhaps climatic considerations still influenced a number of northerners (Arkansas' southern situation contrasted with the more northerly and temperate situation of Missouri). The difference in outcome is certainly far from unimportant, but seeking an explanation for it should not be permitted to obscure one basic fact: the great majority of congressmen voted the same way on both measures. The different result stemmed from a small change at the margin: a mere handful of northerners adopted different positions on the two bills. On 27 February the Senate rejected the anti-slavery clauses in the Missouri bill and passed it, so amended, on 2 March. The House refusing to yield, the measure was carried over to the next session of congress. On 1 March, the Senate passed the Arkansas bill which duly became law.

Glover Moore, the principal historian of the Missouri crisis (*The Missouri Controversy, 1819–1821*), has stressed its apparent suddenness and the extent to which it was unexpected; like him, others have paid little attention to its provenance. But, like the banking crisis, that provenance can be discovered, in part at least, in the economic growth and development of the previous years. The expansion of slavery had been an integral feature of American territorial and economic growth. The invention of the cotton gin had made possible the large-scale cultivation and harvesting of the short staple cotton upon which the British industrial revolution was increasingly dependent. Between 1815 and 1819 the cotton boom in the western portions of South Carolina and Georgia, and in the Southwest, was the subject of almost continuous comment in eastern newspapers and journals; a foretaste of that interest had been seen in the great attention paid to the huge profits made from the cultivation of sugar in Louisiana after the Louisiana Purchase. Associated with the evidence that slavery was a vital and growing institution, rather than the moribund legacy of British colonial rule so often described by Chesapeake planters and northern commentators in the late eighteenth century, was an increasing confidence amongst slaveholders in the legitimacy of their actions. In the debate on the fugitive slave law mentioned above Senator Smith had no qualms about defending slavery in very positive terms, and his example was widely followed during the Missouri debates. But while the new-found, though by no means universal prosperity of slavery fostered pro-slavery arguments, it also promoted a more intense and wide-flung anti-slavery north of the Mason–Dixon line.

Exactly why it should have proved possible in early 1819 to generate such solid northern support in Congress for these anti-slavery measures has puzzled historians. The southern explanation that humanitarian arguments were being exploited quite cynically in pursuit of party and sectional ambition cannot be dismissed out of hand. It was clear, after all, that most proponents of slavery restriction were not, and did not claim to be abolitionists. On the contrary, they insisted that their humanitarian objectives were properly circumscribed by considerations of political realism and constitutional propriety. But since from the very beginning of the dispute their claims to constitutional propriety were hotly contested, their principles also appeared pretty insecure. The constitutional arguments invoked by both sides were complex in detail but simple in substance. Southerners denied that Congress had authority to legislate for states or territories on such municipal issues as slavery. The assertion of a congressional authority was interpreted as a direct attack upon the principles of states' rights and as a clear attempt to create a consolidated union out of the existing federation. However, while the limited anti-slavery commitment of most restrictionists may invite cynicism, it does not require it: the Missouri Crisis was indeed an anti-slavery crisis even if it was other things as well. John Taylor of Caroline's 'fanatical crisis' was not merely a figment of an overheated imagination, however lurid a description it may have been of the anti-slavery of his day. Sincere anti-slavery was a reality, and southerners took it seriously at the same time that they poured scorn on those they pictured as fellow travellers. As Betty Fladeland has noted, the congressional debates appear 'to reflect that the abolition societies of the period, at least in the minds of southerners, were not considered so weak and ineffectual as they have been pictured. If they had even a few southern politicians "running scared", their impact must have been felt'.[14] It was. Increasingly, though, southerners incorporated their concept of the import of anti-slavery within the same framework that contained their fear of political and economic consolidation. It constituted for them an attempt by the supporters of anti-slavery to impose upon the nation a single moral standard. Potentially, that was an even more dangerous centralising tendency than any other. Some southern spokesmen were explicit in their rejection of the Declaration of Independence as a definition of a national morality. They insisted it had no force in law and preferred to interpret the Constitution as a relatively value-free set of legal arrangements. Some advanced arguments which anticipated the popular sovereignty doctrines of a later age, insisting upon local self-determination of slavery-related issues.[15] The southern position, in other words, did not really require a differentiation between cynical and principled opponents: all, in their own ways, were promoting a process of national consolidation at the expense of the states, of property rights and of regional and local variation. Virginians and Old Republicans, in particular, sought to exploit the sensitivity of southerners towards slavery to persuade them to think of anti-slavery in this way; they thereby sought also to alert them to what they deemed the related issues of financial and economic consolidation. The debate on a possible termination of the charter of the Bank of the United States followed immediately upon the Missouri debate.[16]

Thus the roots of the Missouri Crisis have to be sought not only, or directly, in the nation's changing economy, but also in the changing pattern of anti-slavery, itself related to that economic development. In more ways than historians have commonly realised, the situation around the crisis resembled that of forty years later. Anti-slavery and anti-southern feelings were aroused by an apparent resurgence of slavery. Prior to about 1810 it was possible to believe that slavery was not only being contained but had been made to suffer some severe reverses. Its abolition had been achieved, or had been put in hand, in large areas of the United States, and the international slave trade had been outlawed, the first step in the eyes of most abolitionists towards the final extinction of the institution itself. By 1820 more than one in eight blacks in the nation were free, compared to a miniscule proportion at the outbreak of the American Revolution. Moreover, if one compares the images of the South perceived by Federalists after 1800 with those perceived by Republicans after 1854 one is struck by the similarity. Slavery was associated with social poverty and decadence and with economic inefficiency, cotton profits notwithstanding. John Taylor of New York was not alone in comparing Maryland, for example, unfavourably with Pennsylvania.[17] After 1815 it became increasingly difficult to sustain an optimistic view. Slavery appeared to be growing in strength and was becoming more aggressive in its demands. There was mounting evidence that the international slave trade was actually continuing on a large scale, albeit unlawfully. One of the consequences of slavery expansion, moreover, was the stimulation of the internal slave trade. That, in turn, stimulated the kidnapping of free blacks for transportation to the southwestern slave markets. Such kidnapping did not constitute a large portion of the trade. It did serve to focus interest upon the slave trade and to suggest a reinterpretation of earlier attitudes towards it. It had long been popular to argue that slavery depended upon the slave trade; it was the interests of African traders, or so the argument ran, which had first mandated the development of slavery in America. Such a view now seemed hardly tenable. Clearly it was slavery which mandated the slave trade, not the reverse. The iniquities of the domestic trade seemed, moreover, to mirror those of the African trade. It involved the rupture of families and the kidnapping of free persons. Kidnapping had long been a concern of anti-slavery societies. The Pennsylvania Abolition Society, the first of its kind in the United States, had been formed in 1775 precisely in response to such activity. After 1815 the concern about this activity multiplied enormously. The middle states were the most vulnerable and they came under intense anti-slavery pressure to enact harsh legislation designed to deter offenders. All middle states passed such laws between 1816 and 1818. The punishments imposed ranged from the death penalty, to whipping and cropping, to long sentences in penitentaries: all these punishments were, at one time or another, actually administered.[18] But there was a serious weakness in all attempts to prevent kidnapping so long as the federal fugitive slave law of 1793 remained on the statute book. It was easy to use the law as a cover for kidnapping. From 1817 on there were concerted attempts to persuade Congress to revise the law. The ensuing debates were extremely bitter and, as has been seen, involved both open attacks upon slavery and open defences of it. As an example of the 'horrors of slavery' kidnapping was a powerful weapon against slavery; moreover, the denial of any rights to the black defendants in cases brought under cover of the fugitive slave law linked the issue to the general defence of American constitutional rights.[19] Equally, the attempt to involve the federal government in the prevention of kidnapping was seen as further evidence of a centralising tendency.

The expansion of slavery occurred at a time when the mental and intellectual framework within which such expansion would be viewed had altered. During the debates on the Louisiana government bill in 1804 many northern spokesmen had been prepared to concede an expansion of slavery into the Southwest. Even such a man as Senator Stephen Bradley of Vermont, who in 1805 was to have the honour to move the first resolution for the abolition of the slave trade (such abolition to take effect on 1 January 1808), was prepared to concede the southern case. After 1815 such concessions were not forthcoming. What had changed? First, there was an argument about the possibility of white labour in the tropics. But whereas in 1804 the territory in question, namely Louisiana, was at least sub-tropical, between 1815 and 1820 the South appeared to have abandoned the climatic defence of slavery and proposed to expand into temperate areas. Even in the earlier period the legitimacy of any expansion had always been tied to another factor. Early in the century it was possible to argue with some plausibility that the expansion of slavery involved only a geographical expansion, not demographic growth. No more than a redistribution of existing slaves was involved. From about 1811 Malthus was being widely reviewed in the United States. By the time of the Missouri Crisis he was widely quoted by slavery restrictionists to support the view that a geographical expansion necessarily involved demographic growth. An increase in the resources to support the slave population must eventuate in an accelerated growth of that population.[20] One of the most important and influential works to appear at this time was Daniel Raymond's *The Missouri Question*. A considerable proportion of his book was devoted to Malthusian arguments and arithmetic. He was concerned to demonstrate not only that expansion would generate an increase in the slave population, but also that it would generate a relatively larger increase in the black than the white population.[21] The idea that a geographical containment of slavery was an essential component of the fight against the institution was novel. It was not simply a device to restrain the power of the slaveholders.

None of this necessarily implies that the proponents of restriction were abolitionists in the normal sense of that word, although some were. No one was more prominent in the fight against slavery in Missouri than Rufus King of New York. King led the campaign in the United States Senate and his speeches were widely distributed in pamphlet form; yet he was quite explicit, both in his public pronouncements and in his private correspondence, that he was not seeking to advance the cause of abolition. (Having said that, one might yet be cautious about accepting King's protestations at face value: in 1825 he was to move in the Senate a resolution to put aside the proceeds of the sale of western lands, as soon as the national debt had been cleared, in order to purchase, emancipate and settle slaves in the West.)[22] We should beware, however, of being too cynical about the motivations of restrictionists and those who proclaimed anti-slavery sentiments. Our understanding of early anti-slavery in America has been largely conditioned by our knowledge of what came after. In the late 1820s and 1830s the cry for 'immediate' abolition came to dominate the anti-slavery movement and, in the process, that movement became detached from the mainstream of politics.[23] With certain exceptions it was not until the 1840s and 1850s that anti-slavery was again to make a significant impact on national politics. The exceptions are significant: only when anti-slavery was directly related to the defence of white rights could it generate widespread support from practising politicians. The disputes over the gag rule and the censorship of the southern mails are the most obvious examples. It was precisely the passions aroused during the Missouri Crisis, passions which continued long after the crisis itself was resolved, which largely account for this.[24] The possibly disunionist consequences of continued anti-slavery agitation increasingly set the issue aside from other controversial issues. This was a departure from the earlier pattern. Before the 1820s anti-slavery found powerful articulation within the political arena alongside other issues. It found its place as one amongst many possible improvements. It was more or less taken for granted that anti-slavery sentiment and, perhaps, some forms of anti-slavery action were within the legitimate political domain. Thus the expression of anti-slavery ideas was not confined to the abolition societies but, on the contrary, was frequently to be heard in the halls of Congress and elsewhere. Equally, however, this state of affairs reduced the possibility that it would be, for politicians especially, the dominant issue around which they would concentrate their energies. At least in part because of the confidence that the struggle against slavery would be won in the longer term, no such single-minded commitment was required any more than it was necessary to avoid the issue. The commonplace nature of anti-slavery ensured that, along with other commonplace reforms such as temperance, it would be gathered up in the wave of missionary activity and benevolent reform which broke upon the United States after 1815.[25] We should not be surprised, therefore, that in 1819 anti-slavery voting should have so permeated the northern

delegations to Congress. Nor should we be surprised that in the summer
and autumn of 1819 mass meetings across the North should have supported
the anti-slavery positions of their representatives, thereby steeling them to
resist compromise in the coming session of Congress. Although compromise
was in fact achieved, it was only after the most extended and bitter
arguments that a slender majority could be found for it.[26]

While anti-slavery figured frequently, then, in the panoply of northern
political concerns, southerners had from the very first Congress resisted it
as something beyond the political pale. During the Missouri Crisis that
resistance reached new heights as threats of disunion and of a bloody
outcome were thrown at supporters of the Tallmadge amendment.[27] For
most southerners slavery *was* an issue to be isolated from normal political
processes. Some, however, saw the agitation over slavery as but one, albeit
the worst, manifestation of a number of forces all pushing in the same
direction. Much of the strength of the new benevolent reformism was rooted
in the northern middle classes, often urban dwellers, who also represented
the growing commercial and capitalist elements in American society.[28] Just
as the principal opposition to the Bank of the United States, and to
corporate capitalism in general, was articulated by Virginian and other Old
Republicans, so the opposition to compromise over Missouri emanated
from the same sources. Virginians provided over forty per cent of the
hardline southern votes in Congress against compromise. As a result of this
perception of interrelationships Old Republicans were able to build a
powerful and coherent philosophy of resistance, a philosophy which had a
number of important dimensions.[29]

The geographical nature of the division over Missouri pointed to the
necessity for a spatial diffusion of governmental authority. An emphasis
upon states' rights promised the possibility of a local determination of
controversial issues; it thereby suggested a political framework which
permitted the co-existence of divergent moral principles. Given the
breakdown of the superficial consensus on the inherent evil of slavery, this
was vital. The same principle of local self-government could be applied to
other pressing problems. Economic regulation, particularly with respect to
corporations, was the most obvious case in point. Nor was this philosophy
merely negative and restraining: there were positive aspects to the Old
Republican position. A diffusion of authority, by making that authority
more representative, would ensure governmental responsiveness to the
predominantly agrarian nature of American society. The linkage between
slavery and economic issues was important also as a means of re-creating
an orthodox republican party at the national level. When Martin van Buren
and Thomas Ritchie worked together in the 1820s to create a new national
party, shorn of its heretical elements, they did so on the basis of a
republican philosophy which, it was hoped, would have a wide appeal to
agrarians everywhere at the same time that it secured slavery in the
South.[30] It was not an accident that the Democrats, and especially the

radical Democrats of the 1830s and 1840s, should find the roots of their ideology in the published works of John Taylor of Caroline, to a greater extent even than in the ideas of Jefferson.[31]

From 1819 to 1821 the Old Republicans lost all the major battles. The federal courts continued to protect corporations and the national bank; Congress had asserted its right to legislate for slavery in the West; and, in the short term, the Republican party looked to be in as big a shambles as ever. But from a longer perspective their achievements were considerable. In the face of a decay in republican ideology, and its replacement by essentially liberal doctrines, they had resurrected the Republicanism of the eighteenth century. They had shaped it, moreover, to fit their changed circumstances. To the notion of variety stemming from 'interest' they had added a much more explicit concept of moral variation. Their republicanism was less monolithic, more value-free and more legalistic than that of their predecessors. The idea of self-government almost became itself the highest good rather than a means to an end. More to the point, they had demonstrated the survival power of republican ideas. Those ideas were never again to attain majority support in the nation; but as a refuge for the disaffected, for those out of sympathy with mainstream developments, they were to prove valuable. It was eighteenth-century Republicanism, reformulated during the crises of 1819, which was to provide the intellectual framework for the radical Democratic critique of capitalism in the 1830s and for secessionists in the 1850s.

# Chapter 3

## *Moral Suasion, Community Action and the Problem of Power: Reflections on American Abolitionists and Government, 1830–1861*

### by David Turley*

### I

The relationship between reformers and institutions in the United States has attracted much attention from historians of ante-bellum reform. An influential interpretation, developed particularly by Elkins, Thomas and Fredrickson, stresses the anti-institutional character of reform, one aspect of which was the positive hostility of reformers to action through government. In this sense abolitionism has been seen as paradigmatic.[1]

It is argued that under the impact of the religious revivals of the Second Great Awakening abolitionists were filled with millennial hopes both for individual perfection and the reform of society, understood as the successful urging of individuals to cast off sin. This entailed the emancipation of slaves by their masters, who thus ceased to commit the sin of interposing themselves between God and His children. If the experience of conversion was both the model and catalyst of reform, institutions, including government and political parties, given their concern with interests, compromise and limitations, were much more likely to seem obstacles than agents of reform. Yet institutions offer a measure of possibility and a channel through which to handle power. Their substantial absence from reform, Elkins concluded, accounted for the 'wild and unfocussed quality . . . of the various reform impulses of the period . . . and an overwhelming illusion of the individual's power to change society'.[2]

With this in mind it is tempting to accept Salmon P. Chase's distinction of 1842 between abolition, aiming at the ending of slavery everywhere and essentially carried on by moral persuasion, and anti-slavery, a political enterprise seeking the separation of the federal government from slavery and the overthrow of the Slave Power's control of the national government.[3] However it will become apparent that some abolitionists and anti-slavery men are difficult to distinguish one from another, especially in terms of what they thought government action could achieve. It will also be necessary to distinguish Garrisonian abolitionists from others and even to

* Lecturer in History, University of Kent.

locate differences of emphasis within the Garrisonian camp, particularly between William Lloyd Garrison himself and Wendell Phillips.

All abolitionists and anti-slavery reformers, whatever their attitudes to government, found that they were working in a context which presented them with severe problems. William Brock in his fascinating study of the politics of the 1840s, *Parties and Political Conscience: American Dilemmas, 1840–1850*, has argued that by that decade Americans had ceased to regard parties as temporary groupings and saw them as permanent organisations to promote principles.[4] Party stability and party loyalty thus became virtues convincing most Democrats and Whigs that their party's success, and therefore the enactment of beneficial measures that had little to do with slavery, depended on a national electoral base. They thought this required conciliation, or at least no overt provocation of the South. From the abolitionist perspective this conciliation was the core of Slave Power, guaranteeing a firm southern grip on government and compliance of powerful northern interests.

Crucial to the health of the second party system was the refusal to allow slavery to become a major political issue. This was aided by an established federal constitutional consensus on slavery. The Constitution was deemed to embody the agreement that slavery could exist in the states which chose to maintain it; that only individual states could abolish it; and that the federal government would protect the rights of those who held property in men.[5] How much government, particularly the federal government, could do unless prevailing views were changed by abolitionists was doubtful.

By the end of the 1830s all organised anti-slavery activity in the South had closed down. National denominational organisations showed such hostility to the anti-slavery question that a number of them divided along sectional lines. Reformers thus faced the dilemma of how to change a section increasingly closed off to their propaganda and ideas. When they turned to influencing the North they spoke to a people in a section largely free of slaves, most of whom saw little connection between their own local and material concerns and the existence of slavery in the South. Moreover there was a widespread racist sentiment in the free states, expressed in discriminatory legislation against the small free black population. Only when the annexation of Texas and the acquisition of the lands of the Mexican cession inserted the topic of the territorial expansion of slavery into politics in the mid 1840s could the potential material interests of the northern population be engaged.

Yet abolitionists did not work in a uniformly hostile environment. They themselves spoke the language of morality and religion and lived at a time when even the discussion in politics of material interests could be cast in a moral form. This was partly the result of the influence of revivalism on Americans far beyond the confines of anti-slavery societies, but it had other sources too. Professor J. R. Pole has written of Lincoln's 'morally conscious nationalism' based on pride in the principles established at the founding of the republic.[6] Many other Americans shared that awareness of founding principles. Such principles were used to justify different lines of action and argument, and in addition allowed questions of economic development or the role of government to be seen not only in immediate practical terms but also in terms of America's ultimate character, its identity. Abolitionists had their own views on the true nature of their country's identity, as will become apparent, but they used a vocabulary and concepts which connected them with the mainstream of politics and the deepest sentiments of many fellow citizens.[7]

Granted that any serious attack on slavery faced severe difficulties, it might seem obvious that the divisions of the American Anti-Slavery Society in 1840, which left the organisation with the Garrisonians and sent their opponents off to work through the American and Foreign Anti-Slavery Society and the Liberty Party, defined those abolitionists who took government seriously as a reform agency. The Garrisonians shortly came out in favour of disunionism, while other abolitionists participated in electoral politics. Yet reformers, like other men, changed over the years. In the 1830s, before the split in the national society, the future opponents worked relatively harmoniously together so that moral suasion and certain kinds of political action, as well as calls on the federal government to act against slavery under its jurisdiction, were seen as complementary. Both kinds of abolitionist felt the impact of forms of moral perfectionism, which caused them to place fundamental importance on moral suasion. Both faced the difficulty of reconciling their moral commitment to end slavery with the constraints of the Constitution.

With such similarities established, it is now possible to be more precise about the differences between Garrison's Boston radicals and other abolitionists. The strains of moral perfectionism which affected many of them were of rather different kinds, with the consequence that Garrisonians placed almost exclusive reliance on moral suasion after the late 1830s, were sharply critical of third party political action and so impressed by the corrupt dominance of the Slave Power that they turned to disunion. Even so, it will be suggested, moral suasion, particularly as perceived by Phillips, could be used to construct an alternative or equivalent to formal institutions which had failed in the essential task of dealing with the corrupt character of power.

By contrast, the form of perfectionism associated with Charles Grandison Finney and many evangelical abolitionists prompted a more pragmatic approach to action through government. But eventually the yoking together of a moral politics with the aim of electoral advance for a third party, within the limits of a constitutional consensus, could not be sustained. This produced a reconception of federal power in relation to slavery in the South and the development of the basis for a broader anti-slavery politics based on free soil appeals. Yet all abolitionists understood that 'opinion' was both crucial and dynamic in shaping American society from the 1830s and that influence – apart from that wielded by a remarkably coherent planter class – was decentralised. Brief consideration will therefore be given to evidence on abolitionism in northern local communities to offer some minimal test of an analysis based on national spokesmen. Finally, in the strange decade of the 1850s we shall see by what routes all kinds of abolitionists came to sanction the power of the federal government in war.

## II

Garrison began his career as editor of the *Liberator* in 1831 with the conviction that moral suasion on the sin of slavery and the need for immediate emancipation – immediately begun rather than immediately accomplished – had to underpin all other action. Congress and the state legislatures could express the moral power of the nation if they responded to abolition petitions. Washington could end slavery in the District of Columbia, under direct federal control, and revise the representation clause of the Constitution to remove the advantage to the South involved in counting three fifths of the slave population. Raising petitions was itself a form of moral suasion amongst the population and led to direct pressure on government at state and federal level.[8]

How then did Garrison, within a decade, come to reject American government entirely? We shall see the importance of immediate perfectionism upon his outlook by the late 1830s. It is clear, however, that the looming influence by the Slave Power in government provoked Garrison to anger and despair before his perfectionist declarations of late 1837. Congress acted on none of the flood of abolitionist petitions sent in the mid 1830s; the executive sanctioned, unconstitutionally, the removal of propaganda addressed to the South from the mails, and a 'gag' rule was imposed in Congress to table all further anti-slavery petitions without discussion. In addition, when Texas broke away from Mexico, some southerners in particular began efforts to have Texas annexed to the union 'for the express purpose of extending slavery and the slave trade'. It was hard for Garrison and his radical Bostonian colleagues not to believe that the power of federal government was corrupted. When they saw how northern state legislatures and governors considered proposals to restrict abolitionist activities at the behest of the South, they were convinced that the Slave Power had reached right into their own communities.[9] The effect of perfectionism could only be to confirm the need to turn away from the political mire.

The additional feature of Garrisonian perfectionism that startled so many contemporaries was its rejection even of religious institutions.[10] Garrison started his reform career as an evangelical, sure that the conversion experience gave men the power effectively to struggle against their own sin and work to eliminate it in others. This opened up the possibility of an increasingly perfect society, best achieved, Garrison thought, under the leadership of evangelical ministers. By 1836, however, he was sure this leadership was betraying its task. Increasingly sceptical of political authority, and now of religious authority, Garrison received the revelation from the influence of John Humphrey Noyes, the perfectionist communitarian, that authorities of this kind were not necessary. He became convinced that the acceptance of Christ permitted a person to become literally and immediately perfect because Christ spoke through him. There had to be a time span in the purification of society because moral suasion could not be applied instantaneously to everybody. From that time Garrison's whole concern was with the work of regenerate individuals converting the unregenerate to the extreme logic of perfection. Thus not only did Garrison universalise his reform interests, but he also concluded that human government, like slavery, disrupted man's relations with God. His aim was to bring men 'under the dominion of God, the control of an inward spirit, the government of the law of love, and unto the obedience and liberty of Christ'. Love and self control would replace the coercion upon which all governments relied.[11]

Both experience and doctrine led the Boston radicals to reject the agency of government. Garrison's expectation in 1839 of 'abolition at the ballot box' could only follow upon 'a change in the moral vision of the people', achieved solely by moral suasion. To engage in electoral politics was chimerical and could only retard the sweep of opinion which was the only sure means to secure government action for emancipation.[12]

By 1844 the American Anti-Slavery Society went one step further and declared the need to withdraw from the union with slaveholders. The Slave Power was entrenched at the centre of government; its position was sanctioned by the very framework of government, the Constitution. In earlier years the radicals had occasionally hoped that effective action under the Constitution was possible despite its defects.[13] Experience now counselled them otherwise, as did their desire to underline the untenable basis of the political action of rival abolitionists. The familiar litany of the representation clause (Art. 1 sect. 2), the power to suppress insurrections (Art. 1 sect. 8), the requirement of states to return to each other fugitives from labour or service (Art. 4 sect. 2) and the requirement that the United States defend each state against 'domestic violence' (Art. 4 sect. 4) filled the columns of radical publications in the first half of the 1840s as evidence that the Constitution protected slavery. The irony was that this conclusion exactly matched that of the southern slaveholders.

Only a sharp break with the existing situation (parallel to a religious conversion), the project of disunion, offered any possibility of salvation.[14] The call for a break up of the union held in prospect an opportunity, perhaps a final one, for the South to reassess its attachment to slavery should the protection offered by the union be withdrawn. More importantly the new slogan 'no union with slaveholders' was intended to create discussion and agitation throughout the North and 'exalt the moral sense, increase the moral power and invigorate the moral constitution of all who heartily espouse it'.[15] The Garrisonians knew they were in a small minority and did not expect any immediate action towards disunion in the North. But the shock of their demand was intended to reorder the northern frame of thought by dramatising the standard of absolute purity in government. It was also to prompt abolitionists to greater exertions by convincing them that their movement had a continuing dynamic so that political institutions might yet be compelled to register the triumph of moral influence.

Such a distant prospect underlines the conviction of the radicals that the role of government would be simply to execute the established will of the vast majority. They had no sense of government being manned by politicians with experience and specialised skills which might prove useful. On the contrary, politicians and their activities, under the dominance of the Slave Power, were objects of suspicion and hostility. Slave Power's control and the inadequacies of the Constitution demonstrated that power, essentially corrupt and corrupting, was insufficiently subject to formal political and institutional constraints. Organised moral opinion, 'influence', must take the place of inadequate formal checks. Certainty of the true moral transformation of opinion was vital to ensure that the check was effective. Moral suasion, therefore, which in the 1830s was seen as complementary to formal institutional action, became in the 1840s the irreducible requirement to replace formal institutions with a more effective equivalent in organised mass influence. As Phillips put it with characteristic sharpness in 1845:

> This objection, that we non-voters shall lose all our influence, confounds the broad distinction between *influence* and *power*. *Influence* every honest man must and will have, in exact proportion to his honesty and ability. God always annexes influence to worth. The world, however unwillingly, can never get free from the influence of such a man. This influence the possession of office cannot give, nor the want of it take away. For the exercise of such influence as this, man is responsible. *Power* we buy of our fellow men at a certain price. Before making the bargain it is our duty to see that we do not pay 'too dear for our whistle'. He who buys it at the price of truth and honour buys only weakness – and sins beside.[16]

Garrison's critics amongst evangelical abolitionists, especially those influenced by Charles Grandison Finney's revivals in the Second Great Awakening, also had a perfectionist streak in them, yet their reform methods were more pragmatic. Finney, like others who moved away from Calvinist orthodoxy in the United States, believed that man had sufficient free will to seek his own salvation under the sway of the revival preacher. Finney's own 'new measures' as a revivalist produced large numbers of converts who were then likely to express 'disinterested benevolence' towards others. His aim for young converts was that they should 'aim at being holy, and not rest satisfied till they are as perfect as God'.[17] This version of perfectionism was a continuous state of becoming, but the convert was likely to express his own growth in grace by undertaking socially beneficial activity. Such converts envisaged a gradual process of hard struggle towards perfection in which backsliding was possible. Finney's convert, the abolitionist agent Theodore Weld, still feared his frailty after conversion and even questioned Finney's own progress towards perfection.[18]

In contrast to the Garrisonian vision of the automatic spread of sinlessness through moral suasion, the long struggle expected by evangelical abolitionists virtually required the use of a variety of methods to bring about the millennium. The test of what to do at particular moments was the result of pragmatic judgement. During the 1830s the evangelicals worked with Garrison and his colleagues on petitioning, persuading legislative committees, questioning candidates and setting up local societies as a channel for these activities. When they failed to make headway with Congress or state legislatures some of them, particularly Myron Holley, Joshua Leavitt and, a little later, James G. Birney, tried to form a separate abolitionist party. Eventually the balance was tilted sharply towards the pragmatic. Evangelicals like Leavitt and Elizur Wright, who both became allies of the Republicans, constantly sought a way of translating the metaphysics of 'immediatism' into practical action that would appeal to moral but commonsensical northern opinion. In 1840 such political abolitionists saw their establishment of the Liberty party as confirming rather than replacing the moral power of an 'unseduced and determined minority'. Realistic third party men did not initially expect to get more than a slightly increased response to abolitionist pressure from the administration or Congress. Only the very optimistic hoped for a constitutional amendment in the foreseeable future to allow a direct attack on slavery in the southern states.[19]

Modesty invited competitive criticism. The anti-slavery Whig, Joshua R. Giddings, suggested that he and his friends inside a major party were equally seeking disentanglement of the federal government from support for slavery, and had more chance of achieving their aim. This was telling, given the electoral failure of the Liberty party nationally in the early 1840s. Consequently, there emerged a strand of Liberty thinking that made a more explicitly sectional appeal to the North to reverse the advantages the South enjoyed through the Slave Power's control of the federal government, a control that had been possible because the major parties had refused to draw a political division between slavery and freedom.[20] How national freedom might result from an essentially sectional appeal was not clear. Nor could it be clear, since Liberty men talked of abolition yet recognised the federal constitutional consensus on slavery, and restricted their platform to a policy of federal disentanglement. With further electoral failure in 1844, the time had come to distinguish political abolitionism more clearly from general anti-slavery or to merge them.

In the years 1844–45 Alvan Stewart, William Goodell and Lysander

Spooner all published arguments proposing that the federal government had the power under the Constitution to attack slavery in the southern states. Their arguments essentially relied upon the superior character of natural to positive law. Since liberty was a natural right of all men, governments could not abridge it by positive law. If the federal government acted against slavery in the states it would be acting in defence of a natural right enunciated in the Declaration of Independence and taking responsibility for the first time for the basic rights of all Americans.[21] Such action was a proposed expansion of federal power which foreshadowed the Fourteenth Amendment.

By contrast, Chase's way out of the abolitionist dilemma, pointed to significant limitations on the power of the federal authorities as against the states. He provided a sophisticated constitutional argument for the strategy of disentangling the federal power from slavery that abolitionists had already been pursuing. But he took a further step. He agreed with the premise that slavery was contrary to natural law and was able to show that the Founding Fathers had accepted this. He thus inferred that they had not intended to protect slavery in the Constitution. Slavery existed solely by virtue of 'municipal' or state law, which meant that whenever a slave came within the ambit of the federal government he must be treated not as a slave but as a 'person'. Thus the Fifth Amendment to the Constitution which stopped Congress from depriving any 'person' of 'life, liberty or property' without due process, destroyed slavery wherever the federal government had direct authority. A slave's freedom could only be abridged in the free states if the free state itself chose to act to protect property in man. The federal government could not enforce such protection and therefore federal Fugitive Slave Laws were unconstitutional. The argument implied a weakening of federal authority, which did little for the slaves in the South but gave full freedom to the northern states to express their hostility to slavery without federal interference. It was a doctrine amply suited to provide a basis for free soil politics.[22]

It is worthwhile at this point to look briefly at the fragmentary evidence on abolitionism in northern communities in order to give sociological and geographical dimensions to the ideas embedded in the words of national spokesmen. Abolitionists did not have to look far for local evidence of the Slave Power since they faced sharp, often violent opposition from powerful groups from the early 1830s. Violence was intense in the 1830s, though sporadic in later decades. Richards argues that it came in areas and at times when auxiliaries of the American Anti-Slavery Society were being established, and especially when programmes for free black improvement or fears of 'amalgamation' were connected with local reformers. In older, established communities, members of the elite, including city and state officials, tried to crush abolitionism, which they saw as a threat to established authority, customary racial practices and, in places, economic links with the South.[23]

In newer communities, the hostility to abolitionism should probably be seen as part of a struggle to crystallise a social and moral order. Local emergent elites were often split, but opposition seldom expressed itself as simply pro-slavery. It frequently came from respectable racial conservatives who preferred the methods of the Colonization Society, and from members of benevolent societies whose perspective was that of social control and who, though sometimes evangelicals themselves, were alienated by the seemingly subversive implications of abolitionist revivalism.[24]

Local abolitionist activity occurred in communities touched by revivals. Commitment was expressed in local efforts to establish schools for free blacks, lyceums and libraries, and to work through the churches to deny communion to slaveholders. Reformers were seeking to inculcate amongst their fellow whites and free blacks 'those peculiarities, habits, tastes and acquisitions' which constituted, in Theodore Weld's estimate, a homogeneous community.[25]

Associations of abolitionists saw themselves as bands of morally homogeneous brothers and sisters,[26] a pattern of relationship they hoped to transfer to wider spheres, perhaps through Liberty politics in the 1840s; and the Liberty Party in turn could take on a character pointing to a Free Soil and Republican future. In Smithfield, New York, where Liberty men won every state-wide election between 1843 and 1847, support came from a significant number of journeymen, artisans and labourers as well as the agricultural population. The Liberty campaigners attacked northern 'aristocrats' as allies of the slaveholders and forecast class legislation against white labourers unless they banded together to help defeat slavery.[27] Here was a hint of that 'white man's anti-slavery' which placed the actual or potential interest of free whites near the centre of popular Republican hostility to slavery in the 1850s, as the question of slavery in the territories became the prime issue of national politics. But the links were more than in political rhetoric; the evidence of electoral returns indicates that what Liberty men modestly began, Free Soilers and Republicans in much larger numbers and from the same areas carried on.[28] In the 1850s events moved at a headlong pace; after the Fugitive Slave Law of 1850 and the repeal of the Missouri Compromise in the Kansas-Nebraska Act of 1854, many northerners for the first time took the threat of an aggressive Slave Power seriously. In these new circumstances, while usually impotent as independent reformers, abolitionists could in some respects draw closer to the main currents of northern thought and feeling.

Those who moved least, and had least impact, were the remnants of Gerrit Smith's and William Goodell's National Liberty organisation in the American Abolition Society founded in 1855 and the Radical Abolitionist Party. Their view of government was built on Goodell's doctrine of the 1840s that the federal government, given its duty to suppress crime and protect human rights, could destroy slavery wherever it existed in the United States.[29] The group found that its doctrine had as little purchase on opinion as had similar ideas in the 1840s. As Charles Francis Adams remarked, this kind of political anti-slavery seemed abstract to many voters, lacking the appeal of 'temporal absorbing self interest'.[30]

The Republican party, on the other hand, fully recognised that attraction of self-interest. However, abolitionists who gave it their support did not believe they were sacrificing essential principle. As the most radical elements within the party coalition, they settled on Chase's view of the Constitution, yet saw it as leading not to the containment but to the ultimate destruction of slavery. Charles Sumner's programme listed abolition everywhere within the jurisdiction of Congress, prohibition of the entry of any more slave states and the cessation of the interstate slave trade as well as keeping slave holders out of office and denying the use of slave labour on federal projects.[31] Abolitionist Republicans were convinced that at last they had found a way to meet the problem of power posed by the clash of their moral commitment and constitutional limitations. In addition, events were providing them with the necessary political support.

Perhaps the most interesting feature of abolitionism in the decade was that Garrisonians ended up supporting the power of the federal government at war. The Fugitive Slave Law was peculiarly obnoxious to abolitionists. It required northern citizens to cooperate in their own communities in taking alleged fugitive slaves before commissioners, often to be returned to slavery. Federal law thus imposed actions which conflicted with the grass roots growth of abolitionist and anti-slavery opinion. Garrisonians were perfectly prepared to advocate non-cooperation. Non-cooperation, however, sometimes became violent resistance and was justified by Wendell Phillips and Theodore Parker as a defence of justice against a corrupt law. Fellow Bostonians who insisted on the obligation to obey the law, Phillips suggested, mistook government for liberty and sacrificed fundamental principle as well as the reputation of their community. Phillips did not precisely advocate violent popular resistance to law, but he advised fugitives to protect themselves as they judged best. He further indicated that if they were unable to escape to Canada, he would, in their position, risk the consequences of violent resistance. Parker agreed and even more insistently than Phillips drew a parallel with the American Revolution.[32]

This was a constant motif throughout the decade, equally sounded by Garrison and Henry C. Wright. In the context of rising anti-slavery feeling and seeming acts of southern aggression, the parallel between British tyranny and the tyranny of slavery encouraged violent opposition. Although Garrison still insisted on his own pacifism, he too spoke of the American standard set by the Revolution in relation to both the Fugitive Slave Law and slave rebellions within the South.[33] The American Revolution was, of course, seen as a vital part of the heritage of liberty by citizens far beyond the ranks of committed abolitionists. Thus at the moment when they came closest to advocating the violent nullification of federal law, the radicals positioned themselves as protectors of the main moral constituent of

American nationality – the nurture of liberty – and linked themselves with the sentiments of large sectors of northern opinion.

Garrison and Phillips's hopes for a morally purified and homogeneous nation are finally apparent in their responses to Harper's Ferry and the secession crisis. Both men welcomed John Brown's raid, Garrison after some hesitation, as evidence of progress in the will to resist despotism. Phillips went further and saw Brown's blow as struck not against government and law but in favour of civilisation against barbarism; his incursion had revealed the lack of a true moral order in the South.[34] When the southern states began to secede, Phillips welcomed disunion since it marked the loss of the Slave Power's control over the nation. The immediate result in the North was to be 'homogeneous institutions', but secession also made possible the knitting together of a true unity. The 'unripe union' was broken, but it was a temporary rupture for 'we are one in blood, trade, thought, religion, history; nothing can long divide us'.[35] The main obstacle remained slavery, both as an intrinsic evil and as a mark of the South's retarded development in the growth of modern civilisation. When war broke out Garrison and Phillips both supported it, accepting the legitimacy of government because government power could crush evil and pave the way for a better moral order and a more fundamental political unity.[36]

A few more general points remain to be drawn out from the argument. Evidence from local communities referred to earlier indicates abolitionist concern to reshape their communities morally. They were often involved in a complex of improvement activities – including education and temperance – which went beyond questions of race. It was the evangelical impulse at work, a local sign of the drive towards a morally homogeneous national society. Government, they felt, was using its power most appropriately when it was able to express the true moral character of American nationality. The Slave Power was most objectionable in demonstrating the control and use of government for sectional and class purposes: the planters were an anti-republican 'aristocracy'. Yet the moral nationalism of the abolitionist spokesmen also betrayed its class origin. Despite evidence of support for abolitionism from artisans and working men, most abolitionists were unsympathetic to the demands of the incipient labour movement for government action on their own behalf. For the abolitionists, legal freedom constituted self-ownership, the only necessary basis for virtuous progress.[37] With a few exceptions Eric Foner's description of Republicans in the 1850s as confident exponents of their northern bourgeois culture fits abolitionists too.[38]

# Chapter 4

## Federal Power and Economic Policy: Henry Carey and the 1850s

### by Bruce Collins

I

The relationship between economists and politicians has always been a difficult one. The more economists have built up their stock of scientific expertise and indeed have come to view themselves as scientists, the more they have contrasted the rigour of their conclusions and their prescriptions with the messiness and expediency of politics. Yet, for practitioners of macro-economics at least, the political world is the fulcrum upon which the economic world turns. It was the recognition of this fact, and the concomitant if frustrating need to persuade politicians, that drove on the gospeller of lower tariffs, F. W. Taussig, in the late nineteenth and early twentieth centuries; that fuelled the missionary fervour of Keynesians, British and American, in the 1930s and 1940s; and that fires the monetarists of the 1970s and 1980s.[1] Macro-economic theory and government policy have become not merely inter-related but increasingly interdependent. This fact in turn, and the propagandist effort to alter policy, led macro-economists to simplify their own theories, to exaggerate the possible consequences of legislative action, and to denigrate the prevailing political order. Starting as scientists, economists operating in the open market-place of ideas swiftly became utopians and Cassandras. These characteristics of economists' public propagandising were as much in evidence in the mid nineteenth-century age of limited government as they were in the twentieth-century period of extending federal power.

To say that what men thought of reality often transcends in importance what actually was, repeats mere cliché; but at least the cliché bears repetition in considering mid nineteenth-century Americans' attitudes towards federal power. The federal government in the 1850s was weak. It spent well under $100 million a year in that decade, whereas total national output rose to about $4,000 million by 1860. Its expenditures went on defence, debt and interest repayments, and the post-office. Its most important, fully observed and controversial duty was governing the territories until they became states. In terms of social and business policy, of direct investment, and of total spending, the federal government was readily dwarfed by the aggregate efforts of local and state governments – as, in most respects, it continued to be, in peacetime, until 1946.[2] Yet, even if its powers and duties were relatively limited, the federal government enjoyed a moral and political significance far outweighing its practical powers. The most notable, and explosive, manifestation of this significance attached to federal power was southern secession in 1860–61; for secessionists believed that, somehow, the new Republican administration in Washington would act in such fashion as to endanger the South's $2,000 millions' worth of property in slaves. These were large consequences to fear of a government supposedly straight-jacketed in its activity.[3] But the assertion that federal initiatives could have far-reaching repercussions was not confined to southerners fearful of anti-slavery Republicans. It was also a central part of the arguments advanced by America's leading and most distinctively American economist of the 1850s, Henry C. Carey.

Carey's writings in the 1850s exemplified the main characteristics of the full-blooded economic propagandist. Present policies were, to Carey's mind, not simply wrong, but tended to undermine and corrupt a society increasingly wrenched from its pristine origins and its virtuous, earlier days. A change in policy (in Carey's case, the impositions of high, protective tariffs) would reverse the process of decline – a process at the same time moral, material, and political – and open up extraordinary opportunities for economic development and diversification. The sharp reversal of an entire train of historical events lay fully in the power of the federal government. However few its daily responsibilities may have been, the federal government clearly possessed, even in the age of *laissez-faire*, a talismanic capacity to transform society. Its capacity to effect good or ill much exceeded its paltry share of gross national product.

In his work as an economic propagandist, Henry Carey was also a moralist and a critic of his age. He was America's first economist of international repute; but he was also a publicist deeply involved in and keenly committed to party – Whig and subsequently Republican – politics. In this latter role he is often regarded as an optimistic spokesman for an optimistic ideology. In fact, as publicist and partisan he was a Jeremiah of his times. By re-examining Carey's writings in their own context and on their own terms, and not simply as contributions to an evolving economic or sociological theory, we will also remind ourselves of how historically shallow – and how repetitious over time – the economic publicist's intellectual stocks-in-trade really are. For the political requirements of the 1850s, and the moral and social assumptions underpinning Carey's thought, led Carey into a false history and misleading utopianism, all centred upon the federal government's powers and policies. In this respect, his work has a contemporary relevance to the student of federal power; for his arguments, and his cavalier disregard for historical accuracy, suggest how the imperatives of economic theory encourage an exaggerated treatment of the extent and potentialities of federal power. One is reminded here of Milton Friedman's popular treatise *Free to Choose*, with its promise to so apply

federal power as to resuscitate the values of a past that never was, in a
purified future that will never be. When, in doing this, Friedman bemoans
the corruptions and usurpations and fiscal extravagances of an expanded
federal government, his language in general, if not in detail, reminds us how
commonly economists fulminate against the vast effects of policies they
despise, and how imprudently they promise universal improvement as the
consequence of their own pet prescriptions.[4] In understanding Carey in his
own time, we will also understand something of the relationship of
economists to politics.


## II

Historians have generally misrepresented Carey by failing to distinguish
between his contribution to economic and sociological theory and his
contribution to economic and social propaganda. The one word used to
describe Carey's thought – and passed down from historian to historian like
the Olympic torch – is optimism.[5] This is accurate enough as a label for the
assumptions behind his economic and social theory. He rejected and
scorned the gloom of Manchester economics, most notably Malthusian
conclusions about the consequences of population growth, and Ricardo's
theory of rent. He also argued that it would be feasible to create a 'harmony
of interests' in America through social and economic association. Not only
would a utopian future be realized in America; Europe, with the loss of its
over-spilling population to the expanding American economy, would itself
be relieved of pressing social and economic problems. His theoretical work
refuted – at length and with much determination – the notion that man was
trapped inexorably by the unremitting pressure of numbers and the fact
that (according to Ricardo) agricultural land was only in short and very
expensive supply. These arguments led logically to more practical
conclusions. Carey was a robust patriot; his nationalism paraded an
optimistic self-confidence in America's future and in America's separateness
from, and superiority to, Britain. He also envisaged, as the ideal type of
society resulting from a 'harmony of interests', the economic milieu existing
around Philadelphia, where medium-sized industrial towns were implanted
in a rich and highly commercial agricultural setting. These aspects of his
thought, his philanthropic concerns, and his intense belief in the
transforming potential of highly protective tariffs, all gave a practical cast to
his optimistic theory. Not surprisingly, therefore, those historians who place
Carey in his political context – Daniel W. Howe in treating Carey as a
representative Whig, and Eric Foner in more briefly citing Carey's
relevance to an understanding of the Republicans' free labour ideology
– emphasise the economist's optimism as symptomatic both of those larger
creeds and of the North's self-assurance in the mid nineteenth century.[6]

Yet, if Carey's theory was optimistic in assumptions and ultimate
message, it was conveyed to a wider public in language that regretted the

passing of traditional American values, that decried the prevailing economic order, that attacked the political establishment, and that deplored the existence of an overmighty federal government. In two of his most notable works of popularisation – *The Harmony of Interests, Agricultural, Manufacturing, and Commercial* (1851) and *Letters to the President, on the Foreign and Domestic Policy of the Union, and Its Effects, as exhibited in the Condition of the People and the State* (1858)[7] – Carey's view of what had happened to America, and what would continue to happen unless protectionism was introduced to reverse the trend, was pessimistic in the extreme.

Carey saw mid nineteenth-century America as subservient to Britain both economically and ideologically. The very first sentence of *The Harmony of Interests* announced the text of his sustained sermon: 'The tendency of the whole British system of political economy is to the production of discord among men and nations'. Such discord resulted from high rents and oppressed proletarians, two features of economic life justified, or at least explained, by Ricardo and Malthus respectively. According to Carey, free trade impoverished the rural populations of Ireland and India as well as of Britain, and kept British urban wages so low as to foster depravity in city life. The free trade system further propelled Britain to seek overseas sources of cheap raw materials and willing, if not pliable, markets abroad for her manufactured goods. In so far as America accepted and implemented free trade ideas, America too suffered from low prices for her raw materials, destined for British manufacturers, and from depressed wages. And America, like Britain, was forced to seek sources of raw materials and markets for manufactured goods through geographical dispersion.[8]

Where others – especially ante-bellum Democrats – celebrated America's territorial expansion, Carey deplored it. Settlers decamping to California and Oregon depleted the rest of the country of valuable labour. Their movement westwards also disrupted capital markets, for a vastly over-extended railroad system in the 1850s drew off investment, and material resources, from what Carey regarded as more fruitful projects. Yet dispersion, following logically from free trade precepts, was actively promoted by the federal government: 'the policy of the central government looks steadily to the dispersion of our people, to the occupation of new territories, to the creation of new States, and to the production of a necessity for further [rail]roads'.[9] As it encouraged expansionism, so the federal government created further demands: the political pressure for free homesteads to western settlers was especially criticised by Carey, since revenues from public land sales would thereby be forfeited, and such revenues might prove essential to compensate for income lost by the federal government in raising the tariff. But, more generally, Carey argued that the central relationship between territorial expansionism and the economic order was wrong. Under free trade, America expanded its sovereignty and dispersed its people from a compelling need to do so. Under protectionism, Carey predicted, America would prosper to such a degree as to attract the voluntary annexation of Mexico and the British North American colonies:

> With each year, the desire of our neighbours, north and south, to enter the Union would increase, and but few would elapse before it would embrace all North America, and a population of forty or fifty millions of people, themselves consuming far more than all the cotton we now raise.

Prosperity engendered by protection would feed upon itself to create within America an ever-expanding market for the country's every-growing output. But that prosperity could be achieved in the first place only by the closer association of producers within geographical proximity of each other; for while Carey condoned domestic 'commerce', he condemned the waste involved in over-extended international 'trade'.[10] And that greater degree of improving association could be secured only by a dramatic reversal in federal policy.

The use or misuse of federal power was central to Carey's argument. In 1858 he declared:

> For half a century, during which the Federal government was administered by Washington and his successors, down to Jackson, the general tendency of its action was towards carrying into practical effect the Declaration of our Independence. During nearly all that time, there was a general tendency towards increase in the diversity of employments, with constant increase in the power of association, in the strength of local action, and in the steadiness of the currency – no general suspension, in time of peace, having occurred in all that time.

This description disregarded the vagaries of tariff policy from the 1790s to the 1820s, and conveniently ignored the economic dislocation occasioned by the embargo and by the panic of 1819. Moreover, the years of massive growth stretching from the late 1820s to the late 1850s (albeit interrupted from 1837 to 1845) became in Carey's propaganda a period of increasing national dependence upon British markets and British manufacturers, and of increasing federal power.

> In the period that since elapsed [after Jackson's election], the policy of the revolution has been abandoned, with constant increase in the dependence of the planter and farmer on the distant trader. The power of local action, therefore, steadily declines, with constant diminution in the respect of the general government for local rights, and growing instability of the currency – the suspensions of payments, in that brief period, having been no less than three in number.

Free trade had produced a sudden and complete reversal in national policy, for free trade impelled a territorial expansionism that could be effected only by war:

> In the half century from Washington to Jackson – the policy of the country having been that of peace, and of the extension of . . . domestic commerce . . . – the Federal government was economically administered, and the power to

contribute to its support was a steadily augmenting one. Since then – the policy having become that of free trade, annexation, and war – the expenses of the central government have greatly increased, while the power to contribute to its support, or to that of local institutions, has tended to diminish[11]

If this account omitted the Louisiana Purchase, the War of 1812, and a succession of measures to gain land from the Indians – all providing evidence that weakened Carey's general thesis – it amply illustrated the extent to which Carey portrayed America as a country adrift from its early roots and principles, a country, in short, in decline, and in need of immediate regeneration.

Such generalisations showed how far Carey's politics shaped his economics. For the Democrats, as the proponents of free or freer trade, were readily criticised as the advocates and engineers of American expansionism through war. Not only did the Democrats extend federal power abroad; they also persistently exploited it to attack paper money at home. Carey declared in 1857:

> For more than twenty years . . . the Federal government has been engaged in an almost unceasing effort to secure to itself the control of that great instrument of association known as money – the professed object of all its labors in that direction, having been, the establishment of what has been termed 'a hard money currency', to the entire exclusion of the paper circulation.[12]

Here, again, Carey produced a parody of historical reality. The effort to increase the amount of specie in circulation had hardly been as radical or as strenuous as Carey suggested. Nor, during the Democratic 'ascendancy', from the early 1830s to the mid 1850s, did the total number of banks fall regularly. Nor did the *federal* government consistently battle against the banks.[13] Yet the historical record of economic growth and credit extension had to give way to Carey's image of national decline. From 1849 to 1850 he grasped at every shred of evidence of labour unrest, and of nativist jealousy of immigrants competing for scarce jobs, to assert that low wages and lack of work resulted inexorably from the tariff of 1846, which lowered barriers to large-scale imports of cheap British manufactured goods.[14] And he repeatedly dismissed evidence of commercial prosperity and economic expansion – in the shape of growing cities – by insisting instead that great conurbations represented exploitation, not true and virtuous wealth:

> The great cities and towns of the world are built up out of the spoils of the farmer and planter. Looking around in New York, or in Philadelphia, or Boston, it is not possible to avoid being struck with the number of persons who live by merely exchanging – passing from the producer to the consumer – producing nothing themselves . . . as if for the pleasure of doing it.

In addition, for many who merely laboured in the cities the metropolis was a place of defeat in the economic race, not success:

> It is asserted that of all the persons engaged in trade, in our cities, four-fifths fail. The cause is to be found in the fact that so many are forced into trade, for

want of being enabled to apply themselves to production, and that when there
they are exposed to the effects of the enormous changes which result from the
existence of the English monopoly system. Iron sells at one time at ten pounds,
and soon after at five. The man of small capital, who has a stock on hand, is
ruined. Cottons and woollens change in like manner . . . . The consequence is,
that our cities are filled with men who adventured in trade, and failed.[15]

Instead of great trading cities, Carey wanted to see a textile mill established
in every county in the Union, so as to place industrial activities and
agriculture side by side. Instead of population dispersion westwards
through territorial expansion, Carey wanted to see a concentration of
Americans east of the Mississippi. Instead of the regional specialisation that
was a feature of the 1840s and 1850s, Carey looked forward to the local
diversification of economic activities, the creation of a local harmony of all
economic interests.[16]

If protectionism led Carey to attack the consequences of free trade in
their widest manifestations, it also led him to concoct a false economic
history of the United States. This false history in turn gave his writings a
nostalgic quality, fully exemplified in his obeisance to the agrarian myth. It
would be wrong to portray the economist from Philadelphia as simply a
herald of the new economic order of textile mills, railroads, iron foundries
and, on the horizon, Bessemer processors. On the contrary, he yielded to no
one in his deference to rural values and rural wisdom. His words 'of all the
pursuits of many, agriculture – the work of production – is the one that most
tends to the expansion of intellect' laid down his credentials as a worthy
follower of Jefferson's.[17] But his praise of agriculturalists went beyond mere
nostalgia: agriculture lay at the heart of his economic theory.

One of the vital aims of tariff protectionism was to shelter the agricultural
sector from the short-term fluctuations endemic in free trade, and from the
long-term reduction of raw materials prices which British doctrine and
British policy alike sought to achieve. And, just as free trade depressed the
unit price of cotton and wheat, so the dispersion of American agriculture
lowered financial yield per acre. By promoting industrial development,
tariff protection would boost land values, since the proximity of urban
demand for raw materials and foodstuffs would lift prices and expand
agricultural output. At the same time, profits accruing from expanded
output and higher prices would be channelled into investments more
fruitful than attenuated railroads snaking their course across scantily
populated lands in newly opened regions to the far west. In addition, the
more intensive and profitable agriculture became, the higher would the
value of land rise and the more necessary it would become to use skilled
and well rewarded labour to cultivate it.[18] Given this natural process, the
ending of slavery followed on from the greatly enhanced value of land, since
skilled and diligent labour – the sort of labour which would necessarily be
applied to expensive land – was automatically equated with wage-labour.
When land became southern slaveowners' principal asset, then slaves

would steadily be freed, to become paid labourers in field or factory, or tenant farmers on increasingly sub-divided plantations. In this way, protectionist theory met the political requirement that Carey's Republicanism created; for, if Carey was little interested in slavery as a social or political problem in the 1850s, he had yet to escape from the trap caused by the fact that protectionism, by enriching American agricultural producers (and producers of cotton as much as of wheat), would strengthen slavery and slaveownership.[19]

Carey's anti-southernism was not based specifically upon a deeply felt hostility to slavery. It mushroomed rather from southern politicians' powerful opposition to protective tariffs and their support for territorial expansionism. Carry himself was politically sensitive enough, while still a Whig, to try to convince his southern readers that protectionism would obviate the necessity for territorial expansion, by increasing economic diversification within the existing area of the United States, enhancing land values, and promoting highly profitable market farming. He developed this case during the winter of 1849/1850, at the precise time when the congressional dispute over California's fate and that of the rest of the Mexican Cession, together with the possibility of westward slavery extension, was about to explode. His economic argument that southern territorial expansion would be unnecessary under a protectionist regime was as politically timely when written in 1849/50 as was his passionate and merciless attack on twenty years of Democratic rule published immediately in the wake of the financial panic of 1857.[20]

But, while Carey's economics were carefully attuned to a variety of political needs, they were also responsive to, indeed founded upon, a range of social anxieties. Protectionism promised, after all, to regenerate American society.

The social consequences of free trade (or the fairly close approximation to it prevalent in mid nineteenth-century America) were appalling. Because small towns and rural areas offered limited local employment, 'the young men are forced to seek the cities, or to fly to the West, and thousands and tens of thousands of women remain at home unmarried, while other thousands also seek the cities in search of employment, and terminate their career as prostitutes'. The flight of young men to California and Oregon drained settled areas of duitful sons and brothers and prospective husbands, weakening family ties and eastern society generally.[21] And all this social dry rot was caused by mistaken federal policies.

So, too, the over-expansion of federal power and the federal bureaucracy threatened to warp the political system. Carey estimated that, by the late 1850s, the president's patronage gave him power over the opinions of about 60,000–80,000 public officials. These functionaries in turn intervened widely in county and township elections, spreading *federal* influence, eroding local rights. And as government power expanded at all levels, the temptations of business and corporate interests to direct it, or benefit from it grew. The country's legislation had 'fallen almost entirely under the control of navigation, railroad, and other transportation companies; and . . . legislators . . . largely participate with their managers, in the profits of enormous grants of money, and of public lands'. The lobby had become a third house of Congress; and city government had fallen under the sway of men fit largely for the 'penitentiary'. Political corruption was matched by social degeneration; 'we find a rapid growth of rowdyism and intemperance, with corresponding decline in the security of person and of property – frauds, peculations, seductions, murders, and crimes of every kind' rapidly rising.[22] All these disturbing elements thus came together in a picture of woe; low tariffs and territorial expansion had served to depress wages and land values, to distort the true progress of eastern society, to prop up slavery, to subordinate America to British economic interests, to expand federal power and to debase social and public virtue alike. At the end of 1857, following a decade under the low Walker tariff of 1846, 'we witness a decline more rapid, and more pervading, than is recorded in the history of any country in the world'.[23]

Given this ample accumulation of social, political and economic woes, all brought on by the federal government's mistaken policies, it would be one-sided to describe Carey during the 1850s as anything but a pessimistic critic of his times. He exploited every manner of anxiety in order to drive home his advocacy of tariff protectionism. If his economic theory was optimistic in its refutation of Manchesterism and in its promise of what could in future be done, his economic propaganda and his analysis of the state of the Union in the 1850s were full of grim prognostications.

## III

Having placed Carey more precisely, and more accurately, in his context, we may now reflect upon his larger relevance, both to the politics of the 1850s and to the general question of how economic ideas are affected by political practice.

In his political rhetoric, Carey bewailed the recent expansion of federal power and thereby parrotted a cliché of his age. Southern politicians of the 1850s repeatedly groaned about the accretion of federal power. Northern opponents of the Democratic federal administrations of 1853–61 attacked them for extending federal activities and fattening the federal employment rolls.[24] When Carey charged that the president by the late 1850s commanded the loyalties of 60,000–80,000 public officials, he was not exaggerating too wildly, for in 1861 the federal government employed 36,672 civilians; in addition, there were military and naval personnel and various elected officials at state and local level who, through the party patronage system, were to some degree amenable to presidential influence or even control. If we assume that federal civilian employees were adult males, then about one in every hundred (free) adult males in 1860 was in federal service.[25] Even in an age of very limited government, the federal administration was easily the nation's largest single employer. And, as the figures in the following table show, the growth in federal civilian

Table: Federal Civilian Employment and Total U.S. Population, 1821–61[26]

| | Federal Civilian employees | | Total Population of U.S.A. (to nearest 000) |
|---|---|---|---|
| 1821 | 6,914 | 1820 | 9,618,000 |
| 1831 | 11,491 | 1830 | 12,901,000 |
| 1841 | 18,038 | 1840 | 17,120,000 |
| 1851 | 26,274 | 1850 | 23,261,000 |
| 1861 | 36,672 | 1860 | 31,513,000 |

employment outpaced population growth in the period 1821–61. Moreover, federal spending per annum rose fairly dramatically from a total that hovered around the $25 million mark in the period 1839–45 to a total just short of $70 millions in the late 1850s.[27] Even though these bald figures take no account of the overall recovery in the national economy from the early 1840s, when prices and output were depressed, to the far more prosperous mid 1850s, they were quite dramatic enough to sustain Republican complaints against Democratic federal extravagance. Moreover, federal spending was strongly criticised because about half of it (both in the early 1840s and in the late 1850s) went on the army and navy. This meant that spending was directly related to federal initiatives which, as in the case of policing Indian territories, could be questioned and opposed. It was certainly Carey's contention that free trade stimulated territorial expansionism and annexations. Without linking such activity so tightly to free trade, Republicans generally objected to the Caribbean and Central American fixations and ambitions of many, if not most, ante-bellum Democratic leaders. And they pointed to the fiscal consequences – in terms of keeping up a frontier army and expanding the navy – of those Caribbean yearnings.[28]

Westward expansion created – as Carey said it did – additional federal responsibilities. Not only was the federal government increasingly preoccupied from 1846 to 1861 with territorial policy and its related rights and duties respecting slavery in the territories. It was also under pressure to promote railroad building in the western states and territories alike. In 1850 Congress awarded its first land grant for railroad construction. By channelling the federal land to a state government, Congress avoided becoming the direct sponsor of a business corporation operating within a state; instead, the state then passed on lands so granted to a corporation or corporations chartered by its own legislature. After giving 2,595,000 acres to the Illinois Central railroad in 1850, Congress made a few lesser donations in the same year, two awards in 1852, three in 1853, and thirty-two grants, involving 11,500,000 acres, in 1856. After the last-mentioned outpouring of generosity, a number of relatively small grants for railroads in the territory of Minnesota were made before the Civil War.[29] Yet throughout the 1850s, strong demands were also pressed, particularly by politicians from the Mississippi valley states and from the Pacific coast states, for federal land grants and financial aid to be allocated for a railroad linking the Pacific coast to the Mississippi valley. Discussions of a federal commitment to this scheme became bogged down in intricate financial, geographical, and political complexities, and nothing practical came of them before the 1860s.[30] But such proposals clearly focused political attention on the federal government and aroused debate over the legitimate uses and limits of federal power.

In this fashion, Carey's warnings against federal activism were timely. They did not necessarily coincide with Republican policy in detail; many Republicans, for instance, warmly advocated federal aid to a Pacific railroad and free homesteads for western settlers, both of which measures Carey regarded as drains upon the federal Treasury. But, in general terms, the opposition to the Democratic administration of James Buchanan castigated it for excessive spending, excessive activism, and excessive extensions of federal power. Here was what the Old Whig *National Intelligencer* had to say about President Buchanan's message to Congress of December, 1858:

> We must retrench the extravagant list of magnificent schemes which has received the sanction of the Executive.... The acquisition of Cuba...; the construction of a Pacific Railroad...; a Mexican protectorate; international preponderance in Central America, in spite of all the powers of Europe; the submission of distant South American states;... the enlargement of the navy; a largely increased standing army...what government on earth could possibly meet all the exigencies of such a flood of innovations?[31]

These criticisms were widely echoed by Republicans in the late 1850s.

How far all these evils were believed to flow from a defective federal tariff policy was quite another matter. Most leading Republicans by 1860 accepted the need for a more protective tariff. But they did so from the political consideration that Pennsylvania's coal-mining and iron-and-steel-producing areas were economically depressed, had only been captured by the Republicans in 1858 and needed to be held in the Republican electoral camp. In other words, Republican politicians were properly sceptical of Carey's vast and bold claims for protectionism.[32] If this was partly because their principal fear of expansive federal power was the use made of it by southerners to protect and extend slavery, it was also because they simply did not accept Carey's utopian vision of a society transformed by the introduction of protection. While Republicans shared the optimism of Carey's economic theory, and agreed with his notion of mid nineteenth-century America as a country in crisis, in decline (less readily) and at an important cross-roads in its evolution (more certainly), they did not view the crisis as running quite so deep in northern society, or as originating from the same source, low tariffs. Yet all agreed that, however wide-ranging the state governments' functions were, however much state and local governments outspent the federal government, however lively an interest the voters and politicians took in state issues, however prominently state rights and state pride were matters of public concern, it was the *federal* government that gave tone, character, purpose and central direction to American politics. In writing and speaking about protectionism and about slavery expansion and the Slave Power, Carey and the Republicans respectively agreed that it was the federal government, not the states, which guided the destinies of the republic. Despite the recent emphasis given by historians to state political issues and state reform programmes during the age of energetic state governments and ideological *laissez-faire,* the federal government was accorded by contemporaries, in theoretical writings and in public debate, far greater power to do good or ill than the states were commonly deemed to possess.[33] Only when southerners formulated their ideas about ultimate state sovereignty and the justification for state secession did intellectual attention shift weightily back to the states.[34]

## IV

If, in reading Henry Carey, it is worth remembering his Irish forebears and his inherited Anglophobia, it is similarly important to note the political constraints upon his economic preaching. When he wrote the *Harmony of Interests* in 1849/50 he sought to appeal to national sentiments; in opposing *British* trade policy and in allaying sectional tensions he aimed to calm north-south rivalries over slavery extension in the Mexican Cession. So, too, in 1858 he graphically described two generations of wrong-headed federal policy when he attempted to extract the maximum protectionist profit from the economic recession of that year. In trying to advance protectionism's cause, he played up the political evils of Democratic rule, and countered the tendency, expressed most eloquently in Abraham Lincoln's 'House Divided' speech of June 1858 and in Senator William H. Seward's 'Irrepressible Conflict' speech of October 1858, for Republicans, despite the economic recession, to concentrate on slavery extension. By thus essaying to deflect political attention towards his own theories and prescriptions, Carey fell into a number of intellectual bad habits which are commonly found among economic publicists.

Historical truth fell victim to the requirements of theoretical consistency. However carefully Carey laboured to compile and compute his economic data, he saw little reason to lavish similar effort and diligence upon the analysis of past politics. A golden age spreading from Washington to John Quincy Adams and followed by the only briefly interrupted evils of a Democratic ascendancy more or less summed up Carey's view of American political history. And the Democratic ascendancy from Jackson's election to the late 1850s was caricatured as siring the triumph of free trade, a war upon paper money, an annexationist foreign policy and a corrupt and socially debilitating growth in federal power. What in later historical perspective was seen as a period of exceptionally rapid economic growth, was dismissed by Carey as one of economic failure and social disruption.

In terms that remind one almost of the extreme forebodings of Milton Friedman's *Free to Choose* – with its hectoring assertions that federal power had in the 1960s and 1970s grown to the point of undermining individual liberty and wrecking the social fabric[35] – Carey portrayed mid nineteenth-century America as a country in dangerous decline. Yet having by its past mistakes helped initiate and speed on that process of degeneration, the federal government still commanded the means of redress. For by making changes in federal tariff levels, the federal government would succeed in not simply fine-tuning or improving the economy: it would fundamentally re-direct society. This extraordinary messianic faith in the social and political and moral multiplier effects of economic policy was to become, if it had not already long been, a prominent characteristic of the economic propagandist trying to shape policy and therefore simplifying his economic ideas. In this process, the extent, nature, and near-revolutionary force of federal power was constantly high-lighted, and grossly exaggerated, even in the age of circumscribed government and supposed *laissez-faire*.

# Chapter 5

## Beyond the Federal Consensus: A Doctrine of National Power

by S. G. F. Spackman*

Contemporaries recognised that the Civil War and Reconstruction were the crucial experiences of American nationhood and that the outcome guaranteed both the continuance and the character of their national existence; and while subsequent generations of Americans have shared this judgement they have found it much more difficult to agree on any other aspect of the crisis of the 1860s. Yet the conflict would not have taken the course it did without a federal political system that enabled the South to withdraw from the Union in its attempt to preserve a social system dependent on slavery. Nor could the military exigencies (on both sides) of the resulting war have been met without vastly increased governmental activity. The nature and use of federal power, therefore, became as much a central political concern as any particular question of policy when the two basic problems of reconstructing the Union had to be faced. Under what conditions, if any, were the seceded states to be restored? And what, if anything, was to be done for the blacks released from the shackles of slavery?

To solve these problems congressional leaders, faced with President Johnson's refusal to cooperate and with southerners' adamant resistance to even the barest minimum of social change, imposed what is generally described as 'Radical Reconstruction'. This involved military occupation, black suffrage and political disqualification of the Confederate leadership, any one of which would have been an utterly unthinkable assertion of federal power by any received constitutional standard (though in the light of European parallels such actions seem quite remarkably lenient). While this whole episode has become part of the southern myth – the iron heel of the Yankee grinding down upon poor Tara – even historians of northern sympathies have treated it with some embarrassment, unsure of either the radicals' motivation or their goals. Both viewpoints rest, however, upon similar assumptions about the nature of the American constitutional system and the location of the boundaries that ought to exist between the exercise of federal and state power.

Significantly, it was William Brock, making the first major interpretative

* Lecturer in Modern History, University of St. Andrews.

contribution to the historiography of the United States to come from
Britain, who pointed out in *An American Crisis* that the nature of the federal
system itself contributed very largely to the intractability of the Reconstruction problem, of how to square civil rights for blacks with the civil liberties
of other Americans. He showed the radicals, therefore, consciously moving
towards the exercise of national authority within the political structure as a
whole, and towards congressional preponderance within the federal
government as the only way they could see of making the political structure
accommodate the problem of race. Brock summarised the constitutional
issues in the words 'in its assertion of national power and of legislative
supremacy the Radical revolution remained incomplete; great changes in
the constitutional balance of power had been suggested but not driven
home'. This summary still seems valid in spite of a recent interpretive trend
to assert the fundamental continuity of constitutional assumptions during
Reconstruction both with those of the pre-war years and with those of the
late nineteenth century. Brock himself anticipated this line of approach
when discussing why neither the concept of strong national government,
nor the fact itself (which had become the central political phenomenon of
the 1860s) was able to gather sustained public support. In the sheer weight
of tradition and the bogey of 'centralism', he pointed to two major
obstacles. The Radicals' attempt to secure civil rights for blacks in the
South without doing anything to secure social justice for farmers or
industrial workers in the North meant that their concept of national power
was too wide for conservatives but too narrow to attract support from
movements of agrarian or industrial protest. Furthermore, the process of
Reconstruction left behind no institutional legacy through which
bureaucratic inertia and vested interest could knit the Radical ideology into
the social fabric when the emergency had passed that had called it forth
and sustained it.[1]

The 'great changes' noted by Brock were those wrought by the three
reconstruction amendments, the Thirteenth abolishing slavery, the Fourteenth establishing legal equality and the Fifteenth ordaining an impartial
suffrage; but whether they could be driven home depended on what men
made of them once they were ratified and part of the Constitution. The
ratification of the Fifteenth Amendment and the re-admission of Georgia
(the last of the Confederate states to remain outside the Union) in the
spring and summer of 1870 represented, therefore, not only the completion
of a process but a new beginning. The real tests were to come when for the
first time since the war Republicans had a real and not merely a nominal
control of both the Presidency and the Congress during Grant's
administration. Only then was there a real possibility of legislative and
executive authority being harmonised on the basis of a valid and legally
completed congressional reconstruction. At the same time the thrust for
legislative supremacy implicit in the reconstruction clashes between
Congress and both Presidents Lincoln and Johnson seemed to have struck

home. Grant regarded his role as primarily that of an administrator; and a surge of congressional activity took over the making of policy as Congress passed more laws than ever before (the Forty-second alone made more than a thousand), codified the existing body of federal law and systemised its own procedures and internal organisation.[2]

In early 1870 the man of the hour was Charles Sumner, at the peak of his political influence in Washington. His writ seemed to run at both ends of Pennsylvania Avenue. The President and his Secretary of State deferred to Sumner on questions of foreign affairs, two of his intimate political colleagues sat in the cabinet (one of them a candidate for the Supreme Court), and the senator was assured of his fill of patronage. Simultaneously, and for the first time in his Senate career, Sumner emerged as the party leader in terms of domestic legislation when he swung the Senate behind him to impose new and exacting fundamental conditions for the re-admission of Virginia and Mississippi. Only he seemed to have a plan to deal with the South's continued civil disobedience, its resistance to national authority and its refusal to countenance any change in its traditional social patterns. For Sumner the only solution was to sweep away racial discrimination in its entirety and thus transform the nature of southern society. Sumner derived the congressional authority to do this from the recent Amendments, the guarantee clause of the Constitution and, above all, from the Declaration of Independence which, as a result of the war, he claimed should now 'stand side by side with the Constitution and enjoy with it coequal authority'. In terms of conventional constitutional theory these arguments were as extraordinary as the policy they justified. The price of re-admission imposed upon Virginia and Mississippi was ratification of the Fifteenth Amendment, open eligibility for office regardless of race and the maintenance of a system of public education. In the course of debate Sumner, in effect, gained senatorial sanction not only for subsuming the New England system of common schools under the concept of a republican form of government, but also, in the words of Henry Adams, for the theory that 'the powers originally reserved by the Constitution to the States are in future to be held by them only on good behaviour and at the sufferance of Congress'.[3]

The ideas that Sumner advanced in this re-admission debate constituted a coherent doctrine of national power that drew on both moderate and radical anti-slavery constitutionalism, in the light of which it claimed an authoritative interpretation of the reconstruction amendments. This doctrine mounted both an explicit and an implicit challenge to the federal consensus which, out of respect for the police powers of the states, had before the war accepted the jurisdiction of the states over slavery and allowed the federal government an involvement only in peripheral areas; and which after the war was reflected in the commitment of the architects of Reconstruction 'to returning the nation and all states as quickly and thoroughly as possible to prewar arrangements, secession and slavery always excepted'.[4] It was this consensus that received its ultimate endorsement in Justice Miller's majority opinion in the *Slaughterhouse* case, that the traditional structure of American federalism had in no significant way been altered by the recent amendments.

The explicit challenge to this consensus lay in the nature of the legislation that the doctrine of national power was used to justify. The Enforcement Act of 31 May 1870 was a federal law outlawing racial intimidation in state and local elections, which could be overseen by U.S. troops and federal officials. The Enforcement Act of 14 July 1870 included congressional elections in large cities. An act of 28 February 1871 (extended to rural areas the following year) specified written ballots and permitted the appointment of federal election supervisors. And the act of 20 April 1871, the Ku Klux Act, allowed the President to declare martial law and suspend habeas corpus in an effort to break the power of the Klan. Taken together, these measures were intended to ensure minimum standards of personal security and to protect political participation not only for blacks in the South, but also for voters faced with intimidation by the urban political machines of the North. To guard against this political participation becoming a source of social instability and to encourage a responsible use of the widened suffrage, various measures to establish a national education system were considered and passed by the House (though not by the Senate) during the early 1870s. Finally, Charles Sumner's Supplementary Civil Rights Bill, which comprehensively struck down racial discrimination, was before Congress in one form or another continuously from 1870 until the eventual passage of a seriously weakened version in 1875; but even this measure was passed only during the final days of the last session before Republicans lost their fourteen years' control of the House of Representatives.[5]

The implicit challenge to the federal consensus by the doctrine of national power lay in the nature of its arguments – arguments that at one time or another were all advanced from the fringes of the political spectrum and which afterwards, therefore, carried with them radical overtones whether or not these were still justified by substance or context. Throughout, the doctrine laid great stress on ideas of the responsibility and the duty of government towards its citizens, refusing to use the Constitution on its own terms but placing it in other perspectives, whether moral, philosophical or ideological. Its textual bases when taken from the Constitution were rhetorical like the Preamble, or ambiguous generalities like the Guarantee clause; or were even extra-constitutional, as in the case of the most important of them all, the Declaration of Independence.

From the moment of its promulgation the Declaration of Independence was used in the cause of anti-slavery, in spite of a clear presumption that if to be taken literally its words were applicable to whites only; but it was not until the Missouri Crisis that the Declaration as an integral part of anti-slavery ideology became a regular and formidable element in constitutional debate and interpretation. Seen in its light and taken together with the Northwest Ordinance, the Constitution seemed implicitly to deny the legitimacy of the expansion of slavery and its Guarantee clause to gain a substantive content (thus alarming southerners who thought that this might challenge slavery within the states); while Rufus King was understood to have maintained baldly that the Declaration simply forbade slavery. This argument, of course, was absolutely basic to the abolitionist movement as it entered its immediatist phase, being written into the constitution of the American Anti-Slavery Society, even while the Society accepted the federal consensus and recognised that slavery within the *states* was both beyond their own reach and that of the federal government. This train of thought eventually entered the mainstream of anti-slavery politics through, successively, the Liberty, Free Soil and Republican parties. And it received perhaps its most clear and powerful articulation in Sumner's 'Freedom National' speech of 1852, where he hailed the Declaration as that 'Great Charter of our country' embodying 'in immortal words, those primal truths to which our country pledged itself with baptismal vows as a Nation'.[6] On the other hand, during the 1840s radical abolitionists argued that Congress not only had the power but the duty to move against slavery actually within the states. In this fundamental rejection of the federal consensus, the Declaration figured not merely as a statement of principles or intent, but as the Constitution itself until the adoption of the Articles of Confederation in 1782. The Declaration thereafter furnished the elemental standard by which all subsequent legislation, its framework and apparatus (comprising constitutions, laws and judgements of courts) had to be judged.[7]

For all abolitionists, whatever their hue, the war amendments did at last make manifest a textual as well as a spiritual harmony between the Constitution and the Declaration, and gave legal credibility to the old assertion that the Declaration was an accepted part of constitutional law. It was from this perspective that Sumner came to argue (on the Ku Klux Act) that while slavery still existed the Declaration had been in abeyance, and that only since the Civil War could it be regarded as anything more than an aspiration. Now had been realised the basic principle of American life, the conjunction of Unity and Equal Rights, both national in character and both expressed in the Declaration. Sumner defined and sought to secure by his civil rights bill the concept of equal protection that he found in the Declaration. Every person, whatever their race or colour, was entitled to receive the same treatment and service in public accommodation, entertainment and transport, and in any publicly supported charitable or educational institution. He was convinced that only by such a measure could the 'the spirit of caste' (of which slavery had been only one expression) be eradicated from American life, and when challenged on its constitutionality he again appealed to the Declaration.

I insist that the Declaration is of equal and co-ordinate authority with the

Constitution itself.... Show me any words in the Constitution applicable to
human rights, and I invoke at once the great truths of the Declaration as the
absolute guide in determining their meaning.[8]

The problem with this line of argument was demonstrated by Rockwood
Hoar (an ex-Attorney General who had reservations about the bill's
constitutionality). If the two were so closely associated, it was all too easy to
write off the bill as a piece of practical legislation and to regard it simply as
the Declaration itself had been regarded, as an essentially rhetorical gesture
standing as a beacon to the future. Nonetheless, for former abolitionists and
anti-slavery men in Congress during the 1870s, the appeal to the
Declaration still held great resonance. John Bingham and George Hoar
(Rockwood's younger brother) both used the argument in their support of
the Ku Klux Act, and the final round of debates on the Civil Rights bill
were as much a tribute to Sumner's own style of argument and sense of
moral imperative as its passage was a tribute to his memory.[9]

If, in the words of Sumner, the Declaration had been the 'baptismal
vows' of the Nation, then the Preamble to the Constitution might be said to
represent its confirmation. The Declaration and the Preamble, after all,
were the two authoritative statements of national purpose, and the
Preamble was commonly regarded by the radical abolitionists as the route
by which the Declaration was incorporated into the Constitution. It had,
therefore, a vital role to play in constitutional construction. For Timothy
Dwight Farrar, the Preamble was not only an integral part of the
Constitution, but the enacting clause of the document as a whole. Pointing
out that whereas strict constructionists generally tried to water down the
effect of those parts of the Constitution of which they disapproved, the only
thing they could do with the Preamble was to try to construe the words
right out of the document. 'This they rightly considered the only way of
avoiding the full drift of general authority and governmental superiority
included in them.'[10] During the war and immediately afterwards this was a
view to command respect, for Farrar was one of the pre-eminent legal
draftsmen of his day, a former law partner of Daniel Webster and a
publicist who had a direct and important influence on the policy-making of
the federal government through his contributions to the 'adequacy concept'
of federal power.[11]

Perhaps the most literal use of the Preamble in these senses, as a guide to
objects of legislation and as a constitutional justification of a particular
proposal, came from George Hoar. Hoar thought that the Preamble was
particularly important as a guide to construction now that the Reconstruction Amendments had made a 'new departure in the Constitution' and
rendered irrelevant the habits of thought that had bound people's attitudes
before the war. From the Preamble's enumerated objects he derived a
considerable proportion of his argument for a national educational system.
And from this he went on to find a national coercive power lodged in the
Preamble, a duty 'to secure the blessings of liberty and promote the general

welfare by prohibiting the States from doing what is inconsistent with civil liberty, and compelling them to do what is essential to its maintenance'. Legrand Perce, the chairman of the House Education and Labor Committee, inherited this style of argument along with Hoar's bill. Consciously trying to avoid a close constitutional argument, he committed himself to a vigorous defence of broad construction. The Founding Fathers had been building not merely for their own day but for the future, and the Constitution must therefore expand with the growth of the nation. There could be no difficulty in reconciling constitutional text with present reality, for the true principle of construction was that 'every clause vesting power in the United States relates back to the principle stated in the preamble'.[12]

But these were restrained and moderate uses of the Preamble compared with what could be read into it. One of the radical abolitionists, Joel Tiffany, had used it as part of his argument to create a paramount national citizenship, and after the war he was prepared to go even further, asserting that the Preamble gave the people of the United States authority to 'establish a national government in such form, and vest in it such powers in respect to the general welfare, as they deem proper', the state governments possessing only a delegated authority. Indeed, Tiffany reads at times as if he thought that the United States had become a unitary state. The Preamble, he said

> ... By its language, in presenting the authors of the instrument, and the grantors of the powers delegated, [it] abolished state lines and state jurisdiction. State individuality was purposely lost sight of.[13]

The Preamble, therefore, was more than a principle of construction; it was in itself an actual grant of power, and one without which the Constitution was but 'vain and vaporing words'. In the Preamble the national government possessed an 'indefinable reservoir of power', argued Purman of Florida, which he used when speaking on the Civil Rights bill to justify the course of legislation since the Fifteenth Amendment.[14]

These two approaches to the Preamble, the interpretive and the positive, were elided by some former abolitionists in Congress who tended to go behind the Constitution and positive law to link the Preamble directly with concepts of natural law. John Bingham emphasised that the equal protection derived from the Declaration of Independence and the due process clause of the Fifth Amendment was an essential part of the establishment of justice specified in the Preamble. His colleague James Monroe, another Ohio abolitionist and a former professor at Oberlin, made the Preamble the centre-piece of his contribution to the Ku Klux debate, arguing that it enumerated the 'great primal object for which constitutions and Governments exist', and which, therefore, Congress had an inherent power to secure.[15]

A further element in the doctrine of national power was the Guarantee clause of the Constitution, and like the others it owed a good deal of its development to the radical abolitionists. Originally intended simply as a safeguard against the reappearance of monarchy within the boundaries of the United States, the clause's generality and ambiguity made it fertile ground for re-interpretation. As with the Declaration of Independence the Guarantee became a commonplace of the anti-slavery argument from the Missouri Crisis onwards, with the assertion that human bondage was incompatible with a republican form of government. Radical abolitionists extended the scope of the Guarantee by linking it directly with the Declaration (according to William Goodell 'that authenticated definition of a republican form of government') and with Madison's majoritarian definition of republicanism in *Federalist 39*, to make it another buttress of congressional power to abolish slavery actually within the states. The 'guarantee', after all, was mandatory, and its exercise in the hands of the 'United States' was unequivocal.[16]

Although the Thirteenth Amendment finally abolished slavery by legislative enactment, it did so as the result of very different circumstances and on the basis of very different arguments; and by this time the reach of the Guarantee had been further extended. During the wartime controversy over the re-admission of Louisiana, Sumner had used the Guarantee to advocate black suffrage. Speaking on the Fourteenth Amendment with the same object in view, he traced the whole history of the concept of republicanism from 'Plato to the last French pamphlet'; and with the Amendment's failure to include black suffrage he went on with Henry Wilson in 1869 to try to enfranchise blacks by act of Congress rather than by constitutional amendment, but still on the basis of the Guarantee. The lack of support generated by this attempt was caused not only by a hostile view of black suffrage itself, but paradoxically also by fears of the reach of the Guarantee 'because it implied a permanent authority in Congress to regulate suffrage in states'.[17]

Sumner's linking of the Guarantee with the New England common school system in the Virginia debate was not as outrageous as some of his political opponents pretended, given the belief in popular education that has always been an 'archetypal element' in American political thought. New Englanders frequently returned to this theme in the following years, as the educational plans of George Hoar and Legrand Perce sought to root republican government in a nation-wide, informed and responsible electorate. The most trenchant expression of this attitude came in George Boutwell's discussion of the educational implications of the Civil Rights bill. For him the school clause was the crux of the bill because 'the public school is the epitome of life'. While the theory of human equality, the principle on which the national government now was based, could not be taught in the family, it could be inculcated in the school. There, he felt, lay the chief safeguard of republican institutions.[18]

Quite apart from the substance that could be read into the concept of a republican form of government, however, the Guarantee also raised the question of the relationship of the state and national governments. It was one thing to use it as the basis for congressional control of recaptured territory during the war, as Farrar had proposed and as Congress had adopted in the Wade–Davis bill. It was quite another to use it after the confederate states had been restored to the Union. Yet it seemed to have an obvious application when the constant feuds within Louisiana bedevilled both state and national politics from 1872 to 1875.[19] Contested elections, the existence of rival state governments and a breakdown of law and order led to intervention by the Grant administration and a succession of requests from the President for Congress to consider the problem. Whereas the strict constructionist equation of 'republican form' with the state constitution itself militated against any congressional action, it was countered by the argument that that constitution could only be given meaning by a government based on the consent of the people freely given in honest elections.[20] As John Bingham summed up the question:

> The nation does not make a constitutional State government, but the nation guarantees it when made. Louisiana has a constitution republican in form, so far as the letter of that instrument is concerned. But what is a written constitution worth to any State of the Union if the powers of government which are essential to its execution are resisted by an opposing force in the State?[21]

Bingham's stress on national action was taken even further by the New Jersey senator and future Secretary of State, Frederick Frelinghuysen. For him the Guarantee clause operated in the Louisiana case because the United States 'is a nation, and not a general agency of thirty-seven states. By the Constitution the States are denuded of many of the incidents of sovereign power'.[22]

Frelinghuysen's reference to the Constitution meant the Constitution as incorporating the Reconstruction Amendments, and the argument from these Amendments, especially that from the Fourteenth, provided the most explicit challenge to the federal consensus to come from the doctrine of national power. The Fourteenth Amendment was seen as having produced a constitutional revolution and to have remade the legal environment. Carl Schurz remarked in debate on the first Enforcement Act 'we are charged with having revolutionized the Constitution of the country by the amendments recently ratified', an accusation in which he took great pride. 'Yes sir, this Republic has passed through a revolutionary process of tremendous significance'.[23] At the same time (although within two years he was to play a significant role in the restriction of the privileges and immunities clause of the Amendment) Matt Carpenter remarked that the Fourteenth Amendment was 'one of the fundamental, one of the great, the tremendous revolutions effected in our Government'.[24] Since this revolution 'the Government of the United States is the *sovereign*'.[25]

A consequence of this constitutional revolution was to introduce at last a consistency of principle into the confused and controversial subject of citizenship.[26] In theory American citizenship was founded on consent (whether overt through naturalisation or implied by birth), and consisted of a single, uniform, status involving a dual membership of state and nation. In practice the consent was qualified by the denial of a right of expatriation which could parallel the privilege of naturalisation; the uniformity of status was a legal fiction belied by the status of women, Indians and free blacks; while dual membership was an acceptable concept only so long as no attempt was made to define the incidents of either, or the relationship between them. Though generally in the North blacks had been accepted as citizens (with rights to liberty, property and access to the legal system), this was accomplished at the cost of a denial to them of the political privileges which the courts had increasingly come to associate with the concept of citizenship. The acceptance of black citizenship was associated with the priority of state citizenship as expressed in the comity clause (the source of the 'privileges and immunities' phraseology), but the ambiguity and reversability of this clause, together with the need to overcome the limitations being placed on black citizenship, led the radical abolitionists Alvan Stewart, Lysander Spooner and Joel Tiffany to postulate the existence of a paramount national citizenship. Paradoxically, the same result could be reached starting from diametrically opposed premises. The creative ingenuity of the abolitionist legal reasoning which equated citizens of the United States with 'We, the people' of the Preamble and the 'all men' of the Declaration was matched by the equally imaginative historical sociology of Chief Justice Taney's picture of an American population in 1789 in which no blacks were citizens, and from which, therefore, they were to be henceforward excluded. However its substance might be interpreted, the concept of a primary national citizenship was rendered authoritative by Taney's *Dred Scott* opinion:

> It is very clear, therefore, that no State can, by any act or law of its own, passed since the adoption of the Constitution, introduce a new member into the political community created by the Constitution of the United States. It cannot make him a member of this community by making him a member of its own.[27]

In the years after the war the Expatriation Act of 1868 and the amendment of the naturalisation laws in 1870 to include blacks together completed the foundation of adoptive citizenship on volition and consent, while the Civil Rights Act of 1866 gave citizenship to the freedmen and the Fourteenth Amendment established a uniform birthright citizenship and defined the relationship between its national and local aspects. In the early 1870s there was no argument about this. The concept of a paramount national citizenship and its consequences for the reach of the national government had judicial and congressional support. Judge Woods, upholding a series of indictments based on the Force Acts, had remarked that since the Fourteenth Amendment had been adopted 'citizenship in a state is the result of citizenship in the United States', and both his judgement and his opinion had the endorsement of Justice Joseph Bradley.[28] Not only the Force Acts but all the consequential legislation based on the Amendments, including the plans for national education and Sumner's civil rights proposals were justified by members of Congress in terms of a primary national citizenship. Even after Justice Miller's majority opinion in the *Slaughterhouse* case had defined the Fourteenth Amendment in a highly restrictive way and gone far toward emptying the concept of national citizenship of any significant content, Frederick Frelinghuysen's uncompromising nationalism (and it was by no means alone) could be heard asserting 'the Fourteenth Amendment goes much further than the old Constitution . . . A citizen of the United States comes under the protection of the Federal Government as to his fundamental rights'.[29]

Whether this was the intention of the framers of the Fourteenth Amendment is still an open question.[30] There is no doubt that the central focus of discussion was not the civil rights clause but the question of suffrage, whether to include black enfranchisement and the extent of rebel disqualification. Even on the question of civil rights the verbal emendation from the positive form 'The Congress shall have power . . .' to the negative form 'No state shall . . .' suggests that the framers retreated from an unqualified nationalisation of rights to a position consistent with the traditional federal consensus in which the states rather than the national government were the fundamental guarantors of the rights of citizens. Moreover the final form of the Amendment was regarded as a betrayal by many radicals. Charles Sumner voted against it and Thaddeus Stevens admitted that it fell far short of his desires.

Nevertheless, there is no getting away from the fact that the Amendment, as an amendment, was designed to place the Civil Rights Act of 1866 beyond reach. Stevens' comment that 'I will take all I can in the cause of humanity and leave it to be perfected by better men in better times' points to the importance of John Bingham's contribution to both the framing and the interpretation of the Amendment.[31] A long-standing abolitionist from the Western Reserve of Ohio and, significantly, a conservative rather than a radical Republican, it was Bingham who was most committed to a national guarantee of the citizen's 'privileges and immunities'. This insistence linked the civil rights clause of the Amendment with the abolitionist political theory based upon a natural law doctrine of equal rights read into the Constitution by way of the due process clause of the Fifth Amendment.[32] One basic problem with that theory had always been its ignorance of the *Barron* v. *Baltimore* judgement that the Bill of Rights restricted federal rather than state action. Bingham, however, had taken care to negotiate that particular difficulty, as he explained when he did take the opportunity in 'better times' to perfect his own handiwork. Chief Justice Marshall had argued in *Barron* that if the first eight amendments had been intended to apply to the states their framers would have imitated the framers of the original Constitution and written in this limitation. 'Acting upon this suggestion', Bingham said in 1872:

> I did imitate the framers of the original Constitution. As they had said 'no State shall . . .'; imitating their example and imitating it to the letter, I prepared the provision of the first section of the Fourteenth Amendment as it stands in the constitution.[33]

The Fourteenth Amendment then could be used both to restrict the states and to allow the exercise of national power. If the positive draft had been adopted, the national guarantee would be secure only so long as backed by congressional will, susceptible to being ignored and vulnerable to the argument that there was no case for its implementation. The restrictive form therefore was in fact a stronger buttress of national power since it prevented discriminatory state action whatever the congressional attitude might be. And it is a significant measure of what many Republicans did understand the Fourteenth Amendment to have accomplished in the early 1870s, that both the Ku Klux Act which outlawed legal and political intimidation and was enforceable by direct national action upon the individual, and the Civil Rights Act of 1875, as near as Congress would ever come before the last twenty-five years to a comprehensive anti-discrimination measure, were both offered on its authority.

Much of the political debate of the 1870s can be read in terms of the distinction drawn between a 'federal' and a 'national' government. This distinction was expressed most pointedly in the range of opinions delivered by the Supreme Court in the *Slaughterhouse* case. Although the separate dissents of Bradley and Swayne, and the minority opinion written by Field all referred to the 'national' government, Miller's majority opinion (delivered with the concurrence of Hunt, Strong, Clifford and Davis) insisted on the use of 'federal' to describe the government in Washington, as it severely restricted the scope of the Fourteenth Amendment.[34]

The decision, of course, illustrated that on a purely legal level the distinction involved determining in particular cases where the boundaries lay between the central and the peripheral authority. And the distinction tended to coincide with the difference between those who thought of their political system in terms of a structure and those who thought of it in terms of a process; between, for example, those who thought that 'the abuses of our Administration have arisen by reason of a perilous departure from the Federal system', and those who believed that 'all great and secure governments, like Topsy, are not made. They grow'.[35]

The political and partisan context of these distinctions, however, meant that the vocabulary of nationhood could never be free from the vices of its virtues. While it promised unity, active government and a purposeful state, it threatened uniformity, repression and centralism. Age-old bogeys these might be, but in the light of contemporary France and Germany they were still very present dangers. It was, however, the social implications of nationhood that made it impossible for a doctrine of national power to overturn the federal consensus in the 1870s. Whereas in Europe the very idea of a nation was based on the assumption of ethnic homogeneity, that assumption was patently false as a description of society in the United States and therefore had to be taken as a goal. Thus Henry Wilson, in the year before he became Vice-President, drew a picture of America as comprising fragments of the decaying societies of Europe and Asia coming together in the new world. It would not be safe 'to leave the character of the new amalgam . . . to depend upon the chance or natural affinities developed by the fusion'. A positive policy of assimilation was needed.[36] This was precisely the cause in which the doctrine of national power had been forged and used, the assimilation of blacks into American society. Yet Americans were not a homogeneous but a heterogeneous people and 'under the 14th. and 15th. Amendments, this heterogeneous citizenship, this blending of civilization and barbarism, there can be no Local Self-Government; nothing but the strong hand of power can control the irreconcilable . . . elements . . . of such a compound'.[37] Here lay the precise virtue of the federal consensus – it restrained that strong hand yet also controlled those irreconcilable elements.

# Chapter 6

# The 'Weakened Spring of Government' Revisited: The Growth of Federal Power in the Late Nineteenth Century

## by Robert Harrison*

> Thus, from one end of the scale to the other, the constituted authorities are unequal to their duty; they prove incapable of ensuring the protection of the general interest, or even place the power which has been entrusted to them by the community at the disposal of private interests. The spring of government is weakened or warped everywhere.

Such was Moisei Ostrogorski's judgement on the condition of American politics at the turn of the century, a judgement which many later commentators have echoed.[1] In a recent essay entitled 'The Weakened Spring of Government', which examines the relationship between the United States Government and the Union Pacific Railroad during and after the Civil War, Wallace Farnham argues that the corruption and inefficiency that characterised much nineteenth-century government stemmed largely from its propensity to provide lavish subsidies and grants of privilege without an adequate measure of direction and control. Instead, government actions were shaped largely by private initiatives. The explanation, he claims, quoting Ostrogorski, lay in men's expectations: 'The notion of the moral objects of the State grew dim in the public mind, the State was asked only to ensure or assist in the production of wealth'.[2] However, while this picture adequately describes government policy during the Civil War era, it is less appropriate to the period when Ostrogorski was writing.

During the closing decades of the nineteenth century, the activity of both state and federal governments expanded considerably. Much of this activity took the form of measures designed 'to ensure or assist in the production of wealth', including subsidies and tariff protection, as well as a mounting investment in applied scientific research. At the same time, the economic development of late nineteenth-century America gave rise to several conflicts of interest, the adjustment of which increasingly required government intervention. Both Congress and the state legislatures passed a variety of measures regulating private business activity, many of minor significance, many ineffectual, but constituting in aggregate what Morton

---

* Lecturer in History, University College of Wales, Aberystwyth.

Keller describes as a 'gradually thickening system of government supervision', which carried important precedents, and important lessons, for the future. The most significant regulatory measures passed by Congress were the Interstate Commerce Act of 1887 and the Sherman Antitrust Act of 1890. The federal government was also forced by a series of railroad labour disputes to confront the problem of labour relations in industrial society. The further elaboration of this 'system of government supervision' was, however, inhibited by the absence of a strong tradition of public administration, which left responsibility for federal regulation largely in the hands of the courts, and the existence of political institutions which were geared primarily to the expression of local interests and the consideration of more traditional forms of economic policy.[3]

Regulatory legislation denoted a considerable shift in emphasis from the dominant pattern of government-business relations during most of the nineteenth century, when, as Robert Lively observes, 'The substantial energies of government . . . were employed more often for help than for hindrance to enterprise'. Numerous studies have revealed the extent of 'public support for business development'. According to James Willard Hurst, the 'working principles' of public policy were 'to protect and promote the release of individual creative energy' and to 'mobilize the resources of the community' so as to enlarge 'the practical range of choices' open to its members. This was done by creating a legal framework conducive to business enterprise, by granting liberal corporate charters and special privileges such as eminent domain and the right to charge tolls on public highways, by subsidising private businesses 'affected with a public purpose', and by protective tariffs.[4] In other words, economic policy was primarily 'distributive' in character; it involved the allocation of resources and privileges to private individuals and groups. Two assumptions were required to justify such liberality: first, that distributive policies were capable of almost infinite 'disaggregation', so that aid to one locality or group need not necessarily preclude similar benevolence to others; and, secondly, that there existed among the various elements of society a 'harmony of interests' such that policies benefiting one group would ultimately redound to the advantage of all.[5]

I

Federal and state governments continued such policies after the Civil War. Congress furnished generous loans and land grants to the transcontinental railroads, as well as subsidies for telegraph and shipping companies. Although the enormous cost of the railroad subsidies, and the attendant corruption, brought such largesse into disrepute, it continued to appropriate large sums for the improvement of rivers and harbours, a project always dear to the hearts of Congressmen.[6]

The high tariff duties imposed during the Civil War continued throughout the period. Advocates of a protective tariff promised security for manufacturers, the cultivation of a 'home market' for American farmers and protection for American workers against the 'pauper labour' of Europe. The two main themes in Republican tariff speeches were the need to guarantee 'American work for American workmen . . . American wages for American laborers', as William McKinley promised, and the manner in which protection worked to the benefit of all sections and all classes. Tariff-making in practice entailed the accommodation of a multitude of special interests, as many, in fact, as there were items in the bill. Protectionist spokesmen, however, successfully contrived its rhetorical transmutation into a programme of national unity and general prosperity, blending both economic and emotional appeals.[7] H. Wayne Morgan and other members of what might be termed the 'Republican school' of Gilded Age historiography see Republican tariff policy as a creative and innovative response to the problems of a developing industrial society, one which 'provided plausible solutions to the dilemmas of economic expansion'. They exaggerate both the effectiveness and the novelty of tariff protection. Its distributive character and its association with concepts of a 'harmony of interests' were its most obviously traditional qualities.[8]

In many respects government research fits neatly into the distributive pattern of nineteenth-century politics. The late nineteenth century saw a proliferation of agencies engaged in various forms of scientific work. The Department of Agriculture, founded in 1862, had as its primary functions the advancement and dissemination of agricultural knowledge. It experienced rapid expansion during the last two decades of the century in response to growing calls for assistance from farmers, particularly those confronting the novel conditions of the western plains. A Division of Entomology was founded in 1880 to tackle the locust plagues then afflicting the plains, and a Bureau of Animal Industry was created in 1884 to help control contagious livestock diseases like pleuropneumonia and 'Texas fever'. Their substantial success in meeting such challenges greatly enhanced the Department's scientific prestige and political influence. Its budget rose from $199,500 in 1880 to $3,272,902 in 1898. The Hatch Act of 1887 extended federal aid to agricultural experiment stations in the several states, and with federal grants went a growing measure of federal supervision. An Office of Experiment Stations was set up to 'indicate lines of inquiry' and furnish 'advice and assistance'.[9] Other significant developments included the establishment of a National Board of Health in 1879 and the creation in the same year of a consolidated United States Geological Survey, which undertook a nation-wide topographical and geological survey, showing special interest in the problems of irrigation and land use in the arid West.[10]

Many of these scientific bureaux were created and funded in response to demands for assistance with specific practical problems, ranging from the irrigation of western lands to the yellow fever epidemic of 1878. Often these demands came from powerful interest groups, whose members became both clients and political supporters. Sometimes their calls for advice and assistance proved irksome. Staff at the agricultural experiment stations, for example, were obliged to spend much of their time analysing soil samples and answering miscellaneous requests for information from individual farmers, rather than conducting research. The scientific activity of government consisted largely of services performed for, and at the request of, specific groups in the population. Charles Rosenberg describes agricultural research as 'a pork-barrel issue easily clothed in the neutrality of science'. However, as they accrued prestige and influence and widened their political alliances, the scientific agencies became better able to set their own objectives and priorities. The growing professionalisation of the scientific community enhanced the *esprit de corps* of their staffs and gave them access to sources of authority and prestige that originated outside the political arena. The gravity of the problems that they were required to deal with sometimes compelled them to assume regulatory functions. For example, the Bureau of Animal Industry was authorised to make regulations concerning the shipment of livestock, while the National Board of Health was temporarily entrusted with the administration of a national quarantine law. As Hunter Dupree points out, 'regulation meant the yoking of science to the fundamental operation of the government. Indeed, it opened the way for the belief that the rational way of science could solve the problems of the nation more efficiently than the chaotic clash of political interests'. Such a belief exerted a growing influence in several areas of policy after the turn of the century.[11]

## II

The development after the Civil War of a complex and integrated national economy with a high degree of functional specialisation and interdependence, the rise of big business and the reorganisation of industrial production gave rise to a variety of conflicts of interest that were difficult to resolve within the framework of the traditional nineteenth-century polity. Reformers like Henry George and Josiah Strong drew attention to the widening extremes of wealth and poverty, while the incidence of industrial conflict bore witness to the mounting tensions between capital and labour. Of greater political importance in this period were conflicts between competing groups of businessmen, for example between railroads and the shippers whose goods they carried, between dairymen and the manufacturers of margarine, or between petroleum producers and refiners. As the market system became 'too remote and massive to be influenced by individuals', notes Samuel Hays, many such groups organised to advance their common interests.[12] They naturally turned to government to redress their grievances, forcing it, in Richard L. McCormick's words, 'to take explicit account of clashing interests and to assume the responsibility for adjusting them through regulation, administration, and planning'. What Hurst calls 'a new disposition of calculation' increasingly entered the policy-making process.[13]

Railroad policy offers a clear illustration of this process. While state legislatures reserved the right to regulate the charges imposed by the railroad companies that they had chartered, before the Civil War they proved reluctant to do so in practice, preferring by the grant of subsidies and liberal charters to encourage transportation development.[14] By the 1870s the discriminatory pattern of rates had created conflicts of interest that made railroad regulation a major political issue. Shippers complained of rates unduly favouring their competitors. 'It is simply in effect letting one man steal another man's business', protested one of their number. Merchants in the Iowa river towns resented low through rates on grain shipments to Chicago, the independent oil refiners criticised the rebates enjoyed by Standard Oil, while New York City merchants protested against the rate differentials favouring rival seaports that had been agreed by the trunk-line pools. In each case the aggrieved parties turned to the state legislatures for redress, but from the mid 1870s they also turned to Congress. The Hopkins and Reagan bills of 1876 and 1878, direct ancestors of the Interstate Commerce Act, were introduced on behalf of the Petroleum Producers' Union, while the New York merchants, if not necessarily, as Lee Benson claims, 'the single most important group behind the passage of the Interstate Commerce Act', were among its most influential and persistent advocates. However, different groups of shippers had different grievances, and, indeed, their grievances were as much against each other as against the carriers, which detracted from their collective influence on legislation.[15] There is much truth in Gabriel Kolko's suggestion that the railroads themselves supported regulation in order to 'establish stability and control over rates and competition', but this is not to accept that they shaped the resulting legislation nor that it necessarily reflected their desires. Pooling agreements, which they wished to be legally enforceable, were roundly prohibited.[16]

The demand for regulation was not merely a product of the aggregation of business pressures but reflected also a public opinion aroused by widespread suspicion of corporate power and fears of 'Monopoly', which at that date was most potently exemplified by the railroads. Benson notes the propensity of New York merchants to don the garb of 'Anti-Monopoly' in their crusade for favourable freight rates. Most Congressmen by 1885 clearly believed that there was widespread public support for regulation, a 'general desire', said Nelson Aldrich, 'that Congress should exercise its unquestioned power over interstate commerce'.[17]

The need to accommodate a variety of interests and points of view produced a measure which contained serious ambiguities and inconsistencies. The Interstate Commerce Act of 1887 prohibited various forms of discrimination in rates but also prohibited pooling agreements which might mitigate the cut-throat competition that was largely responsible for it. It required that rates be 'just and reasonable' but did not stipulate precisely how 'just and reasonable' rates were to be determined.[18] The Interstate Commerce Commission (I.C.C.) created to enforce the act exerted, in its early years, a fairly broad discretion in these matters, permitting certain forms of collusive rate agreement and assuming the right to set rates in place of those that, upon complaint, it found unreasonable. For a while at least, the new law had a discernible impact on the incidence of personal and place discrimination, and it brought a much-needed publicity for railroad affairs.[19] However, the power and influence of the I.C.C. were drastically curtailed by a series of adverse court decisions, particularly that of the Supreme Court in the Maximum Rate Cases of 1897, which denied that the Commission had been empowered to set rates. Equally damaging were earlier court decisions which insisted on a full judicial review of I.C.C. rulings, turning hearings before the Commission itself into mere formalities; the final authority was seen to lie with the courts. By 1900 its impotence was generally acknowledged.[20]

Its troubles stemmed largely from the reluctance shown in the language of the Interstate Commerce Act to vest wide discretionary powers in the hands of an administrative commission, still a fairly novel governmental device. Indeed, it was the proponents of a more stringent railroad regulation who were most hostile to the establishment of a commission, fearing, like John Reagan, that its members would become 'the salaried apologists of the railroads'. 'The people prefer to trust the courts rather than a commission', proclaimed a Grange leader. Americans of this era felt more familiar and comfortable with judicial procedures. The failure of the courts, after the emasculation of the I.C.C., to provide adequate protection for shippers' interests or a sensible and systematic resolution of economic issues of this complexity persuaded many of the need for a powerful commission to administer the law. The experience of 'the first Interstate Commerce Commission' did much to shape the regulatory measures of the Progressive Era.[21]

In response to public alarm at a sudden burst of industrial combinations, Congress in 1890 passed the Sherman Antitrust Act. This made illegal 'every contract, combination . . . or conspiracy in restraint of trade or commerce among the several states or with foreign nations'. The newness of the issue and the 'experimental' nature of anti-trust legislation, together with their own uncertainty as to how far they wished to penalise industrial combinations, left them little alternative, as Senator John Sherman recognised, but 'to declare general principles'. The principles enunciated were not new ones but the 'old and well-recognized principles of the common law', which were now written into the federal statutes, enabling offenders to be prosecuted in the federal courts. The ancient doctrines of restraint of trade and monopolising, however, were neither unambiguous nor easily applicable to the world of modern business.[22] No administrative machinery was provided to enforce the law, so that the federal courts acquired responsibility for the development of anti-trust policy. Despite the discouraging effect of the Supreme Court's dismissal of the government's suit against the sugar trust in 1895, responsibility for the failure to apply the law lay principally with the laggardly presentation of cases by federal law officers. Their indifference, however, was matched by that of Congress and the public, until the combination movement accelerated after 1897. Even then, enforcement was hampered by the ambiguities of the act and the ambivalent attitude towards big business that lay behind it.[23]

Several more specific aspects of interstate business became subject to regulation during this period. To protect the interests of dairy farmers Congress in 1886 imposed a tax on the manufacture of margarine. A series of acts regulated interstate shipments of livestock, and in 1890, to protect overseas markets, a system of federal inspection was introduced covering meat bound for export. Congress also enacted national trade mark and bankruptcy laws and, in a spate of moral enthusiasm, barred lottery tickets from interstate commerce.[24]

The last quarter of the nineteenth century experienced several serious industrial disputes on the railroads, notably the extensive strikes of 1877 and the Pullman boycott of 1894, which forced the development of a federal labour policy, albeit in rather piecemeal fashion. President Hayes dispatched federal troops, at the request of the governors of Maryland, West Virginia and Pennsylvania, to quell disturbances associated with the railroad strikes of 1877. The maintenance of law and order was only one reason for federal intervention. More important was the obligation to keep open the highways of interstate commerce. The Supreme Court, in condoning the Pullman strike injunctions, declared that 'The strong arm of the National Government may be put forth to brush away all obstructions to the freedom of interstate commerce or the transportation of the mails'. The effect of the Pullman boycott, noted Judge William Howard Taft, was 'to paralyze utterly the traffic by which the people live'. The drastic repercussions of major railroad stoppages demanded government action. Until late in the century policy consisted of a series of *ad hoc* responses to critical situations. As in many other areas of policy, responsibility fell primarily upon the courts, who turned increasingly to proceedings in equity as a means of minimising the 'nuisance' created by strike action, issuing injunctions ordering those involved to cease and desist from 'unlawful' actions. The idea of 'nuisance', comment Felix Frankfurter and Nathan Greene, was 'not a very happy or adequate concept from which to evolve law for regulating the clash of conduct in modern industrial relations'. It was also highly prejudicial to the interests of labour. Indeed, the whole drift of federal policy was strongly anti-labour, partly because of the anti-union beliefs of many judges and other government officials, but also because of its reactive nature and its reliance on judicial procedures. Not until 1898 did Congress provide arbitration machinery as an alternative method of resolving railroad labour disputes, but this was rarely invoked.[25]

## III

Although state governments passed a great volume of regulatory legislation during this period covering a wide range of subjects, in certain crucial areas federal power expanded at the expense of the states.[26] Thirty state railroad commissions were in existence by 1903, but their scope was limited by the interstate character of most railroad business. It was estimated in 1885 that three-quarters of all traffic was interstate. Even before the Supreme Court decision in *Wabash, St. Louis and Pacific Railway Company* v. *Illinois* (1886) withdrew interstate traffic from state control, these limitations were becoming clear. The political influence of the railroads combined with the fear of discouraging future investment to lessen the impact of state regulation.[27] By 1890 thirteen states had passed anti-trust laws. Here also legal considerations took second place to the desire for industrial development. Standard Oil, for example, resisted a series of anti-trust suits in Ohio, Texas, Missouri and Kansas by deploying its political influence and legal talent to frustrate prosecution, but also by exploiting the unwillingness of state officials to drive the company to take its business elsewhere.[28] In certain fields the inability of the states to control the importation of articles from beyond their borders made federal legislation necessary to complement state regulatory laws. For example, the federal anti-margarine law followed upon state laws which were frustrated by imports from elsewhere. Congress legislated against lotteries for similar reasons.[29]

Just as advocates of more effective regulation sometimes turned to the federal government, so, in a rather different fashion, did business interests troubled by local laws. Kolko's assertion that railroad managers favoured federal regulation as a benign alternative to 'communistic' state laws does not appear well-founded. Most state commissions were no stricter than the I.C.C. Railroad managers and railroad journals showed no strong preference for either. However, they did show a pronounced disposition to appeal to the federal courts, which they believed to be relatively invulnerable to local opinion and parochial interests. The federal courts were also seen as more sympathetic to employers' interests in labour disputes, so that those who could prove diversity of citizenship sought to transfer cases there.[30]

Despite its supposed attachment to *laissez-faire* doctrines and its supposed fondness for private property rights, the Supreme Court accepted most extensions of federal power during this period. It allowed Congress wide scope in the regulation of interstate commerce, although uncertainty existed as to how inclusively commerce should be defined. In *U.S.* v. *E. C. Knight*

(1895) it drew a distinction between commerce and manufacturing: 'Commerce succeeds to manufacturing and is not a part of it'. Control of the latter lay with the states. On the other hand, in *Champion* v. *Ames* (1903) the Court acknowledged a federal ban on interstate movement of lottery tickets as the only way to crush 'an evil of such appalling character', opening the possibility that control of interstate commerce might permit wide-ranging federal social legislation. In endorsing federal anti-margarine laws the Court appeared also to countenance an equally liberal application of the taxing power.[31]

At the same time the federal courts imposed limits on state legislation. In the *Pensacola Telegraph Company* (1877) and *Wabash* cases the Supreme Court invalidated state laws regulating interstate telegraph and railroad services. 'This species of regulation', proclaimed Justice Miller in the latter case, 'is one which must be, if established at all, of a general and national character, and cannot be safely and wisely remitted to local rules and local regulations'. In several cases federal courts overturned state taxes and regulations which discriminated against out-of-state business. One of their main objects in imposing constraints of this kind was to prevent varying state laws from imposing inconsistent burdens on nation-wide business operations. Interstate commerce, declared Justice Field in *Welton* v. *Missouri,* 'is of national importance, and admits and requires uniformity of regulation'. Local variations in promotional policies imposed no burden on business enterprise. But when governments turned towards more stringent regulation of business activity local variations were potentially damaging. In the long run, the need for uniformity tended to enlarge the role of the central government.[32]

Supreme Court Justice Samuel Miller declared in 1874 that 'there are limitations on power which grow out of the essential nature of all free governments'. A similar belief in 'inalienable rights' animated Field and many of his colleagues. Such 'natural-law' beliefs informed the Court's interpretation of the due process clause of the Fourteenth Amendment as a restriction on state interference with property rights and freedom of contract, a doctrine which was fully developed by the late 1890s. Even then, most state regulatory legislation passed scrutiny on the grounds that it covered matters 'affected with a public purpose' or protected 'public health, morals or safety'. However, the federal courts themselves claimed the authority to determine whether specific measures entered these categories, thereby involving themselves in the consideration of substantive, as well as legal, questions. This is yet another example of the assertiveness of the federal judiciary.[33]

The courts showed little reluctance to assume jurisdiction over complex questions of economic policy, such as industrial relations or the structure of railroad rates. 'The great body of judges are as well versed in the affairs of life as any', claimed Justice Brewer, and well equipped to unravel the 'scholastic verbiage . . . of expert witnesses'. A feature of the developing pattern of regulation was a dependence on judicial processes to adjust conflicts of interest. The uncertainty and hesitancy of legislators, and in some cases, like labour policy, their failure to legislate at all, left large areas of discretion to the courts, who, in the absence of a developed tradition of public administration, filled the resulting 'void of governance'. Only gradually did the employment of expert administrative agencies suggest itself as a desirable alternative.[34]

IV

'The respectability of laissez-faire economic theory, and a pervasive American individualism and localism, worked against any state economic policy'. So argues Morton Keller in his magisterial *Affairs of State*. Certainly the late nineteenth century saw *laissez-faire* and Social Darwinism elevated to the status of almost unimpeachable orthodoxy in American intellectual life.[35] But by such standards most businessmen and politicians were regrettably heterodox. American businessmen showed little hesitation in calling upon government aid or regulation, and American legislators showed themselves frequently willing to oblige. 'Our statute book is filled with provisions which utterly disregard the let-alone theory of government', observed Henry Cabot Lodge, 'and every time we dredge a harbor or deepen a river or open a canal we set it to naught'. The 'release of energy' and enlargement of individual opportunity, not *laissez-faire*, were the principal goals of nineteenth-century economic policy.[36]

Localism was another matter, pervading as it did the entire structure of nineteenth-century politics. It was a powerful force in Congress. 'The members of the Senate and House', observed a Democratic senator in 1881, 'are the advocates and representatives of different local interests all of which naturally seek to influence the transactions of the government on their own behalf'. A Congressman's 'continued success', notes William Brock, writing about the period just after the Civil War, 'depended upon the degree to which he was able to make national influence serve local interests'. Congressmen were highly attentive to their constituents' views on matters of legislation and tailored their votes and speeches accordingly. Their constituents' views were most often expressed with references to local interests in the narrowest sense, and it was these to which many congressmen devoted most of their time and attention. A Pennsylvania congressman, whose legislative proposals were all of local application and whose sole contribution to debate during the Forty-fifth Congress was to offer an amendment doubling the appropriation for a new post-office at Harrisburg, was far from untypical. He was reported to enjoy 'marvelous popular strength'. Congressmen were expected also to attend to demands for patronage, pensions, government publications and other time-consuming departmental business. Even the dignity of the Senate did not provide immunity. 'I am so engrossed with the routine work, and errands and pensions and the like, that I find little time to read, or to study great questions', lamented John C. Spooner. Although some complained of such tedious duties, the rank and file probably relished them as a means of improving their local standing. Since few could expect to spend more than one or two terms at Washington – the average during the 1870s was 2.05 – or think in terms of a career in national politics, their standing at home mattered more to them than their standing on the Hill. Indeed, given such limited expectations regarding the duties of a congressman, it was hard to resist demands that the office be subject to rotation, as was the practice in much of the rural North.[37]

The rapid turnover of members and the parochial preoccupations of many contributed to the legislative incapacity of Congress. Allan Nevins describes the House of Representatives in 1875 as 'a Laocoon struggling against the serpentine constrictions of bad rules, organized obstruction, and lack of responsible leadership'. The rules offered immense scope for dilatory tactics. They were, said William Frye in 1880, 'a body of rules calculated better than anything else to disturb the legislator and to obstruct legislation'. No party leaders had the authority to plan strategy or determine the order of business. What organisation there was was provided by the committee system, but this created a dispersion of power and responsibility among the several committee chairmen. The same lack of party organisation detracted from the legislative efficiency of the Senate, where neither party caucus nor guillotine threatened the individual Senator's freedom of action. Congress convinced many of its incapacity. Charles Francis Adams Jr., as president of the Union Pacific, had many dealings with Congress. 'The fact is', he concluded, 'that in Washington unless there is some great popular demand for a given measure, so small an amount of obstruction suffices to complicate the wheels that it seems almost hopeless to do anything'.[38]

The profusion of essentially administrative business that came before Congress, including such matters as private pension claims or the exact location of mail routes, tended to crowd out the consideration of questions of general policy. That Congress devoted so much time to such detailed business, however, was not so much a distortion as a true expression of its function in the political world of the nineteenth century. Most of its business was distributive in character, consisting not so much of general policies as accumulations of 'highly individualized decisions' catering to the needs of specific groups, which in the disarticulated society of the nineteenth century were usually highly localised. Robert La Folette recalled that in the 1880s

> most of the lawmakers, and indeed most of the public, looked upon Congress and the government as a means of getting some sort of advantage for themselves or for their home towns or home state. River and harbor improvements without merit, public buildings without limit, raids upon the public lands and forests, subsidies and tariffs, very largely occupied the attention of Congressmen.[39]

Another obsessive concern was with the distribution of patronage. Gideon

Welles's oft-quoted comment on post-war congressmen – 'With them all the great and over-powering purpose and aim are office and patronage' – could be applied to the whole structure of party politics. Patronage served as the currency of politics: its allocation was central to the art of party management. This, too was a form of distributive politics, catering to individual demands for the emoluments and prestige of government office.[40]

The party system of the Gilded Age was best equipped to deal with the traditional issues of distributive politics. Party differences had meaning in these terms, with the Republicans pronouncing the virtues of an active national government, ready to use its resources to protect and promote the development of industry and agriculture, a programme still enunciated largely in Hamiltonian terms. Democrats condemned the enlargement of national power and its 'unwholesome progeny of paternalism' in language inherited from the time of Jefferson and Jackson. The party, says Carl Degler, was 'still steeped in the Jeffersonian conception of the limited role of the federal government'. These ancestral ideologies retained meaning with reference to the issues which for so long had provided the substance of national economic policy.[41] This is why the tariff did such yeoman service during this period as a defining issue. As Keller points out, it accorded well 'with the traditional Republican stress on the active state'. In the decades after Reconstruction tariff protection became the central item in Republican appeals to the national electorate, while to the Democrats it served as a common cause to unite its disparate and discordant elements.[42] Party leaders were more at ease with distributive policies, whose impact was widely diffused, than with regulatory policies, which tended to cut across party lines in accordance with sectional and other economic divisions. Voting in Congress on railroad and anti-trust legislation bore little relationship to party identification. Reformers of various persuasions, ranging from Mugwumps to Populists, frequently denounced party politicians for their neglect of the 'living issues of the day'. Some recent historians, such as Morgan, see this view as narrow and biased, arguing that real and important policy differences existed. It depends, of course, which set of issues is under discussion.[43]

Nineteenth-century political parties reflected the localistic character of American society. The hierarchical structure of party 'machines' and the contemporary fascination with 'bossism' obscured the extent to which their strength lay at the grass roots, in the willingness and ability of local party workers to 'get out the vote' at election time and in the loyalty of their electoral support, which, as we now know, was an expression of the group life of American communities, particularly of their religious and ethno-cultural allegiances. They were therefore highly responsive to 'community impulses'. On the other hand, as Robert Marcus has shown for the Republican party, they were notably unable to forge durable national organisations. R. Hal Williams describes the Democratic party of the 1880s as 'a loose grouping of state parties'.[44]

The late nineteenth century was a period of intense party competition.

The narrowness of popular majorities in presidential elections and the continuous alternation of control of Congress and the Presidency militated against positive or consistent decision-making and induced in party leaders a cautious attitude to men and measures. The 1890s, though, was a time of 'critical realignment'. A severe depression during Cleveland's second term combined with debilitating sectional and ideological divisions to produce a sharp and permanent fall in the Democratic vote, leaving the Republicans in a commanding position for a generation. This they read, however, as a mandate for traditional Republican policies rather than as an opportunity for policy innovation.[45] The archaic and anarchic rules of the House of Representatives were substantially revised in 1890, reducing particularly the scope for obstructive tactics by the minority. The Committee on Rules during the 1880s and 1890s was given considerable power to organise the business of the House, acting in effect as a 'steering committee' chaired by the Speaker. These changes created the conditions for responsible party government. David Rothman has traced a similar tightening of party organisation in the Senate around 1890. The aim in both cases was to enable small Republican majorities to enact an ambitious legislative programme. Their programme, however, was decidedly traditional in its composition, including tariff legislation, generous river-and-harbour appropriations and a liberal pension law, as well as a bill to prevent intimidation at the polls. The concentration of power in the hands of a Senate oligarchy composed of men like Nelson Aldrich and William Boyd Allison and a House 'machine' headed by Tom Reed and later, of course, 'Uncle Joe' Cannon did not lead necessarily to innovative extensions of federal power or creative responses to the problems of an urban-industrial society. The regulatory legislation of the Progressive Era was passed by bipartisan majorities.[46]

Regulatory measures cut across party lines. Therefore, political parties proved most unsatisfactory vehicles for their attainment. As Hays observes, pressure groups, or 'functional organizations', as he calls them, offered 'an alternative form of political expression' to political parties. A multitude of interest-group organisations, reform associations and professional bodies appeared during the last decades of the century, and particularly around 1900, ranging from the National Association of Manufacturers to the Anti-Saloon League, both founded in 1895. The growing number of pressure groups seeking regulatory legislation developed a range of lobbying techniques that were largely independent of party organisations, involving the cultivation of close relations with relevant congressional committees and administrative agencies, and the launching of propaganda campaigns appealing directly to public opinion. With experience, they developed a strong preference for bureaucratic procedures over the vagaries of congressional 'log-rolling', which was all too susceptible to constituency and partisan pressures. Hence they welcomed the creation of powerful administrative agencies, like the I.C.C. in its second incarnation. The growing importance of regulatory issues created in time 'a new political order' in which the force of localism and the influence of political parties were substantially diminished. What Walter Dean Burnham calls 'the onward march of party decomposition' was well under way by the first decade of this century, with sharp falls in electoral turnout and straight party voting, and numerous manifestations of political independence and anti-party feeling. While this is a complex, and as yet largely unexplained, phenomenon, it owes much to changes in the issue content of politics.[47]

The late nineteenth century was a period of exceptionally rapid social and economic change, in the face of which American politics seemed stagnant and unresponsive. The period, said Henry Adams was 'poor in purpose and barren in results.' However, Keller remarks that 'American governance was not so much stagnant as it was held in suspension between old and new social values'. It 'felt the effect of industrialization and its social consequences. But . . . traditional values and established modes of governance checked the forces of change'. The clash of interests in an industrial society gave rise to new types of political demand which proved difficult to accommodate within the 'established modes of governance'. Political institutions geared to the politics of distribution coped uneasily with the politics of regulation. Nevertheless, several important measures of this type passed Congress during this period, and the experience gained in drafting and enforcing them was to prove invaluable in the shaping of later policy. The 'spring of government' was significantly stronger at the close of the nineteenth century than it had been a generation earlier.[48]

# Chapter 7

## Means to What Ends? Government Growth and Liberal Reformers, 1910–20

### by John A. Thompson*

The growth of the federal government obviously forms one of the major themes of twentieth-century American history. Although much of the growth is due to the vastly heavier demands of foreign policy and defence, the chief reason for it is the great extension of the government's role in the economic and social life of the United States. This development has generally been attributed by historians to the influence of that tradition of liberal 'reform' which encompasses the progressive movement, the New Deal and the Great Society. 'The twentieth century has produced phenomenal advances in coping with the problems which the nineteenth century transformation of the United States created', writes John Buenker, for example, adding 'Most of the progress can be legitimately attributed to a phenomenon roughly called twentieth century American Liberalism, a development which had its origins in the first two decades of this century'. Otis Graham agrees that, as 'a reformist-humanitarian-pragmatic political creed, ... liberalism has been the most conspicuous force shaping our politics. And, using political power as a lever, it has helped transform American society in the twentieth century'.[1]

That this reform tradition has been both diverse and in some ways ambiguous has been demonstrated by several scholars, not least Graham himself.[2] Nevertheless, it has generally been seen as possessing certain basic characteristics. One is a wish to extend the role of government, which has involved challenging the orthodoxies of free market economics. A second is a desire, in Arthur Schlesinger's famous phrase, 'to restrain the power of the business community'.[3] A third is an avowed commitment to the principles of democracy, equality of opportunity and social justice. Putting these together, Arthur Link has defined 'progressivism' as 'the popular effort, which began convulsively in the 1890s and waxed and waned afterward to our own time, to insure the survival of democracy in the United States by the enlargement of governmental power to control and offset the power of private economic groups over the nation's institutions and life'.[4]

The view that it is, indeed, the gradual advance of this progressive

* Lecturer in History, Cambridge University

movement that accounts for the growth of the interventionist and welfare state in twentieth-century America has been challenged in recent years by historians of the so-called 'organisational' school. Such writers as Samuel Hays, Robert H. Wiebe, Louis Galambos and Ellis W. Hawley have questioned the assumptions of progressive historiography concerning the dynamics of change, the lines of political conflict, and the effects of 'reform'. In seeking what Wiebe has called 'another lens' for 'the proper angle of historical vision', they have concluded that 'the fundamental issue at stake in the history of the progressive period is modernisation'.[5] From this perspective, the rise of the large corporation and the growth of government are seen as parallel, not opposing, developments. As Hays puts it, they both represent 'technical systems' in which decisions are made in an impersonal, 'scientific' way by highly specialised professionals operating in centralised, bureaucratic organisations.[6]

Not only is it 'logical', in Wiebe's words, 'to see these revolutions in power as a single social process', but, according to these writers, there was not in fact an antagonism between the corporate managers of private business and the effective proponents of increased government.[7] A number of monographs and special studies have highlighted the part played by organised business interests in shaping federal economic intervention.[8] 'Such measures as antitrust laws, or railroad, banking, and agricultural legislation in the years from the 1880s on to the Great Depression of 1929', concludes Hays, 'were not so much attempts by the general public to restrict private business in the "public interest", as devices of some segments of private business to restrict other segments when their objectives could not be reached through private accommodation. The results of such legislation should be interpreted as governmental co-operation with private groups in the development and maintenance of a political structure and a decision-making system'. In such areas as transportation and pure food and drugs, 'nationally organised businesses and other interests beyond the confines of a single state actively promoted national regulation'.[9] The progressive interpretation was thus misleading as an analysis of the political process because, as Galambos complained, it 'had isolated businessmen, leaving them an essentially negative role as opponents of the reform measures which (in the liberal view) shaped our modern society'.[10] It was also, according to Hawley, deficient as an approach to the history of political ideas since it had 'assumed a business-government dichotomy' and thus overlooked 'a kind of liberalism standing apart from both laissez faire and welfare statism' that 'articulated organisational ideals having both pluralist and corporative features'.[11]

If the growth of government was promoted by private business interests and organised professionals, conceived in terms of efficiency, market stability and corporate pluralism, and managed by technical bureaucrats, it is not surprising that its effects should neither weaken capitalism nor enhance democracy and equality. That such agencies as the Federal Trade

Commission have generally served the industries they supposedly regulate has become an historiographical commonplace.[12] Similarly, according to Hays and others, the democratic rhetoric of those who pressed for municipal reform was deceptive. 'While reformers maintained that their movement rested on a wave of popular demands, called their gatherings of business and professional leaders "mass meetings", described their reforms as "part of a world-wide trend toward popular government", and proclaimed an ideology of a popular upheaval against a selfish few, they were in practice shaping the structure of municipal government so that political power would no longer be broadly distributed, but would in fact be more centralised in the hands of a relatively small segment of the population'.[13] Hays, indeed, has frequently stressed the inherently elitist implications of the whole process of modernisation, centralisation and specialisation. 'The spirit of science and technology, of rational system and organisation, shifted the location of decision-making continually upward so as to narrow the range of influences impinging upon it', he has argued. Furthermore, 'reason, science, and technology are not inert processes by which men discover, communicate, and apply facts disinterestedly and without passion, but means by which, through systems, some men organise and control the lives of other men according to their particular conceptions as to what is preferable'.[14]

Just as historians in the progressive tradition exaggerate the conflict between business and government, so, Hawley claims, they tend to neglect the conflict 'between the new organisational order and those resisting it'.[15] As Hays sees it, 'a major element of political conflict' was 'a continuous tension . . . between those at different points of the community-society continuum'. 'Local community impulses became increasingly traditionalist and conservative', as was shown by the changing social and political commitments of evangelical Protestantism, and they found effective expression in local legislatures and the geographically-decentralised political parties. But, in the long run, 'one observes a gradual exclusion of local community leaders from the decision-making process which, in turn, involved a gradual exclusion of direct representatives of lower socio-economic groups'.[16]

This revisionist interpretation has secured many adherents in recent years and has given rise to interesting work on professionalisation and reform movements outside the traditional sphere of politics.[17] It does, however, appear vulnerable to the criticism that the concept of 'modernisa-tion', though an attractive characterisation of a broad social change, is not in itself an adequate explanation of any particular course of events. From a world-wide perspective, the process of modernisation has admitted of many variants, of which the American is only one. Therefore, the peculiarities of the American experience require more explanation than can be provided by a simple, homogeneous model of the social implications of modern science and technology. Significantly, one well-known comparative essay sees the

United States as a deviant case of modernisation precisely because of the relative weakness of its central government bureaucracy.[18] This was particularly true before the First World War when, as Robert Cuff has pointed out, there was a 'striking disparity . . . in the pace and level of bureaucratic development between the private and public sectors of American society. Big business outdistanced all others in organisational achievement . . . A federal government which numbered only 256,000 civil servants by the turn of the century could hardly compete with the bureaucratic power available in private hands'.[19]

There are other relevant variables besides the sheer size of government in considering the particular course that modernisation took in the United States. Both the nature and the purpose of government activity are also matters of some importance, as Wiebe himself recognises in *The Search for Order*. 'To what end – or, better, by what inclination – was it all moving?' he asks at one point. 'Bureaucratic management lent itself equally to social control and to social release. In fact each of the new reforms involved a blend of the two'.[20]

On the question of how far these alternatives were clearly perceived at the time, Wiebe is somewhat equivocal. With regard to municipal reform, he suggests that they were. 'By 1905 urban progressives were already separating along two paths. While one group used the language of the budget, boosterism, and social control, the other talked of economic justice, human opportunities, and rehabilitated democracy. Efficiency-as-economy diverged further and further from efficiency-as-social-service'.[21] Elsewhere, however, Wiebe contends that ambiguity of purpose characterised progressivism and that 'its plastic center invited . . . contradictory experimentation'. 'It was not that the exponents of bureaucratic thought sacrificed ends to means but that they merged what customarily had been regarded as ends and means into a single, continuous stream, then failed to provide a clear rationale for the amalgam. Endless talk of order and efficiency, endless analogies between society and well-oiled machinery, never in themselves supplied an answer'.[22]

In order to explore this question further, it is necessary to examine more closely the views of progressive reformers themselves. My focus here will be on the way the question of the role of government was discussed by some of the most prominent progressive publicists in the early twentieth century.[23] In a brief account it will be possible only to outline the general character of their views, but this may help to indicate the broad contours of contemporary political debate and thus provide a context for the detailed arguments over particular legislative proposals and measures upon which some studies have concentrated.[24] I shall pay particular attention to the years around the First World War, since during the war the activities of the federal government grew in a manner that some revisionist historians have seen as both a natural culmination of pre-war trends and portentous of future developments.[25]

There is no question that progressive publicists did seek an extension of the scope of government activity. Indeed, they desired a much greater extension than was to take place. One sphere in which this was so was social welfare. The various state laws that were passed during the Progressive Era regulating the conditions of work of women and children and establishing workmen's compensation by no means satisfied many reformers. As well as the campaign for a federal child labour law that seemed to meet success in 1916,[26] there were several calls for national systems of insurance against sickness, old age, and unemployment.[27] As for 'the industrial program' of progressivism, when Walter Weyl in 1912 sought to sum it up, he had no doubt that its 'most characteristic feature' was 'the emphasis which is laid upon the state in industry'.[28] In this area, too, much more was demanded than was accomplished. There was a good deal of support not merely for regulation but for a fair measure of public ownership. This was particularly true in the case of the municipal ownership of public utilities, which had long been advocated by city reformers like Frederic Howe.[29] At the national level, the government ownership of the railroads was endorsed by an impressively large number of reform journals and writers.[30] Together with that other legacy from the Populist programme, the nationalisation of the telegraph and telephone, it was proposed by Gifford Pinchot in 1916 as a central plank in the platform upon which he sought to rally a number of the leading members of the Progressive party after the body blow inflicted by Theodore Roosevelt's defection.[31] Indeed, many believed in principle in the public ownership of all natural monopolies and natural resources.[32] This specifically included coal mines, and during the serious labour troubles in Colorado in 1914 several well-known progressive publicists, including Weyl, Amos Pinchot and Hamilton Holt, editor and proprietor of *The Independent*, (which had developed from its origins as a religious weekly into a middle-class magazine on current affairs) advocated government ownership as the only solution.[33] Later that year, the newly-launched *New Republic* declared roundly that 'a party which proposes to make itself the custodian of the economic well-being of the American people cannot redeem its promises without undertaking a frankly socialistic programme of industrial reorganisation'.[34]

The grounds upon which this extension of state control were recommended varied and reflected most of the concerns usually attributed to progressives. Municipal ownership, for instance, was seen as a means both of securing more efficient services and of eliminating corruption. For more than a decade after the publication of *The Shame of the Cities* in 1904, Lincoln Steffens used the fame it had brought him to preach to presidents and lecture-audiences alike the lesson that 'municipal ownership would put an end to nearly all the wrong influences that now control many cities'.[35] On the broad question of public ownership, there were within the ranks of reform some with clearly-defined positions. A number of well-known publicists were avowed socialists (at least for a time) and thus theoretically committed to the complete abolition of the capitalist system, although most of those whose writings reached the largest readership consigned the achievement of this goal to the distant future and confined their immediate demands to more limited proposals that attracted broader support. On the other hand, there was an articulate school of thought, the core of which was the Single Tax movement and its weekly journal, *The Public*, that advocated the government ownership of natural resources and of natural monopolies (including the railroads) largely in order to purify the working of the competitive system in the rest of the economy. This position was based on opposition not to size as such but to monopoly, as Amos Pinchot, one of its most tireless advocates, explained. 'We merely want to give everybody, large and small, equal opportunity, and then let business develop to whatever proportions efficiency may dictate'.[36] Progressives of a less doctrinaire bent commonly shared both the predisposition in favour of state intervention in the case of monopolies and the emphasis on the importance of efficiency. 'For some industries you may have to use public ownership, for others the co-operative society may be best, for others the regulating commission', concluded Walter Lippmann. 'It will depend on the nature of the industry which instrument is the most effective'.[37]

Yet if differences of view existed among progressives about the precise nature and limits of government intervention, there was general agreement upon what its basic direction and purpose should be. This was to democratise the control of the economy and to achieve a more equal distribution of its product.[38] The enemy was what Steffens called 'the System', which had been created by a 'revolution which has turned our representative democracy into a plutocratic oligarchy, with Big Business, corrupt and corrupting at the helm'.[39] And, to a remarkable degree, the battle was seen as being simply over who got what. 'The Progressive Movement is radical because it deals chiefly with a more just distribution of wealth', declared Amos Pinchot. 'The whole political question in America seems one of making the poor man richer and the rich man poorer. That is all there is to it'.[40] In 1910, Howe calculated that 'the annual wealth produced in America amounts to $1,170.20 for every family of five, which is just about two and a half times the average wage as ascertained by the census', and concluded that 'there is, therefore, wealth in abundance were it justly distributed'.[41] Citing the report of the Commission on Industrial Relations, George Creel pointed out that the wages received by 'workers in the basic industries' rose only half as much as national income in the years 1890–1912.[42] Such facts constituted the heart of the indictment of the doctrine of *laissez-faire*. 'The automatic fulfilment of the American national Promise is to be abandoned, if at all', wrote Herbert Croly in his ponderous style, 'precisely because the traditional American confidence in individual freedom has resulted in a morally and socially undesirable distribution of wealth'.[43] When in his *Autobiography*, William Allen White felt called on to explain progressivism to a younger generation, he too, concentrated on this issue. 'Our social philosophy simmered down to this: The national income must be shifted so that the blessings of our civilisation should be more widely distributed than they were ... And the shift or redistribution of national income should be achieved by using government where necessary as an agency of human welfare'.[44]

This instrumental view of the role of government did involve challenging an ideology of economic individualism which enjoyed both intellectual authority and popular appeal. But it did not lead either to an uncritical approval of all extensions of state control or to an *insouciance* about the dangers of bureaucracy. That regulatory commissions were, as Amos Pinchot put it, 'likely to become the safeguard of the corporations rather than of the public' was a point made by anti-monopolists and Socialists alike.[45] Nor was there a lack of awareness about the possible conflict between the granting of authority to experts and the principle of democracy. Even such a committed exponent of the claims of scientific knowledge as Chester Rowell, who was perhaps understandably infuriated by the insistence of Californians on their right to choose their own 'healer', proposed only that 'experts ought to have very liberal power of proposing legislation, and a very general duty of reporting on legislation referred to them, and no power whatever of enacting anything ... Whenever the expert fails to convince the inexpert legislators that a certain thing is right or necessary, the conclusion is that the time is not yet right for that thing'.[46] For Howe, one of the virtues of municipal socialism was that, 'with the unit reduced to the city, and with its functions determined by popular control as is done in the New England town meeting, the dangers from bureaucratic or distant control are reduced to a minimum'.[47] Lippmann's journey away from his youthful Socialism owed something to his fear that it had 'within it that great bureaucratic tyranny which Chesterton and Belloc have named the Servile State'.[48]

This did not, however, obstruct Lippmann's recognition that 'without a vivid sense of the possibilities of the state we abandon the supreme instrument of civilisation'.[49] While opposed in principle to bureaucracy, progressives did not generally see it as so immediate a threat to the freedom of ordinary Americans as the power of vested economic interests. As Weyl pointed out, 'what is often interpreted as a limitation of freedom is in effect an increase of liberty, through the protection of some individuals from the hitherto permitted aggressions of others'.[50] Characteristically (but not typically), William Allen White pinned his faith in the racial heritage of the Anglo-Saxon. 'The fact that the surrender to the state of many of the things of life which individuals have hitherto enjoyed, has proved harmful to the Latin races, proves nothing as to the American people', he observed. 'They have an extra supply of individualism, of love of personal liberty, and will guard the liberties they surrender as closely as those they hold'.[51]

In general, then, in the years before the First World War, progressive publicists provided emphatic but discriminating support for the growth of government. There were, of course, differences between them in the extent of their commitment to collectivism and the depth of their anxieties about state bureaucracy. These, however, were not always along predictable lines. In warning against the undemocratic character of 'State Socialism', no one outdid the Socialist writer, William English Walling,[52] while when Amos Pinchot attacked the *New Republic* in 1915 it was for the half-heartedness of their commitment to government ownership. It was the editors of that journal, the ideologists of the New Nationalism, who in their reply stressed that 'the more alert radical thought of Europe and America is profoundly distrustful of this vast extension of government, unless accompanied by an equally vast increase of democratic control'. But both parties to this debate shared the same basic objective, as the editors implied by asking of Pinchot, 'when he had got the railroads into the government's hands, and United States bonds into the safes of the investors, how much nearer would he be to the ending of economic exploitation?'[53] And, with even Walling conceding by 1914 that the state which would result from progressive reforms would be 'very much freer in every direction than any previous society',[54] there was no dissent from the general proposition that accomplishing this objective would require a much greater extension of the role of government than had yet been achieved.

The First World War absorbed much of the attention Americans devoted to public affairs even before most of them had seriously contemplated the possibility that their own nation might become involved in the conflict. Of course, the initial reactions were predominantly those of shock and distress, and, on the part of a good many, of strong sympathy for one side or the other, but there was also a more detached interest in the progress of the war and the performance of the various belligerents. By 1915, a widespread impression had developed that Germany was doing remarkably well and England rather badly, and progressive publicists of all varieties had no doubt that this demonstrated the superiority of collectivism to *laissez-faire*. Before the war, several of those who had visited Britain had been struck by the strength of the class system, and to Croly in *The Promise of American Life*, England illustrated the inadequacy of the principle of individual freedom as a basis for 'national cohesion'.[55] So it was not surprising that the *New Republic* regarded Britain's difficulties in the war as 'retribution'. 'To their dismay, the English are discovering that a business anarchy which never served any purpose, which was simply an individual struggle of caprice, habit, accident, privilege and speculation, cannot suddenly be transformed into an organization national in scope to serve a definite end'.[56] By contrast, Germany had long been cited as a model by reformers, and not only in respect to municipal government.[57] Howe, for example, was engaged when the war broke out in writing a book which, after describing the wide measure of public ownership and social welfare there, concluded that 'the experience of Germany disproves many of the arguments against the possibility of a socialist state'.[58] When it was published, he sent a copy to Colonel House with the note that 'it explains the efficiency of Germany at war'.[59] This idea was widely promulgated. 'The one thing that is keeping Germany on the war map today, with civilisation practically united against her', White explained in April 1915, 'is the fact that for the fifty years last past Germany has followed a consistent program which has made the living standard of the poor higher and has developed strong hard men to stand the impact of war'.[60]

In a more immediate sense, the view that the efficient mobilisation of a nation's resources required an extension of government power seemed amply confirmed by what the *New Republic* called 'the landslide into collectivism' in all the belligerent countries.[61] Reports from Britain on the measures by which the government was asserting its authority over industry and showing a new concern for the condition of the workers were received by progressive journals with particular satisfaction.[62] The lesson seemed obvious. 'If in a great crisis, private initiative and the motive of self-interest needs to be replaced by governmental initiative and the motive of common interest, how do we know that there might not be a corresponding advantage in ordinary times from the exercise of public control?' wrote Edward T. Devine, associate editor of the social work journal, *The Survey*. 'This huge laboratory of trench and submarine and munition factory is trying out experiments pregnant with instruction for us'.[63]

There might well appear to be no more telling indication that progressives were at heart elitists who worshipped at the shrine of efficiency than such wholehearted endorsements of war socialism on the grounds that it was conducive to success in the Darwinian struggle between nations. However, there are reasons for doubting that this would be the correct interpretation. One is that the more authoritarian features of the model were specifically repudiated. 'It is a grim collectivism which Europe has established', the *New Republic* observed. 'It is dominated by a class and operated in the main by a bureaucracy. It has scant respect for liberty, it works through fear and compulsion'.[64] Devine agreed that 'the centralized despotism made necessary by military extremity is, of course, no real precedent for industrial democracy'.[65] Similarly, even those most enthusiastic about aspects of the German system emphasised that 'it is not the socialism to which the Social Democratic party aspires; it does not involve control by the working classes. It is the socialism of the ruling caste, the great estate owners and the capitalists'.[66]

Moreover, there seems little doubt that this whole line of argument was mostly tactical. By pointing out that German success was largely owing to a system of industrial organisation and social welfare similar to that advocated by the Progressive party in 1912, White suggested to Theodore Roosevelt 'you could inject a vast amount of social and industrial justice into the people rather hypodermically'.[67] This element became even more evident during the debate over 'preparedness' which developed in 1915 and 1916. Progressives of all varieties argued that the war in Europe had demonstrated that 'real preparedness' must involve the social and economic reforms they had long been advocating.[68] The *New Republic* urged reformers to use the issue as a 'Trojan Horse'. 'Nor is there anything double-faced about the idea', the editors maintained. 'A planless society cannot suddenly become purposeful, a disrupted people cannot achieve a lasting unity, a nation corrupted by bitter feuds, by rankling injustice, by thoughtless education will reveal itself hideously in time of war. Those who are complacent about the horrors of peace . . . may at least be ready to deal with it for the sake of military preparedness'.[69] A nationalist like Croly could reasonably claim a certain consistency, but there was surely something a little disingenuous about such a noted anti-militarist as Amos Pinchot extolling the example of Bismarck in the pages of *The Public*.[70]

Nevertheless, Pinchot's argument showed that there was a good deal of agreement among progressives over the domestic implications of belligerency despite their differences on the issue of military preparedness. To some extent this survived even the much deeper division of opinion which arose in the spring of 1917 over American entry into the war. It is true that those who opposed intervention emphasised that it would strengthen reactionary forces within America. Apart from the threat of conscription, which some insisted was 'in essence slavery',[71] civil liberties, particularly freedom of the press, were likely to be severely curtailed.[72] Moreover, the requirements of mobilisation might be made an excuse for reversing some of the advances, particularly in the field of minimum labour standards, that had already been made. 'War will check the forward movement of labor', Amos Pinchot warned Samuel Gompers, 'suppress the radical impulses of the nation and put the average citizen in his place – the place that the industrial absolutist and bureaucrat wants him to occupy'.[73] Some of this case was conceded by supporters of intervention. The *New Republic*, for example, acknowledged that 'war always brings with it a tendency to intolerance' and advocated the establishment of a national organisation for the protection of free speech.[74] But in common with most pro-war progressives and socialists it emphasised the opportunities the war would bring to extend the role of government and improve the standing of labour. 'Liberals who can gain public attention will have a chance to put to good use the forced draught of patriotism', the editors added. 'The financing of the war offers an opportunity of redressing some of the inequalities in the distribution of wealth against which social reformers have long been protesting in vain'.[75] The energetic and moderately successful lobby that was set up to press this cause, the American Committee on War Finance, was, however, headed by the anti-war Amos Pinchot.

The wartime experience did much to confirm both the fears and the hopes of progressives. Although these publicists differed in the extent to which they expected civil liberties to be maintained inviolate in a nation at war, it was not only those who had opposed intervention who were disturbed by the censorship and the prosecution of dissenters under the Espionage and Sedition Acts. On the other hand, the extension of government control, through the War Industries Board, the Food and the Fuel Administrations and the take-over of the railroads in December 1917, was seen as a vindication of their long-held views[76] and a turning-point in American history. 'What war impels us to now we will learn to value too much to throw away', prophesied *The Independent*, which called for a sweeping extension of public ownership: 'after the railroads, the coal mines, the telegraph and telephone lines – in fact every natural monopoly of national scope'.[77] There were some qualifications to this enthusiasm. Both *The Independent* and the *New Republic* saw this wartime collectivism as too 'bureaucratic' and authoritarian,[78] and Croly became persuaded of the need to build up 'class, trade and professional associations which will compete with the state for the loyalty of its citizens'.[79] Some had their doubts about the motives of those managing the new agencies. 'The Big Businessmen have been running things absolutely', Gifford Pinchot reported to White. 'They are true to type and have been making large profits for themselves in certain cases'.[80] 'I am myself very fearful of government price-fixing', Amos Pinchot wrote a year later. 'That is what the Steel Corporation has been longing for since 1908'.[81] However, others were more optimistic. 'The Big Businessman', Weyl noted in his diary, 'has become in places the servant of the public'.[82] The activities of the National War Labor Board were a particular source of satisfaction. The new attitude of the government towards labour, Howe thought, 'exceeds anything the most optimistic reformer felt could be achieved in a quarter of a century'.[83]

This optimism persisted briefly beyond the Armistice. Not only the institutional innovations but the cooperative spirit engendered during the war seemed to many progressives to provide a rare opportunity for a decisive advance. The plethora of proposals they produced for 'reconstruction' were very much in line with their pre-war ideas, and were similarly designed to move the United States in the general direction of social democracy. But the rapid dismantling by Congress of the wartime agencies and the reactionary political climate of the post-war years produced disillusionment. In some it aroused misgivings about the way government would use its power. Howe, much affected by his experience as Commissioner of Immigration in New York during the Red Scare, became, in his words, 'distrustful of the state'.[84] It was, he wrote in 1921, 'little more' than 'an agency of an economic class' and 'an agency of suppression'.[85] Similar views were expressed not only by Amos Pinchot,[86] but also, more remarkably, by Croly, who in December 1919 concluded that 'the state, as now organised, is essentially the embodiment of power rather than justice', and pinned his hopes on the emergence of some form of pluralism.[87] On a more specific level, when the labour disputes of 1919–20 led to proposals for compulsory arbitration laws, several progressive publicists were to be found stressing the arguments for freedom from government interference.[88] None of this, however, involved a fundamental re-appraisal of their social ideal. 'I made one reconciling discovery: my dreams – the things I wanted – were still alive under the ruins of most of what I had thought', recalled Howe. 'I wanted a world of equal opportunity . . . and all of the wealth that human ingenuity could create, dispensed as its creators desired'. 'I still wanted all this', he concluded. 'But I had been wrong about the way to get it'.[89] One way that seemed unpromising in 1920 was that of the ballot box. 'In this abominable election', Croly complained in October, 'every attempt . . . to give effective political expression to the aspirations of a progressive to make his vote count on behalf of human liberation . . . becomes pale with unreality'.[90] 'What a God damned world this is!', wrote White to Ray Stannard Baker following Harding's triumph. 'If anybody had told me ten years ago that our country would be what it is today, I should have questioned his reason'.[91]

One could reasonably conclude from this account of the attitudes of progressive publicists to government growth that they were, indeed, among the apostles of modernisation. They insisted that the traditional American practice of unregulated market competition was outmoded, and one of the grounds on which they did so was that it was inefficient and disregarded the claims of expert knowledge. As Samuel Haber has pointed out, several of them were enthusiastic about scientific management.[92] But although, as we have seen, they invoked the claims of efficiency in, for example, pressing the case for municipal ownership, determining the appropriate form of public control in different industries, and preparing the nation for war, it is surely clear that it was not their fundamental value or concern. This might be described as being to realise 'the promise of American life', as it had traditionally been conceived, in terms of democracy and opportunity for the average man, and they sought to exploit the potential of technological advance to this purpose. The major instrument for achieving this programme was, of course, government, but their support for an extension of its role was conditional on its being egalitarian in effect and democratic in method. In short, it was a means to an end, and, in Wiebe's dichotomy, the end was 'social release' rather than 'social control'.

However, a further conclusion which emerges from this review of the writings of progressive publicists is that for the most part they failed to achieve their goals, and they knew it. Before the war, they were strong critics of the status quo, which they believed required fundamental reforms that would include a substantial increase in the sphere of government. Their attempt to exploit first the preparedness movement and then American intervention in the war to promote such reforms gained at least some of its impetus from a general recognition that, with the demise of the Progressive party and the steady gains of a Republican party under 'standpat' control, the prospects of achieving them through electoral politics were not bright. Despite its more repressive and undemocratic aspects, which caused some of them to reassess somewhat their commitment to the enhancement of government power, the experience of the United States during the war generated hopes that a drastic and lasting transformation of the American political economy had been initiated. But these hopes were to prove illusory and by 1920 most of these men were in a state of despair. Neither the extent nor the nature of the government's role in the economy in the 1920s reflected their aspirations.

These conclusions bear upon the conflicting historiographical approaches to the growth of government in this period. The sense of failure of these progressives, and the good grounds they had for it, suggests that their responsibility for the sort of changes that did occur in the United States in these years was much less than traditional accounts implied. It is true that some critics of the revisionist historiography have recently argued that the way government intervention came to operate in practice did not necessarily reflect the goals of those who established it. 'What the organisational thesis mainly lacks', Richard L. McCormick has concluded, 'is the sense that political action is open-ended and unpredictable. Consequences are often unexpected, outcomes surprising when matched against origins'.[93] However, even surprising outcomes still have to be explained. They may, indeed, result from confused thinking on the part of the initiators of change, but the evidence here suggests that in this case they generally reflected the simple fact that other actors on the political scene were more effective than liberal reformers, both electorally and behind the scenes. This possibility might be directly confronted more often were it not for the common use of the term 'Progressive Era', which creates an expectation that those who were indubitably 'progressives' played a dominant role.

Nonetheless, these publicists were energetic contributors to the political debate of the time and the views they expressed played a substantial part in shaping the issues as contemporaries perceived them. It would, however, be hard to place these views unequivocally on either side of a battle 'between the new organisational order and those resisting it'. The case of these progressive publicists reminds us that not all history's losers were clearly associated with 'the past'.

One might say, therefore, that traditional progressive historiography provided a reasonable guide to the contours of political debate and conflict, but an inadequate account of the historical process. By contrast, the 'organisational' school may well offer a more illuminating analysis of the long-term changes in American society, including the growth of government that actually occurred, but a misleading perspective on the political issues of the time. To see political divisions as between 'the future' and 'the past', as both these interpretations essentially do, is usually a mark of a teleological philosophy of history. Perhaps the tendency to conflate the issues of political conflict and historical change is further testimony to what J. R. Pole has called 'the persistent force' of 'the American extension of the Whig interpretation of history'.[94]

# Chapter 8

## At the Gates of the White House:
## The Washington, D.C., Race Riots of 1919

### by Adrian E. Cook*

In the summer after the Great War ended, the capital of the United States was a confused, uncertain place. The dollar-a-year men who had come to Washington to run the war effort were going home to their businesses in Pittsburgh and Detroit and Akron, and the temporary civil servants who had staffed the emergency bureaux could see their jobs slipping away. The makeshift huts that had served as offices still dotted the Mall, and the hastily erected 'tempo' blocks of war workers' housing still filled the plaza outside Union Station, but every day there were more empty desks, more vacant spaces. The very fabric of war-induced federal power suddenly looked impermanent.

The War was over, but peace was not yet established. Newspapers told of a world in chaos: kings and empires, dynasties and thrones were falling like rotten apples in a high wind. There was a Bolshevik government in Moscow, and another in Budapest. In Germany, an insecure republic was beleaguered by forces of the Right and the Left. All over Central and Eastern Europe there was fighting and *coups d'état*, and White Terror succeeded Red Terror.

Corresponding waves of hysteria swept the United States, as Americans were gripped by fearful dread that bloody revolution was imminent. In paroxysms of fanatical superpatriotism and xenophobia, radicals, socialists, communists, Wobblies, anarchists, foreigners – any kind of dissident or social deviant – were attacked, beaten, jailed, sometimes killed. Their parades and processions were mobbed, their offices were wrecked, their journals and newspapers were suppressed.[1] Behind the mob frenzy and the lynch law, there was an ideology: Americanism. The nation was purging itself of alien influences and foreign values, reasserting the standards of late nineteenth-century northeastern WASP culture, and experiencing a grass-roots cultural revitalisation movement[2] that can be aptly compared to the fall of the Shah and the rise to power of the Ayatollah Khomeini in Iran. From 1919 to 1920, the United States underwent a successful counter-revolution.[3]

There were other things that upset Americans' psychic equilibrium in

---

* Reader in History, University of Reading.

those months. A great influenza pandemic had just swept over the land, killing between 400,000 and 500,000 people.[4] 'H.C.L.' – the high cost of living – was worrying everyone, as the wartime inflation continued, and wages fell further and further behind prices. The sudden cancellation of war orders, and other problems of converting the economy back to peacetime, led to serious unemployment. Returning veterans were cheered in the victory parades – and then found themselves jobless.[5]

No city in the nation was harder hit by this problem than the federal capital itself, Washington, D.C. As well as coping with its own ex-servicemen, the city had to play host to numbers of young men who received their discharge at one of the many military bases ringing the District of Columbia, and then decided that they had no desire to go back to their homes. Though they might not have seen Paree, they could not be kept down on the farm after they had seen Brest or New York, or even Camp Meade or Fort Myer. Other veterans came to the city because their wives were 'government girls', temporary civil servants hired during the war.[6] Throughout 1919, Washington was full of demobilised soldiers and sailors, hanging around the streets and the near-beer saloons, often still wearing their uniforms because they had no other clothes.[7] The presence of so many bored, resentful and restless young men, trained in violence, added a dangerously combustible element to the city's life.[8]

Another was the tension between Washington's 340,796 white inhabitants and its 114,632 Negroes. In the 1870s and 1880s, Washington had been the cultural capital of black America, the best town in the nation for able and ambitious Negroes. But the worsening state of race relations in the country allowed the prevailing Southern folkways of the surrounding states to invade the District of Columbia, and by the first decade of the twentieth century white and black Washingtonians lived completely separate lives. There was not a single white hotel, restaurant or cafe that would admit Negroes, and theatres confined them to the 'buzzard roost'.[9] The District civil rights law was not repealed, but it was never enforced. The Negro members of the Washington Board of Trade, knowing that they were not welcome, resigned. Negro ladies withdrew from the local Womens' Christian Temperance Union chapter, at the request of the whites.

It is in the context of worsening race relations that the Washington of 1919 becomes a fitting case-study in the exercises of federal power. In 1878, at a time when forces of localism and individualism were predominant in the United States, the federal government had enlarged its activities in an unusual way. In one of the very few examples before the 1930s of federal power expanding without the stimulus of war, Congress made itself into a municipal, as well as a national, authority: it suppressed all local democratic institutions in Washington and set out to rule the national capital directly. Under the Organic Act of 1878, three commissioners, appointed by the President, were to govern the city, under the eye of House and Senate Committees on the District of Columbia. Two of the commissioners were to be civilians who had lived in the District for at least three years, and their appointment required the advice and consent of the Senate; the third was to be an officer of the U.S. Army Corps of Engineers. To console Washingtonians for their loss of home rule, Congress promised to pay half the cost of governing the District. In the main, this system worked well. Washington was a medium-sized city which did not have to absorb large numbers of immigrants, or cope with vast, growing industries; the Commissioners provided honest, efficient, economical and unadventurous administration, and the federal capital won the (not altogether justified) reputation of rivalling Milwaukee as America's best governed metropolis.

It remains true that neither whites nor blacks enjoyed the right of self-government in the District, and that the blacks suffered much more from the effect of 'Congressional colonialism'. Very few Washington Negroes objected to the Organic Act when it was first passed. In 1878, there were still black Representatives and a black Senator who could look after black Washingtonians. But as the Southern delegations in Congress became all white, and as Americans forgot that their country had once pledged itself to ideals of racial equality, the Commissioners and the District Government became utterly indifferent, if not actively hostile, to the interests of the city's Negroes. By 1912, Washington, with a black population of 94,446 (20,000 of whom were taxpayers), employed barely 900 Negroes, half of them unskilled labourers earning $500 a year or less, and most of the others teachers in the segregated schools.[10]

The inauguration of Woodrow Wilson as President the following year made matters still worse. Wilson's southern Cabinet members, such as Albert Burleson, Josephus Daniels and William Gibbs McAdoo encouraged the adoption of segregation in their departments, and Jim Crow invaded the federal Civil Service. At the same time, southern senators did everything possible to bar Negroes from the dozen or so diplomatic and second-rank administrative posts traditionally reserved for them by Republican administrations. By the end of Wilson's first year in office, most blacks had concluded that the New Freedom was for white men only.[11]

Wartime housing problems made racial tensions worse. The vast expansion of the federal bureaucracy meant that the population of Washington jumped from 359,997 people in 1916 to 455,428 in 1919, but the stock of housing did not increase at all: indeed, because of the slum clearance that was part of the scheme to realise L'Enfant's original plans and construct 'monumental Washington', there was already a shortage of cheap accommodation before 1917. 'The great Union Station swarmed, day and night', wrote one observer of wartime Washington. 'Young women arrived by every train to do 'war work', coming with the magnificent trustfulness of youth without a thought as to where they should lodge or how they were to be fed after they arrived. It was literally true that householders who lived on a car line might answer a ring at the door-bell late at night and find standing on the step an obviously 'nice' girl, suit-case in hand, who was at the end of her physical and emotional resources and begged to be taken in for the night'.[12]

Not much of the increased population of the city was black. The only major employer in the District of Columbia, the federal government, had little need for unskilled labour, and so the Great Migration of Negroes from South to North in the years 1915–18 mostly passed Washington by. Only about 16,500 blacks came to live in the city, but so desperate was the housing shortage that even that number of new residents helped to give the impression that a black tide was sweeping over the capital. As always, Negroes were a highly (and tragically) visible minority, but although there were some neighbourhoods, like South West, Anacostia and the quadrilateral in North West of New York Avenue, 1st Street, Florida Avenue and 14th Street, where the population was between one-third and one-half black, there was no distinct Negro ghetto in Washington. Negroes lived all over the city, in the alleys behind the huge old houses occupied by the whites.[13] Only in the newer suburban areas across Rock Creek Park and in North East, beyond Florida Avenue, was the Negro population less than $12\frac{1}{2}$ per cent of the whole.[14] In most neighbourhoods, it was easy for whites to get the impression that blacks were about to swamp them.

The press, which might have been an ameliorating force, inflamed the racial crisis. None of Washington's four daily newspapers – the *Post*, the *Times*, the *Herald* and the *Evening Star* – showed any sympathy for blacks. All put heavy emphasis upon reports of increased crime, especially crime committed by Negroes, in the first six months of 1919. It would have been strange indeed if the social upheavals of wartime and Washington's swollen population had not led to a rise in crime; other American cities had the same experience, and the District's crime rate was no worse than most. Crime by Negroes had actually diminished during the war years. But this did not stop the newspapers from talking of a Negro crime wave, and splashing lurid stories of black attacks on white women on their front pages day after day in late June and early July, 1919.

Public indignation over these reports led the Washington police to conduct energetic sweeps and searches in predominantly Negro areas of the city. As usual in any lower-class area of any city in any country, patrolmen acted with a great deal more zeal than tact, and rarely bothered about such niceties as search warrants or probable cause for arrest. Relations between the police and the capital's blacks had never been good, and since Prohibition had come to Washington at the end of 1918,[15] they had been deteriorating further: in the familiar pattern of a spurned minority group finding wealth and opportunity by supplying illicit services to the majority, Negro boot-leggers had wasted no time expanding their activities, and had, inevitably, fallen foul of the police. By midsummer 1919, most Washington Negroes had concluded that they could expect nothing from the police: no justice and no protection.[16]

This was a blemish on a generally good reputation. By American standards, the District of Columbia Metropolitan Police was an honest and efficient force. It enjoyed great advantages over other U.S. urban police departments: it operated in a city of manageable size, with a fairly homogeneous and law-abiding population. The only major employer, the federal government, did not pay graft (did not need to, since it could draft the laws to suit itself), and the absence of local politics removed another source of corruption. And, above all, it was organised on a paramilitary basis, the only possible way of maintaining discipline in the lower ranks of a police force in the materialistic and socially-mobile American democracy. The force even used military rankings: the chief of police had the rank of Major, and the patrolmen were privates.

In 1919, the quality of the Metropolitan Police was not as high as it had been before the war. Like other public services, its wages had not kept pace with inflation, and there were 140 vacancies on the force. In April 1919, the chief of police, Major Raymond Pullman, admitted that 'with our present rates of pay, we cannot hope to attract the sort of man we must have in sufficient numbers'. And although the population of Washington had grown, the police had not. In order to protect the city properly, and provide an adequate guard at the White House and the foreign embassies, the Metropolitan Police needed at least twice as many men, if not three times as many, as it could muster in July 1919. Finally, only thirty-one of the 856 men of the D.C.M.P. were Negroes, and the local black newspaper repeatedly charged that only rampant prejudice prevented the recruitment of more.[17]

By the middle of 1919, the press, the police and the black community were all convinced that Washington was a racial powder-keg with a desperately short fuse.[18] The tinder was soon struck. About ten minutes past ten o'clock on the evening of Friday July 18, a nineteen-year-old girl called Elsie Stephnick left her job at the Bureau of Engraving and Printing, and started to walk home down D Street, S.W. On the corner of 12th Street, S.W., two Negroes jostled her and tried to grab her umbrella. She refused to let go, and the two took to their heels when several of Mrs Stephnick's fellow workers came to her help. The Negroes were not caught, but Major Pullman, probably anticipating strong public reaction to such an incident on a brightly-lit street in the heart of the city, ordered his patrolmen to stop and question any young man, white or black, seen loitering in suspicious circumstances or in lonely parts of the city.[19]

Next day, the streets of Washington were crowded with soldiers, sailors and Marines on weekend leave or liberty, as well as the usual groups of ex-servicemen and civilians seeking relaxation and entertainment. Mrs Stephnick's husband worked in the Naval Aviation Department, and after hearing of the attack on her, a couple of fliers decided to exact revenge. Led by Petty Officer Eugene Paul Shafer of the Naval Reserve Flying Corps at Anacostia, and Private E. H. Moore, an Army airman stationed at Bolling

Field, a group of sailors and Marines began to buttonhole servicemen outside the Knights of Columbus Hut[20] at Pennsylvania Avenue and 7th Street, N.W., urging them to join in a 'clean-up'.

Just after 10 p.m., about a hundred servicemen, joined by three hundred or more civilians, moved off to the South West section of the city in search of a Negro called Charles Linton Ralls, who had been interviewed by a detective that afternoon on suspicion of being one of Mrs Stephnick's assailants. Ralls was found on 12th Street, S.W. between C and D Streets, and given a merciless thrashing. As some of the mob began shouting that he ought to be lynched, Ralls managed to break away from his captors and ran for dear life towards his home, 1209, Carlin Court. Several servicemen drew their revolvers and fired at the fleeing man. Negroes in the area began to barricade their houses, and prepare an attack on the mob, but a strong force of police and seventy-five men of the provost guard (ordinary G.I.s serving as federal military police) arrived in the nick of time, and persuaded the whites to disperse. Shafer and Moore were arrested half an hour later, outside the Knights of Columbus Hut. Police patrolled the streets of South West for the rest of the night, but there was only one serious incident. Private Frank McGrath, accompanied by another policeman, challenged a Negro who was standing at the mouth of an alley at $4\frac{1}{2}$ and D Streets, S.W., at 2.15 a.m. The Negro, who obviously had strong reasons for not wanting to be questioned or searched by the police, drew a gun, fired and seriously wounded McGrath, before making his escape.[21]

Sunday July 20, was a searingly hot day. It was ideal rioting weather, but the city remained calm all day, and if Major Pullman had only taken the precaution of keeping large reserves of police near Pennsylvania Avenue further trouble might well have been avoided. But, as he told reporters, the police chief was convinced that the march on South West the night before was nothing serious, merely the work of 'a few hot heads'. An hour after Pullman's press conference, a veteran policeman took a different view: 'hell', he said, 'was popping'.

Just before ten o'clock in the evening, a young Negro called Isaac Payne was arrested at 9th Street, N.W. and Pennsylvania Avenue. A crowd of soldiers, sailors and Marine gathered, harsh words about Negro criminals were exchanged, and Payne was seized and beaten over the head. Luckily, the First Precinct patrol wagon arrived on the scene and Payne was rescued, but the men in khaki and blue were aroused now, and they were spoiling for trouble. Two blocks down the Avenue, on the corner of 7th Street, N.W., they spied a group of Negroes, and there was a brief fight. Three Negroes were knocked out, and the rest scattered. The mob marched on, into Lafayette Square, attacking every black they saw. The few policemen in the area were helpless. For the first time in American history, a race riot was motorised, when taxi-cabs were commandeered and used to search for targets. A couple of moving streetcars were boarded, and Negroes inside roughed up, as white passengers watched. In the often surreal fashion of civil disorders, some social conventions and discipline were still observed, in the midst of all the law-breaking. When rioters invaded Childs' Restaurant in search of Negro busboys, they were persuaded to leave on the ground that they would upset the ladies who were enjoying their dinner there, and towards midnight, things quietened down in the streets, as many of the servicemen returned to barracks because their weekend leave or liberty was over. Some gangs of rioters remained active, though, and in the early hours of the morning one group clashed with some Negroes at 10th and L Street, N.W., and then met over 100 blacks at 7th Street, N.W. and Florida Avenue. Here, in the darkened alleys of the slums, one era ended in the grisly record of American racial violence, and another began: for the first time, substantial numbers of Negroes fought back against white attack. The rioters got the worst of it, and had to retreat. There was another running battle on E Street, between 9th and 8th Streets, N.W.[22]

On Monday morning, Louis Brownlow, the dominant figure amongst the Commissioners of the District of Columbia, issued an appeal for order, and asked Washingtonians to keep off the streets, unless their business took them downtown. Others had different intentions. Pushing the protection of the First Amendment to its uttermost limits, the *Washington Post's* front-page story on the riots included a section headed 'Mobilization for Tonight', reading:

> It was learned that a mobilization of every available serviceman stationed in or near Washington or on leave here has been ordered for tomorrow evening near the Knights of Columbus Hut, on Pennsylvania avenue between Seventh and Eighth streets.
>
> The hour of assembly is 9 o'clock, and the purpose is a 'clean-up' that will cause the events of the last two evenings to pale into insignificance.
>
> Whether official cognizance of this assemblage and its intent will bring about its forestalling cannot be told.

The authorities did bestir themselves. The Secretary of War, Newton D. Baker, and the U.S. Army Chief of Staff, General Peyton C. March, promised Commissioner Brownlow soldiers for provost guard duty in the city, including a troop of cavalry.[23] Josephus Daniels, the Secretary of the Navy, ordered Marines in from Quantico, Va., and gave instructions to his officers at the Washington bases 'to spare no effort to prevent participation of men wearing the uniform' in the rioting. Both Baker and Daniels ordered all leave to be cancelled at bases in and around Washington.

A cordon of troops was thrown around the downtown area where trouble had begun on Saturday and Sunday nights, from 7th Street, N.W., to 15th Street, N.W. and from the Mall South of Pennsylvania Avenue up to H Street. About a thousand whites gathered on the Avenue as the sun went down, and made desultory efforts to march through the cordon down to South West. They were easily turned back, but some of the more determined amongst them headed up 7th Street, N.W., planning an attack on the Negroes of U Street. A cavalry charge as they reached H Street sent them helter-skelter back to Pennsylvania Avenue, however, and there they stayed. Any Negro fool enough to show his face on the Avenue received a savage mauling for his pains, with little interference from the police and soldiers, who were content to keep the mob from breaking out of the area. A relaxed, good-natured atmosphere prevailed, partly because some members of the forces of law and order had a great deal of sympathy with the white rioters, and might even have been amongst them on previous nights. 'Ain't it hell how things change', a cavalry trooper mused to a reporter on the corner of Pennsylvania Avenue and 15th Street, N.W. 'Here I was last night down here with the boys. Tonight I'm supposed to shoot them down if it becomes necessary. But – it's orders'.

The real trouble on Monday night was elsewhere in the city. Early in the day there were signs that the Negroes of Washington were in a bitter, vengeful mood, and were ready to take the offensive. Just before noon, four blacks in a car drove past the Naval Hospital at 23rd and B Streets, N.W., and fired eight wild shots at a sentry on guard outside and at convalescent sailors sitting on the lawns. This motorisation of riot was repeated after night fall. Eight or nine cars careered through the streets of North West, their black occupants taking pot-shots at whites on the sidewalks. Throughout the day, the Metropolitan Police pawnshop and second-hand shop bureau received reports of Negroes buying up all the revolvers, knives and blackjacks they could get, and the black mobs were very well armed. Trouble centred on U and T Streets, between 7th and 14th Streets, N.W. where a dozen whites were badly beaten, and on streetcar stops near Negro sections.

A group of Negroes attacked a streetcar at 4th and N Streets, N.W. One of them, Randall Neal, was killed by a member of the Home Defence League who was assisting the police (the H.D.L. was a home guard under federal command). Negroes' houses were barricaded and turned into fortresses. A fusillade from an alley house at 220, G Street, N.W., brought the police there. Officers broke in and began searching the darkened rooms. Suddenly the silence was broken by two loud reports, and Detective-Sergeant Harry Wilson fell dead, shot by a seventeen-year-old Negro girl who was hiding under a bed. Other detectives fired back, and both the girl and her father were badly wounded. Another Negro, Thomas Armstead, drove a car up 7th Street, N.W., with his passengers firing at soldiers and police. They shot a cavalryman's horse from under him at 7th and M; a policeman had a lucky escape when a bullet meant for him went through his hat. A police car overtook Armstead's vehicle, and in a shoot-out he was killed. July 21st was Washington's bloodiest night.[24]

President Wilson had been ill with acute dysentery, but rioting on such a scale so near the White House made him leave his sick-bed and call Secretary Baker to the Oval Office. Baker left with instructions to take strong measures, and with the cooperation of Josephus Daniels, he brought 1,200 soldiers, sailors and Marines into Washington to help the police. Major-General William G. Haan, head of the War Plans Division of the Army General Staff, who had led the 32nd Division in France, was put in command. Truck loads of arms and ammunition were hurried over to Metropolitan Police Headquarters, and by early evening the Federal troops were assembled and ready for duty. General Haan kept two thirds of his force in reserve at the Washington Marine Barracks, Potomac Park and Camp Meigs, with plenty of trucks ready to speed them to any trouble spots. The rest of the men were distributed amongst the seven inner-city police stations, or sent out on patrol with the police.[25]

During the day, there were a few clashes between whites and blacks in North West; two Negroes were shot and wounded, and a gang of twenty-five or thirty blacks stoned passing cars on Rhode Island Avenue between 9th and 10th Street, N.W., but there was little trouble that night. The only serious incident was a double shooting at 9th and M Streets, N.W., shortly after 10 p.m. Isaac B. Halbfinger, one of the thousand members of the Home Defence League who had been called out by Major Pullman, and Benjamin Belmont, a civilian volunteer helping the police, approached a Negro who was alighting from a streetcar. Perhaps the black thought the two special officers were white rioters bent on attacking him; they were both wearing civilian clothes, with only a badge to show their authority. He drew a revolver, and shot Halbfinger through the heart. Belmont grappled with the Negro, who shot and seriously wounded him, and made off down a dark alley between M and N Streets.

There were plenty of riot calls on Tuesday night, and both police and troops were kept busy driving around the city. But most alarms were caused by over-wrought nerves. Small knots of whites in the area bounded by Pennsylvania Avenue and H Street, 7th and 9th Streets, N.W., and little groups of Negroes along 7th St., N.W., above H Street (nearly all boys and young men between fourteen and twenty years old in both cases), were kept moving along, and there was no disorder. After meetings with Commissioner Brownlow, Captain Peck of the Second Precinct police, and Captain Doyle of the Eighth Precinct, leading Negroes agreed to try and persuade their fellow blacks to stay indoors that evening, and most of the movie houses, near-beer saloons and poolrooms that catered to blacks were closed. The evening papers were full of stories about the heavy fines and maximum sentences imposed in the Police Court that day. But much more important than either of these factors, the weather broke, and rain, the finest riot control agent of all, began to fall. Heavy showers cleared the streets like magic. The Washington race riots were over.[26]

Several theories have been offered to explain the peculiar fact that rioters, who are quite prepared to risk being clubbed, bayoneted, shot, or arrested and sent to prison, are not willing to get wet. The least convincing explanation argues that rioters usually belong to lower income groups, who live on the edge of destitution, and who cannot afford to miss a day's work or lose a day's wages. Since they only possess one set of clothes, they are trained from childhood not to get those garments wet and risk losing money by catching a cold or chill, which would then force them to stay in bed and take time off from work. When the rain begins to fall, their early training reasserts itself: they leave the riot and go home. Rather more convincing is a psychological interpretation. This theory points out that rioting is fun; it is a carnival, a Roman holiday, a time when people lose their inhibitions and forget themselves, swept away in the warm community and sense of togetherness of the mob. When the rain starts, the discomfort of getting wet recalls people to a sense of their own individuality – and peril from the forces of law and order.

Personally, I would advocate still another idea. Modern Western societies tend to nourish a spirit of optimism and a gamblers' ethos. No rational person, calculating the odds on being involved in a road accident in present-day Western Europe or North America, would ever buy a car, still less a bicycle. But everyone believes that disaster will strike other people, not themselves. And during a riot, few take the threat of deadly force seriously until firing actually begins. But rain is certain; once it starts, everyone knows that they will get wet unless they seek shelter (and, therefore, stop rioting).

Seven people died in the Washington race riots.[27] Besides Detective-Sergeant Wilson, Randall Neal, Thomas Armstead and Isaac Halbfinger, the dead included Kenneth Crall, a seventeen-year-old white boy who was shot during the fighting at 7th Street N.W. on Monday night, by a twenty-five-year-old Negro janitor called William Laney. Crall died at Emergency Hospital late the same night. Also on Monday night, Amos Green, a Negro, got into a fight in a near-beer saloon at 1233, 7th Street, N.W. Two U.S. Marines, Sergeant Richard Kelly and Private Alfred Krieyer, who were on guard in the street were called in to break it up, but Green pulled out a gun and wounded the Sergeant in the neck. Kelly and Krieyer both fired back, hitting Green, who died in Casualty Hospital on Saturday July 26. Another U.S. Marine was shot on Monday evening, but this time accidentally. Theodore Micajah Walker, a black night-watchman at the Treasury building was riding to work on a motor cycle when he ran into a hostile crowd at 15th St., N.W., and New York Avenue. He swerved desperately to try and get away, and fired a wild shot as he did so. The bullet struck Marine Louis Havilchek, who was standing on the corner waiting for a streetcar to take him home, and he died of head wounds in the Naval Hospital two days later.[28] Ninety-three people were injured badly enough during the riots to receive hospital treatment, including nine members of the District of Columbia Metropolitan Police. Fifty-three of these hospital cases were white, and forty were Negroes. Thirty-nine had gunshot wounds (twenty-five whites and fourteen Negroes). Five whites and three Negroes were under the age of twenty-one, and six were women, two white and four black.[29] As always during American race riots, many of those lightly injured, especially Negroes, probably did not seek professional medical attention, but relied upon their own treatment, or the ministrations of friends and neighbours with some nursing knowledge.

Like the Atlanta, Ga. race riot of 1906, the Washington, D.C. disorders were due in some part to an irresponsible and inaccurate press.[30] After the city had been pacified, the National Secretary of the N.A.A.C.P. wrote to the Attorney-General asking if he intended to prosecute the *Washington Post* for incitement to riot. 'In view of the fact that the 'mobilization' announced by the Washington Post had not been ordered by any authority, military or civil', he pointedly enquired, 'does not the passage show intent by the Washington Post to bring about such 'mobilization'?' But the Justice Department wasted no time in replying that it did 'not regard the article to which you call attention as warranting judicial proceedings either civil or criminal'.[31] Perhaps the Attorney-General genuinely believed that no challenge to the constitutional guarantee of free speech could succeed; perhaps he was also thinking of the political power of Ned McLean, the *Post's* wealthy editor and owner, who was showing distressing signs of falling away from the rock-ribbed Democratic faith of his father.[32]

Here, once again, 1919 marked the passing of an age. After the popularisation of radio in the mid 1920s, fewer and fewer Americans relied on the press for their supply of news,[33] and no newspaper ever again played a major part in causing civil disorder. Radio broadcasts provided the authorities with a quick and compelling method of killing rumours, and two-way mobile radio revolutionised police communications. The introduction of tear-gas soon gave the police even greater power to repress disturbances. The troubles of the 'Red Summer' of 1919 were the last pre-technological riots.

On Thursday 24 July, the number of troops kept in each of the seven inner-city police stations was reduced from fifty to twenty, and on the 26th, all the soldiers were withdrawn to two reserve locations, Potomac Park and Camp Meigs. That same day, the Marines and sailors were relieved from duty.[34] Washington returned to normal. Both groups of rioters obviously felt that they had made their point. The whites had reasserted the sanctity and inviolability of white womanhood: most American race riots before the Harlem outbreak of 1935 began as attempts to uphold the accommodative structure of black–white relations established in slavery times and minimally revised after the Union victory in 1865, and the Washington riot was no exception. For their part, the blacks had on this occasion shown that they could defend themselves, and even mount a counter-offensive.

Classifying riots as follows:

(1) the pogrom;
(2) the one-way battle: white aggression and black defensive reaction;
(3) the two-way battle: white aggression and black counter-attack;

(4) the territorial-commodity disturbance (e.g. the U.S. ghetto riots of 1964–1967); and

(5) the manifestation (e.g. the troubles caused by British Union of Fascists' marches in Cable Street, Stepney, in October 1936, and in Bermondsey in October 1937; or the U.S. campus riots of 1963–1968; or the May 1968, events in France);

then the troubles in Washington, D.C., were a pogrom, which turned early on Monday morning first into a one-way battle, and then into a two-way battle.

Blacks had shown a readiness to resist white and mob violence before, in the New York City Draft Riots of July, 1863, and in the Atlanta disorders of 1906.[35] But it is true that the Washington race riot was the first occasion on which Negroes fought back on a large scale, and even carried the war to the whites. In most race riots before 1935, the Negroes suffered much more heavily than the whites, but the numbers of dead and wounded in Washington show the extent and fury of the black counter-riot. In Washington, Negroes were well-armed and numerous enough to make successful resistance a genuine possibility, and there was a fresh spirit abroad amongst American blacks in 1919. Woodrow Wilson's rhetoric about making the world safe for democracy, the new horizons and new opportunities opened up by the war, the unprecedented prosperity many blacks enjoyed, thanks to the cotton boom or a move up to work in a northern factory, all created an upsurge of self-confidence and a mood of assertiveness. The 'New Negro' was the result. 'Behold the day, O Fellow Black Man!' wrote W. E. B. Du Bois. 'They cheat us and mock us; they kill and slay us; they deride our misery. When we plead for the naked protection of the law, there where a million of our fellows dwell, they tell us to "GO TO HELL!"

TO YOUR TENTS, O ISRAEL! And FIGHT, FIGHT, FIGHT, for Freedom'.[36]

A white woman who talked to the Negroes of Ledroit Park on the evening of Tuesday 22 July found them determined to stop a repetition of the humiliating East St. Louis riot of 1917:

> They were armed, most of them, and were quite frank about it . . . As one put it: 'A man would be less than a man if he didn't fight for his family and his home'.[37]

The *Boston Post*, commenting on the interracial battles in Washington, called it a national disgrace that such scenes should disfigure the avenues of the country's capital.[38] Others, however, thought that it was better to have a race riot in Washington, D.C., than in any other city, for the stories of Negroes being mobbed and beaten outside the White House would stir the nation's conscience, and break the iron hand of segregation.[39] Unhappily, nothing of the kind occurred; Negro life in the United States remained much the same as before. Like all the other bright hopes of change and liberation that were raised at the end of the war, this dream died, crushed by the counter-revolution of the Red Scare. 1919 was a turning point about which American history failed to turn.

# Chapter 9

## *The New Deal and the Localities*

### by Anthony J. Badger*

The New Deal produced an unprecedented expansion of federal power and government interference in the daily lives of individual Americans. Early New Deal historiography was essentially Roosevelt- and Washington-oriented, concerned with the national impetus to, and dimension of, those changes in government power. The 1950s yielded the major biographies of Roosevelt, and Arthur Schlesinger, Jr.'s study, which largely concentrated on the ideological clashes among policy-makers in Washington. Schlesinger's last volume, however, appeared in 1960 and it took Frank Friedel a further thirteen years to advance his biography of Roosevelt over the eight months from the 1932 election to the end of the hundred days.[1] The focus of New Deal historiography in the meantime shifted. New Deal programmes were rarely dictated from Washington and implemented by an army of federal officials loyal only to their New Deal masters. Historians became less interested in New Deal policy-making and more concerned with the execution of particular government programmes at the local level and the effect of local administration on the new federal powers.

The book which served both to isolate and identify this historiographical shift and to point the way forward for further studies was James T. Patterson's *The New Deal and the States* (1969). Patterson's lead was followed in the 1970s by a plethora of published and unpublished case studies of individual New Deal programmes in action and the impact of the New Deal in specific communities. The purpose of this essay is to draw some general conclusions from this disparate and largely undigested material. Have these local studies significantly contributed to our understanding of the nature of the changes in American society wrought by the New Deal? Or have they simply confirmed in greater detail what was already known, so that conventional generalisations about the New Deal can now be bolstered by the evidence from Holly Springs, Mississippi, or Montpelier, Vermont?

Patterson's argument can be briefly stated. He was in little doubt as to the conservatism of state governments prior to the New Deal. In the 1920s reform at the state level had been, at best, 'business progressivism' with little welfare or labour legislation, progressive taxation or utility regulation. State governments confronted the depression with first complacency, then

* Senior Lecturer in History, University of Newcastle upon Tyne.

bewilderment, but above all with conventional policies of retrenchment, balanced budgets and regressive taxation which gave little scope for providing relief for the unemployed.[2]

It was precisely the New Deal's provisions for relief and welfare that gave Patterson the classic interaction of federal and state policies. The Federal Emergency Relief Administration (F.E.R.A.) was administered by the states themselves and the social security scheme in its provision for unemployment compensation and categorical assistance provided federal stimulus and matching funds for state programmes. Patterson examined the problems caused by personality clashes, rivalries between states, local politics under both the F.E.R.A. and the Works Progress Administration (W.P.A.), state reluctance to contribute financially, conservative administrators, and the wide variations and low benefits tolerated in the social security system. Despite these limitations he believed that the New Deal caused dramatic changes in welfare provision, a conclusion he has recently re-affirmed: 'the welfare state under the pressure of emergency responded with a level of public aid scarcely imaginable in 1929'.[3]

Patterson, however, found no evidence that this transformation in welfare was parallelled by a desire of governors to follow the Washington example and launch 'Little New Deals' in their own states. Floyd Olson and Phil LaFollette had given dynamic leadership to Minnesota and Wisconsin, a handful of governors like Herbert H. Lehman, George Earle and Frank Murphy had brought New Deal liberalism to major northern industrial states, but the majority of governors were 'nobodies, moderates, undramatic, yawn-inspiring men with legislative programmes as pedestrian as they were unhelpful'. Federal largesse was accepted as a means of balancing the budget; new federally-inspired obligations were an excuse to impose regressive taxation.[4]

This uninspiring record at the state level reflected the persistence of conservative political strength. Liberals in the 1930s and, more recently, political scientists like James McGregor Burns, argued that such strength could have been permanently eroded if Roosevelt had made a long-term strategic commitment to party re-alignment and had systematically directed federal patronage towards building up pro-New Deal factions in the states. Patterson examined Roosevelt's involvement in state politics and argued that the obstacles to such a re-alignment were formidable. He argued that Roosevelt's opportunistic policy of helping progressive non-Democrats in some cases, sustaining liberal Democratic factions in others, and working with the conservative established forces in yet others, was about the best that could be expected. Conservative Democratic factions were too entrenched and liberal alternatives too weak for a more systematic policy to have been pursued.[5]

This emphasis on the constraints which limited the New Dealers' freedom of action paved the way for Patterson's conclusion: 'What could the Roosevelt administration have done to ensure a more profound and lasting impression on state policy and politics? Very little ... the most striking feature of federal–state relations during the 1930s was not the failure of New Dealers, but the limits in which they had to operate'.[6]

Patterson's work has served to sharpen considerably the analytical quality of local case studies of the New Deal. Authors no longer content themselves with a catalogue of local New Deal activities that is of simply antiquarian interest. They have also moved away from what might be called 'the celebratory mode' of local history where state pride dictates that the politicians of the past are treated as the heroic disinterested public servants they saw themselves as.[7] Nevertheless, the case studies have not yielded surprising results. They have not uncovered unsuspected power, for example, for black southern sharecroppers in the farm programme. The case studies, as might be expected, tend to re-inforce the main trend of New Deal historiography since the 1960s which stresses the essentially limited nature of New Deal change. Within that context, however, the studies have subtly changed some emphases, thrown new light on some major areas of controversy and opened up some areas of enquiry that were outside the scope of Patterson's investigations.

Patterson's picture of a conservative state–government response to the depression through retrenchment and a balanced budget is amply confirmed. Indeed it has received additional emphasis. First, it is clear that some of the most effective grass-roots political pressure came from organisations of taxpayers anxious to cut government spending in order to relieve their tax burdens. Whether it was from farm organisations in Kansas, the Chamber of Commerce and the National Economy League in Boston, the Farmers and Tax Payers League in South Carolina or farm women storming country courthouses in Colorado, politicians usually found themselves under greater and more immediate pressure from these groups, seeking in particular to ease the burden of property taxes, than from armies of unemployed demanding spending for relief.[8] The budget director in Oregon described the consequences of such pressure when he called the 1933 legislature 'the worst' in the state's history, consisting of 'a lot of wild jackasses who believed they heard the call of the people and were willing to destroy anything and everything so long as they could make a show of saving a nickel'.[9]

Secondly, when voters did express their dissatisfaction with the existing conservative political establishments, they often elected colourful and demagogic politicians who, for all their rhetorical denunciations of the corporations, Wall Street and the 'fat cats', offered conservative remedies to economic ills. William 'Alfalfa Bill' Murray in Oklahoma was prepared to use the National Guard to curb the over-production of oil, but was hostile to the very idea of unemployment relief.[10] Mayor James Curley in Boston toyed with expensive public works programmes, but feared the dole and unemployment insurance.[11] Robert R. Reynolds in North Carolina won election to the Senate preaching a doctrine allegedly 'so strange and radical

that it had never been heard before by this generation in North Carolina',
but his programme simply called for the repeal of Prohibition, the insurance
of bank deposits and the payment of the veterans' bonus, not increased
government spending and regulation for unemployment relief or industrial
and agricultural recovery.[12] Eugene Talmadge in Georgia rejoiced in the
title of 'The Wild Man from Sugar Creek' and vowed 'Sure I'm wild and
I'm going to stay wild' but his red-gallused appeal to the small farmers was
for rigid economy against high taxes and high government spending. [13]
Often local elections did not focus on the major question of how to tackle
the depression. In Idaho, for example, in 1930 the main issue in the
gubernatorial election was the use of a state car for campaign purposes.[14]
Prohibition remained in many areas the salient issue. As late as 1933 high
school students in the most devastated state in the nation, Mississippi,
could list pressing national issues in order of importance as strong drink,
illicit sex, idleness, gambling, narcotics and pornography and, last of all,
poverty.[15]

Given this local climate, it is not surprising that the case studies bear out
Patterson's account of the difficulties caused by state and local administration of relief and social security. Examples of state government miserliness
and local conservatism and corruption abound. The sheer magnitude,
however, of finding the necessary trained personnel to run relief and welfare
programmes at the local level can now be better appreciated. In a city like
New York relief administrators could draw on social workers from many
private agencies and could capitalise on the experiences and expertise of a
massive private charity effort at work relief and the state's own Temporary
Emergency Relief Administration. Consequently, by September 1933 a field
investigator could report that she 'found relief administration and adequacy
so far ahead of what I had seen in other states that there just isn't any basis
for comparison at all'.[16] But in some southern states it was a different
matter. In Georgia the relief director, Gay Shepperson, had to overcome
formidable local political and male opposition to appoint trained women as
county relief administrators. 'Many counties [in Georgia] that had never
seen a social worker now had one permanently stationed within their
borders' notes Michael Holmes.[17] South Carolina and Mississippi were not
so lucky. In South Carolina a Washington investigation of the Relief
Administration uncovered an administrative nightmare of inadequately
supervised, untrained personnel on poor salaries. Nepotism and faulty
accounting were not the least of the problems of county administrators who
were described as 'conscientious, hard-working, sincere and incompetent'.[18]
The absence of social workers in Mississippi meant that trained county
relief directors would have had to be imported from outside the state.
Mississippi politicians had no intention of tolerating that.[19]

Such problems were perhaps highlighted most in operating the W.P.A.'s
service and professional relief programmes. In cosmopolitan New York it
was relatively easy to find the writers, artists, actors and musicians to run

the various arts projects, although even in New York the requirement that ninety per cent of the musicians came from the relief rolls handicapped the supervision of the Music Project. But whereas in New York there was a waiting list of 1,800 for the Writers Project, in Georgia it was difficult to find enough unemployed writers to fill the quota. New York provided forty per cent of the painters employed on the Federal Art Project in 1938, Georgia only employed one artist a year. Tensions between the bureaucratic demands of a government agency, the need to provide relief, and professional and artistic standards appear to have been universal. Incompetent writers could plague the New York project at the same time as it was employing the distinguished black novelist, Richard Wright. Drunken supervisors and unskilled workers could ruin archaeological digs in Georgia.[20] Nevertheless, Mississippi could boast the distinction of an all-blind W.P.A. orchestra in Vicksburg![21]

Local studies also show how restrictions on spending compromised the quality of the work relief programmes. Work relief could not cater for all the needy employables. No more than forty per cent of New York's unemployed were employed by the W.P.A.[22] The dictates of economy also precluded conditions of work that would have given work relief the legitimacy, on a par with private enterprise, that Hopkins sought in order to avoid the stigma of charity and the dole. No matter how much local unions or W.P.A. directors protested, wages were not allowed to compete with prevailing private wage levels. The requirement that workers came from the relief rolls meant that W.P.A. workers had to undergo the very degradation which Hopkins wished to avoid: the means test. The need to spread the benefits of limited funds meant that skilled workers could not be employed in jobs commensurate with their skills: in Pennsylvania sixty-one per cent of W.P.A. workers were given work assignments different from their usual occupation.[23] The unpredictability of funding not only made long-term planning impossible, restricted the type of project that could be funded and hindered completion of projects, but also caused wide fluctuations in the relief rolls. Sudden cutbacks meant the arbitrary laying-off of workers irrespective of the quality of work of the individual worker or of the overall level of the economy and the availability of alternative jobs in the private sector.[24]

Defenders of the New Deal who claimed that relief was not exploited politically by the New Deal but rather that local politicians brought politics into the administration of relief, and that many who benefited were opponents of the New Deal, can find support in the case studies. In North Carolina, for example, Senator Josiah W. Bailey, arch-conservative opponent of the New Deal, illegally secured lists of key W.P.A. supervisory personnel in his re-election campaign of 1936 and his henchmen openly solicited campaign contributions in W.P.A. offices. Within a year Bailey was denouncing the W.P.A. as a gigantic political machine run by the federal government. In the same year the state director of the W.P.A. was given $25,000 in a brown bag to distribute on behalf of the conservative gubernatorial candidate Clyde Hoey in his fight against a liberal pro-New Deal challenger.[25] Nevertheless, as Lyle Dorsett and Bruce Stave have shown, New Dealers were not always innocent by-standers in the politicisation of relief. The political coercion files of the W.P.A. indicate that in cities like Pittsburgh, Memphis, Chicago and Kansas City, Washington administrators were only too aware of the illegal pressure on relief workers exerted by local Democratic organisations. Hopkins and his associates were perfectly willing to turn a blind eye to such activities as long as the offenders were administration supporters.[26]

The local studies' most important evidence on relief serves to modify the argument by radical sociologists, Frances Fox Piven and Richard Cloward, that New Deal welfare policies were prompted by the threat of serious disorder and radicalism and the desire of elite policy-makers to defuse that threat.[27] There is a much greater awareness now of the activities of radical Unemployed Councils organised by Communists, Socialists and Musteites, and their existence is an important antidote to simplistic pictures of the apathetic unemployed. But even sympathetic studies show how few of the unemployed belonged to these groups – no more than five per cent – and how few of the members shared the radical views of the organisers who were, in any case, too busy with their clients' immediate grievances to inculcate in them longer-term radical opinions.[28] Studies of relief in New York show that, although there were unrest and demonstrations – and an awareness of them by local and national administration – the implementation of relief programmes was not primarily a response to 'the specter of cataclysmic disorder'. It could be equally well argued that radical protest was stimulated by the New Deal relief programmes. It was proposed wage levels and cuts in New Deal spending that triggered off strikes and demonstrations by the unemployed in the summer of 1935, the spring and fall of 1936 and the fall of 1937.[29] In South Carolina it was the levels of relief wages and the quality of relief administration that provoked unprecedented demonstrations by the Richland County unemployed.[30] Similarly in Colorado it was Hopkins' decision in the depth of winter to cut off federal money until the state legislature contributed its share that led the unemployed to take to the streets and force the legislature's hand.[31] Not that the New Deal was unaware of, or unconcerned about, radical threats. Lorena Hickok's tough-minded and evocative reports for Harry Hopkins on relief conditions in the field in 1933 and 1934 show her concern, and that of local relief officials, that the unemployed might go communist. But this concern did not necessarily mean the perception of an actual and immediate radical threat. The spectre of radicalism was useful to convince economy-minded conservatives of the need to raise levels of relief spending. Hickok's concern was less to defuse a revolutionary situation but more to prevent conditions worsening, which might finally break the patience of the unemployed.[32]

Little has emerged in the more recent case studies to alter Patterson's picture of the mediocrity and conservatism of most state governments during the New Deal years. In the first flush of New Deal enthusiasm the response of the states was often in the hands, even in northern industrial states, of men who had not been elected on a New Deal mandate, like Governor Joseph Ely of Massachusetts, or conservative Republican legislatures, as in Pennsylvania. Even in 1934 Oregon Democrats could elect as governor Charles Martin, who saw no need for any relief for the able-bodied unemployed and thought it a pity that the aged and feeble-minded could not be chloroformed. Those governors who sponsored 'Little New Deals' were often opportunists who lacked a genuine commitment to reform. Eurith D. Rivers in Georgia promised a New Deal, but he was simply an office-hungry former ally of Gene Talmadge. His trusted adviser recalled that the governor-elect called him one morning shortly after his election with a problem: 'I got elected because I said I was going to provide for an old age pension and a lot of other welfare programs, but I don't know a damned thing about it. How about fixing me up a welfare program.'[33]

In the northern, urban, industrial states which offered the most fruitful soil for 'Little New Deals' it still required a combination of particularly favourable circumstances to bring one to fruition. In New York, as Robert Ingalls has shown, it needed not only the state's wealth and urban base but also a tradition of progressive governors, strong liberal pressure groups, radical agitation in New York City, and, finally, the decisive leadership of Herbert Lehman, to make reform possible. This combination produced welfare, health, housing and labour legislation which represented a genuine attempt by the state government to guarantee its citizens as a matter of right a minimum standard of living.[34] Yet, at the same time, in Ohio a combination of rural representatives and spokesmen for the business community sustained Democratic Governor Martin Davey in his steadfast refusal to recognise the relief and welfare needs of the unemployed or the unemployables.[35]

Conservative state government epitomised the conservative constraints that checked Roosevelt's reforms in the late 1930s. Could Roosevelt have avoided these constraints by systematically exploiting the New Deal's popularity and the vast expansion of federal patronage to fashion a major party re-alignment in American politics, rewarding progressive politicians of other parties and pro-New Deal factions within the Democratic party? The evidence would appear to sustain Patterson's argument that the obstacles to such a realignment were too formidable to be overcome even by the long-term strategic commitment that critics like James McGregor Burns believe Roosevelt should have adopted.

Roosevelt intervened in local politics more than is sometimes acknowledged. He did not simply work with the existing Democratic organisations, despite the fervent wishes of that supreme party loyalist, Jim Farley. He was prepared to help progressive politicians who were not Democrats against the wishes of the local Democratic party – Floyd Olson in Minnesota, Robert LaFollette Jr. in Wisconsin, Fiorello LaGuardia in New York City, George Norris in Nebraska. If he was cautious about embracing too warmly some of the western Republican progressives, their attitudes to the New Deal after 1936 suggest he may have been wise to be careful.[36] He was prepared in some cases to insist on the nomination of a progressive Democrat as in the case of Frank Murphy in Michigan in 1936.[37] Roosevelt was also prepared to direct patronage against conservative or corrupt Democratic organisations. A. Cash Koeniger has recently shown that New Dealers even attempted to undermine the machine of Senator Harry F. Byrd in Virginia by directing patronage through anti-Byrd congressmen Norman Hamilton and John Flanagan and the pro-New Deal governor James H. Price.[38] Roosevelt's refusal to work with Tammany Hall and his desire to cut Huey Long out of any federal patronage are well known.[39] He also supported Governor Louis Stark's efforts in Missouri to undermine the machine of Thomas Pendergast and Charles Edison's efforts to free New Jersey from the grip of Frank Hague's organisation in Jersey City.[40]

The difficulties of getting involved in local factional struggles in the Democratic Party were, however, formidable. The obstacles facing attempts to build up pro-New Deal factions were most obvious in 1938 when Roosevelt unsuccessfully tried to purge leading southern conservative senators. But by then there had been a conservative reaction against the New Deal in any case. The obstacles were equally daunting earlier when the New Deal was riding the crest of the wave of popular acclaim. First, conservatives often refused to allow themselves to be identified as anti-New Dealers. As an adviser to a conservative candidate in South Carolina pointed out, 'There is no use for me . . . to advise you that to win an election in South Carolina you must pedal softly (very softly) on the New Deal. In fact whether you are in favor of the many philosophies that the New Deal has had, or not, you must go along with them . . . I believe you will feel like opposing some of the things that have been done, but be sure to keep those to yourself. Do not express them on the STUMP'.[41] Before 1936 few Democrats seeking election admitted to be anything other than enthusiastic New Dealers.

Secondly, national issues were not always the salient ones at the local level. Studies of local congressional elections suggest that primary battles were rarely fought on an ideological pro- and anti-New Deal basis. Personality clashes and factional disputes frequently led to supposedly loyal New Dealers fighting each other in Democratic primaries: S. Davis Wilson against Earle in Pennsylvania, Burnet Maybank against Johnston in South Carolina, Marland against Josh Lee in Oklahoma. Thirdly, it was not easy to find liberals who were genuinely liberal and had local political strength. The candidacies of Lawrence Camp and David Lewis in the Georgia and Maryland primaries of 1938 were prime examples of the difficulty of finding

electorally attractive liberals to challenge conservative incumbents. In
Virginia opposition to the Byrd machine did not emerge for the New Deal
to cultivate until 1935 and 1936 when two congressmen and Lieutenant
Governor Price defected. By 1938 one of the congressmen had been
defeated, Price as Governor had been thwarted in his reforms by a
conservative legislature, and Carter Glass and Byrd were as entrenched as
ever in the Senate.[42] All too often politicians who embraced the New Deal
enthusiastically were not liberals but simply politicians out of favour with
the existing state organisation and anxious to use federal patronage to climb
back into power. When Roosevelt cut off federal patronage from Huey Long
in Louisiana and directed it towards Long's opponents, he was not building
up liberalism in the state. Some of Louisiana's most notoriously corrupt and
conservative politicians benefited. It was little wonder that Long himself
viewed the New Deal's activities not as punishment for his corrupt use of
federal funds but as a purely politically motivated personal attack.[43]

What justified Roosevelt's opportunistic strategy, and supports Patterson's contention that the long-term goals of party re-alignment were not
attainable, was the conservatism of the electorate. There simply was not the
raw material with which to shape the sort of re-alignment on ideological
lines that the political scientists wished for. In the northern, urban and
industrial states the potential for re-alignment was clear. The interaction of
New Deal welfare programmes, the needs of lower-income constituents and
the self-interest of urban machine politicians has been amply documented.
The result was not only to cement the allegiance of new immigrant voters to
the Democrats and win over the blacks, but also to create a powerful
pressure group for the expansion of the New Deal towards a permanent
welfare state.[44] But this extension of the New Deal on liberal lines,
envisaged by Roosevelt himself after his smashing victory in 1936, was
not necessarily wanted in the rest of the country. The midwestern farmbelt,
the western mountain states and the South had all benefited immensely from
the New Deal and had shown their gratitude by unprecedented support for
Roosevelt and the Democrats through the 1936 elections. But, in contrast to
the northern industrial states, the voters in these regions, once the worst of
the depression was over, did not want to push to sustain and expand the
New Deal.

John Allswang's county-by-county voting analysis has charted how the
rural midwest swung towards the Democrats in gratitude for the benefits of
the New Deal farm programme, but he noted not only that votes for
Roosevelt did not necessarily extend to a partisan commitment to the
Democrats at the congressional level, but also that after 1936 the rural
counties shifted back to the Republicans.[45] In Nebraska, for example, the
New Deal had been the salvation of the state: in the short-term through
massive A.A.A. and relief payments which offset the effects of five summers
of drought, in the long-term through its development of the state's water
resources to secure its farming future. In the 1936 elections Roosevelt and

Senator George Norris were supported accordingly. But Norris, who believed that Roosevelt had done more 'for the farmer of this great middle west than any president ever had' was appalled to find that as agricultural prosperity returned in the late 1930s and early 1940s Nebraska farmers detested the New Deal and hated the President. Farm programmes that had been their salvation new seemed burdensome and restrictive, and the urban New Deal was unresponsive to their needs. Their defection paved the way for Norris's defeat in 1942 and the long-term triumph in the state of a particularly conservative brand of Republicanism.[46]

The hold of the New Deal on the electorate of the mountain West and the South was equally tenuous. In many ways no areas of the country benefited from the New Deal as much as these two regions. Because of the expanse of public lands and because of droughts in the 1930s, western states received more per capita from New Deal spending than any other states. Because of the South's poverty and the matching requirements of so many New Deal programmes, the South did not fare so well on a per capita basis. But as a percentage of the spending on relief and welfare in the southern states, the federal government's contribution was far greater than in any other region and the farm programme undoubtedly rescued the rural South from disaster.[47] Federal aid became the largest single source of revenue for the state of Mississippi in the 1930s and remained so until 1972.[48] The resulting popularity of the New Deal among southern and western constituents meant that it was almost a *sine qua non* for politicians in both regions to support the New Deal before 1936. But in the West there were neither lower income ethnics nor powerful organised labour pressure groups to push for the extension of the New Deal. After 1936 even apparently enthusiastic New Dealers like Burton Wheeler of Montana and Joseph O'Mahoney of Wyoming began to desert the liberal cause. All the studies of the mountain states agree that while the 1930s saw a Democratic and liberal upsurge, the New Deal did not permanently change the states' long-term political configurations. States'-rights philosophies and traditions of individualism survived the New Deal largely intact despite the federal largesse the states had received.[49]

Similarly, in the South, most southern politicians who had loyally supported the New Deal through 1936 were unhappy with what they perceived to be the nature of a non-emergency New Deal that seemed geared to the need of the northern cities and organised labour. Harvard Sitkoff has also shown how important the race issue was to conservative southern opposition to the New Deal, even in the late 1930s when the New Deal was still steering clear of civil rights issues in deference to southern sensibilities.[50] Roosevelt always had faith in a new generation of southern politicians who would provide liberal leadership and ignore the politics of race. Even in the Deep South New Deal liberalism infected governors like Olin Johnston in South Carolina and Paul Johnson in Mississippi. Its influence could be seen in the 1940s with younger politicians who advocated

liberal economic programmes to appeal to the disadvantaged in southern
politics.[51] But it was a tepid and fragile liberalism, vulnerable to the race
issue, that fell far short of the aggressive New Dealism of the Southern
Conference for Human Welfare (S.C.H.W.) with its advocacy of raising
mass purchasing power, extending democracy, and protecting organised
labour.[52] The fate of New Deal pressure groups like the S.C.H.W. which
never gained mass support showed the fundamental conservatism of the
southern political scene. Given the absence of black voters, the failure of
organised labour and an electorate that still excluded many lower-income
whites, there were simply not the pressures for change that the New Deal
could exploit to shake the power of the southern conservatives. A long-term
strategic commitment to party re-alignment by Roosevelt and the
systematic direction of New Deal patronage could not have altered that.

New Deal case studies, therefore, have tended to confirm and amplify
Patterson's conclusions. But they have also moved into areas which were
not Patterson's prime concern. His main focus was on those programmes
which were actually administered by state government agencies. But New
Deal programmes which by-passed state governments were nonetheless
significantly affected by local decisions and administrative practices. Public
works programmes often required local community initiative and spon-
sorship. The National Recovery Administration (N.R.A.) was administered
by national and local code authorities consisting largely of businessmen
themselves. The Agricultural Adjustment Administration was administered
by county and community committees of farmers. New Deal labour
legislation could only protect unions if the workers themselves in fact
organised at the local level.

Case studies of these areas of the New Deal often yield results that are
unsurprising. There are countless examples of the ability of local
conservative pressure groups to thwart New Deal projects. Power
companies attempted to obstruct the Rural Electrification Administration
by building so-called 'spite lines' that 'skimmed the cream' of the rural
market in order to pre-empt the efforts of the local rural electrification
cooperatives.[53] The New Deal's minimal commitment to low-cost housing
under both the Public Works Administration and the United States
Housing Authority was further weakened by the influence of local real
estate interests and slum landlords with local councils which they used to
try to prevent the establishment of the necessary local housing authorities.[54]

Similarly, it is not surprising that case studies of the N.R.A. have shown
how business dominated its administration in particular industries. The
studies have also helped clarify the answer to one of the central questions
relating to the N.R.A. Why was an agency, which, according to revisionist
historians, was designed to protect and conserve corporate capitalism and
was administered by businessmen themselves, so massively unpopular with
the business community? Studies of particular industries have confirmed

the accounts of national policy which show that in fact relatively few businessmen positively wanted the N.R.A., in the first place, even in the 'sick' industries like coal and textiles which were clearly over-competitive and atomised.[55] The operation of N.R.A. codes also reveal sectional and regional tensions within the business community and the irritation of businessmen at the bureaucracy and paperwork that government regulation generated. Henning Prentiss, head of Armstrong Cork – the largest producer of floor coverings and bottle closures in the nation who had benefited from the depression-inspired boom in preserving jars – was exasperated by the thirty-four codes under which his vertically integrated firm had to operate.[56] While small retailers generally favoured the N.R.A., the opposition of hardware stores could be explained by the fact that they functioned under nineteen codes – including one for air-conditioning units and one for upward-outward opening doors.[57]

It is also no shock to find that local studies highlight the failure of the New Deal farm programmes significantly to aid the rural poor, like the southern tenant farmers and the California farm labourers.[58] Nor did long-term rural reform and planning goals carry much weight at the local level: a study of the Dust Bowl shows that farmers were sold on the idea of soil conservation only as a means of growing more wheat in the future, thus creating recurrent Dust Bowls in the 1950s and 1970s.[59] Two conclusions can, however, be drawn from these studies to put the limitations of the farm programme in a different context. First, it is striking how marginal New Deal farm programmes were in relation to the major changes that have transformed American agriculture since 1930 – mechanisation, the increase in size of farms, diversification and the flight from the land. Rather, the New Deal was a rural holding operation, freezing the structure of agriculture and keeping people on the land until the urban prosperity of the 1940s enabled farmers to move to the cities. Second, the farmers themselves did not want the radical alternatives that the New Deal has been criticised for failing to provide. Farmers on submarginal land did not want to move to resettlement communities. Farm labourers on the factory farms of California, as their communist union leaders acknowledged, simply wanted better pay and working conditions, not a change in the economic system.[60] Members of the Southern Tenant Farmers Union, as their leaders also admitted, wanted the chance to own their own farms, not to participate in the collective farms which their leaders were advocating.[61]

This conservative dimension of 1930s rank and file militancy is brought home finally in the study of local union organisation during the New Deal. In the 1970s a much greater emphasis has been placed on the activities of the workers themselves rather than on the New Deal's own labour legislation and the activities of union leaders. As a result an interpretation has developed of a heroic labour past in which radical workers forced union leaders, management and the New Deal to respond. It is argued that this radical militancy was unfortunately deflected into conservative and safe trade union channels by sophisticated corporate liberals, cautious union leaders and the conservative New Deal.[62]

It is important to acknowledge the role of rank and file worker militancy in the 1930s. One has only to look at the coal miners in 1933, the textile workers in 1934 and the autoworkers in 1936 and 1937 to appreciate the release of the pent-up rage of the work force which hurried union leaders into militant action.[63] Radical and communist organisers played a key role in encouraging this militancy. It is salutary also to remember that the Wagner Act was not responsible for the crucial break-throughs in the mass-production industries at General Motors and U.S. Steel.[64] But an interpretation that sees rank and file militancy as solely responsible for labour gains and sees the government role as simply one of containing the labour movement is inadequate. First, a 'corporate liberal' interpretation of labour history in the 1930s fails, as Howell Harris has stressed, to account for the almost total business hostility to the Wagner Act and unionisation. New Deal labour policy may have directed the union movement into outlets that ultimately provided stable industrial relations for corporate capitalists, but the capitalists themselves did not see it that way at the time.[65]

Secondly, rank and file militancy could not succeed without government support. When such protection was lacking, as in the car and textile industries under the N.R.A., rank and file militancy led to explosions of labour unrest, premature strikes and the collapse of militancy as fast as it had erupted.[66] Even the sit-down strikes could not have succeeded if community sentiment and state and federal officials had allowed employers to use their customary anti-union tactics. The National Labour Relations Board was also able to do what no amount of rank and file militancy could: protect union gains during the recession of 1937–8 and break down recalcitrant employers like Little Steel and Henry Ford.[67] Thirdly, as Robert Zieger has observed, many workers did not get involved in union drives, and even for union members the union did not necessarily play the central role in their daily working and social life that some historians have suggested.[68] Fourthly, radical orginisers admitted that while they succeeded in winning workers to the cause of unionism they did not succeed in interesting them in wider political aims.[69] Rank and file militancy was directed at essentially limited union goals – union recognition, seniority, collective bargaining – not at changes in the basic economic and political structure.

What the rural and labour case studies point to is a trend toward a wider social history of the 1930s: a history of the unemployed, farmers, industrial workers, blacks and women that will complement the classic sociological studies of John Dollard, Robert and Helen Lynd and E. Wight Bakke.[70] Such studies will help explain the central paradox which underlies James Patterson's work and the case studies which followed. Patterson, I have suggested, rightly stressed the constraints which limited the New Deal, curtailed its impact and restricted its options. At the root of so many of these constraints – the impact of localism on welfare, the inertia of state governments and the obstacles to party realignment – was a pervasive conservatism, a persistent commitment of many Americans to a business-oriented individualism. Businessmen who had extracted many concessions from government wanted to end government regulation. Farmers, who had been rescued by massive government subsidies and price-supports, believed they simply wanted a fair price in the market place. Dust bowl farmers, whose plight had been caused by their passion to plant wheat, wanted to grow more wheat. Despite the chronic over-population of the land, submarginal farmers and tenant farmers wanted to own their own land. Despite an unparallelled economic disaster, industrial workers just wanted some greater control over their work place. Mississippians who had been saved by unprecedented federal aid increasingly stressed their commitment to states'-rights. Westerners received more largesse than anyone else and proceeded to elect again conservative Republicans. Despite the depression, despite the New Deal, most Americans continued to elect men who deferred to conventional business wisdom and traditions of individual self-reliance. James Patterson and his successors have amply demonstrated this. What we need now is someone to explain it.

# Chapter 10

## *1945, 1984: Government Power in Concept and Practice Since World War II*

### by Rhodri Jeffreys-Jones*

I

Both during and after his Presidency, Franklin D. Roosevelt's opponents denounced him as a dictatorial figure, even as a socialist autocrat.[1] The claims of the opponents he kept out of office for so long are understandable. What is particularly striking is the fact his admirers, while using emollient language, have drawn attention to a similar point.[2] The notion that federal power reached a peak by FDR's death in 1945 is widespread and bipartisan.

FDR's exercise of power was controversial in his day, and remains so. The vigour of the debate fails to obscure, however, his popularity with the electorate. Elected President an unparalleled four times, FDR can be regarded as a symbol of the faith reposing in strong government in the years 1933–45. This chapter is about the period from Roosevelt's death in 1945 to the Reagan Presidency of the 1980s. In that period, there was no major palpable erosion of federal power. In the 1960s, Americans actually displayed a revived faith in initiatives from Washington. Yet, by and large, federal authority and power had fallen into disrepute by 1980.

Anti-governmental feeling since 1945 has run in diverse streams, welling at times from contradictory sources. FDR's successor Harry S. Truman provides an early instance of contradiction. He seemed, at first, to be the champion of the small man against big government. For example, he had opposed the idea of a peacetime national intelligence agency because it might lead to an all-powerful fascist state.[3] In 1947, nevertheless, he welcomed the institution of the Central Intelligence Agency (C.I.A.). Reviewing George Orwell's novel *Nineteen Eighty-Four* in 1949, the sociologist Daniel Bell asked whether 'the creation of a central intelligence agency in the U.S. – voted recently by Congress – with the power to plant agents in every voluntary association in the country, including trade unions', was 'another step toward' the totalitarian state Orwell feared?[4]

By the early 1950s, McCarthyism was a movement whose animosity was directed against the idea of an assertive federal government. The new

* Lecturer in History, University of Edinburgh.

Republican President, General Dwight D. Eisenhower, had recognised that there was no mandate for running down the welfare state of the 1930s, which now, through his inaction, received bipartisan blessing for the first time. The eponymous Senator Joseph McCarthy complained of 'twenty-one years of treason'.[5]

In the early 1960s, Senator Barry Goldwater reopened the anti-governmental campaign. He claimed that the New Deal represented 'an unqualified repudiation' of the American Constitutional 'principle of limited government'. He declared that 'the federal government spends too much', and that 'liberty depends on decentralised government'.[6] He had a fine instinct for the contradictions in his opponents' philosophy. This was particularly evident in the case of defence, the one area in which, inconsistently with his own general philosophy, he did advocate large-scale public expenditure. By 1970, it was plain that the Vietman War was sapping the economic and social welfare of the nation, so defence expenditure had become the target of a revived, *liberal* anti-governmentalism. Goldwater acidly remarked 'We are today witnessing an amazing new development in the ranks of the American liberal . . .'. He 'is for a change becoming an apostle of Federal thrift . . . aimed almost exclusively at defense-related activities'.[7]

Even before the Watergate and C.I.A. scandals of the mid 1970s, there were, then, signs of an incipient anti-Washington consensus welling from contradictory sources. During Richard Nixon's first term as President, criticism of 1960s federal-aid programmes became strong enough for Congress to change the law. In 1972, President Nixon signed the Revenue Sharing Act, which returned five billion dollars' worth of federal tax revenue to the states, to spend as they pleased.[8] The Watergate scandal led to the threatened impeachment of a President, and to the actual resignation of Nixon: an event which dealt a hammer blow to the prestige of federal government. As if that were not enough, 1975 proved to be the 'year of intelligence'. The C.I.A. was depicted as the uncontrolled instrument of an 'imperial Presidency' in foreign policy, legally protected as it had been from congressional supervision and journalistic exposure.[9] Even more worrying to the majority of Americans was the C.I.A.'s importation to the United States of methods hitherto used only abroad: political surveillance, burglary, and the whole paraphernalia of 'dirty tricks'. The journalist David Wise wrote of an impending police state and the slightly premature arrival of an Orwellian '1984'.[10] His opinions did not seem extreme in the climate of the mid 1970s, and the C.I.A. was subjected to a plethora of restrictive legislation.

In the late 1970s, Americans demanded that their federal government should do less, and do it better. Within that general expectation, politicians showed their usual and necessary propensity to disagree with one another. The real and imagined errors of the C.I.A. were a useful campaign issue for Jimmy Carter in 1976, when he defeated the incumbent president, Gerald

Ford. On the other hand, conservative advocates of minimum government argued that the C.I.A. was indisputably part of the minimum, and should be revived; the issue helped the Republican Ronald Reagan defeat Carter in the 1980 presidential election.

Many advocates of reduced government thought defence as a whole should be immune. Carter, however, asked for defence cuts of five to ten billion dollars.[11] In a television debate with President Ford in October 1976, he hinted that government as a whole needed to be infused with a new asceticism: in the 'aftermath of Vietnam, Cambodia, Watergate and the CIA, people have felt that they have been betrayed by public officials'.[12] In April 1977, *Business Week* devoted a special issue to 'Government Intervention'. Its staff writers recalled: 'President Jimmy Carter took office last January pledged to reverse the 200-year trend toward more government intervention in the U.S. economy'.[13] Wishful thinking or not, their recollection reflected a powerful expectation no politician could afford to ignore.

In office, Carter attempted to satisfy some of the expectations he had helped create. The journalist Lewis J. Lord described the President's efforts as a 'War on Big Government'. But what Carter called 'the centerpiece of government reorganisation during my term of office' proved to be an innocuous attempt to make the civil service more efficient.[14] The Democrat from Georgia encountered congressional obstruction, and remained vulnerable to the propaganda of those who wished to capitalise on anti-government feeling.

As governor of California, Ronald Reagan had, in 1973, failed to win the voters' endorsement of a tax-and-expenditure reduction measure. But, in June 1978, the state's voters endorsed by referendum the famous 'Proposition 13', reducing property taxation in California. Reagan's day had come. In his unsuccessful bid to become the Republican presidential candidate in 1976, he had already declared: 'The most effective thing that can be done to improve government is to limit permanently the amount of money it gets'.[15] Very early in his administration – on 8 April 1981 – he appointed a committee to review the relationship between federal, state and local government. In his first 'State of the Union' address on 26 January 1982, he called for a 'New Federalism'. This entailed the return of over forty governmental functions to the states, together with $47 billion per annum in revenue. The President also pressed his demand for the 'deregulation' of industry.[16]

II

It is clear that the prestige of federal government had declined sharply by the 1980s. But one should expect neither clarity nor consistency in explanations of the decline. Those explaining their hostility to big government often glossed over fundamental distinctions. For example – as

Goldwater pointed out – liberals did not reconcile their attacks on federal spending on defence and the police with their support for federal regulation of the economy, business and welfare. One might take this a step further, by asking why liberals who had supported federal domestic spending in the 1960s lost faith in its efficacy as a way out of the problems of the 1970s? A second fundamental distinction is that between the growth of federal power in general, and that of unaccountable presidential power. Though anti-governmental criticism from both conservatives and liberals was sometimes couched in terms of general hostility to Washington, it was as often occasioned by the actions of the Executive alone.

Why did the notion of a powerful federal government lose so much of its acceptability? Was it because federal power was already too great in 1945, or because it increased further thereafter? Certainly, the Cold War of the late 1940s and early 1950s thrust upon the President further responsibilities and powers that encouraged the development of assertive government. But Congress obstructed Truman's 'Fair Deal' domestic reforms, so perhaps the full consequences of enhanced presidential prestige were felt a little later. Some critics of government expenditure have argued that the growth of federal bureaucracy developed a specially dangerous momentum in the 1960s.[17]

On the other hand, it could be that federal power has decreased since 1945. Perhaps the President was not equipped to make all-important decisions based on advanced technology, and had to rely too heavily on civil servants. Perhaps the federal bureaucracy exploited its indispensability and slipped out of control, expanding into a self-protecting impediment to effective government. Perhaps the federal government simply made political mistakes, and was discredited. It would follow that people lost faith in the U.S. government because it no longer worked.

Or was it the other way around? Did the U.S. government find itself incapacitated by a public hostility based on misconceptions about the role of government before and after the 1930s? Did the President find himself the prisoner of an absurd conspiracy theory once entertained only by lunatics, now believed in by a majority of the electorate?

In this chapter, we will focus on three aspects of the exercise of federal power: the safeguarding of the Constitution and federal law, the intelligence issue, and the problem of federal expenditure. We shall deal with them in the order in which they became contentious issues over the years, beginning, therefore, with the federal government's role in safeguarding the Constitution and federal law.

## III

It will be recalled that the Goldwater of the 1960s was a devotee of constitutional government. Even the most avid critics of federal power did not question the President's duty, as Chief Executive and Commander in

Chief of the armed forces, to be the ultimate enforcer of federal law. In his oath of affirmation administered on Inauguration Day by the Chief Justice of the United States, every President undertook to 'preserve, protect and defend the Constitution of the United States'.[18] Nevertheless, the Second Amendment to the Constitution guaranteed 'the right of the people to keep and bear Arms', not, as is sometimes supposed, to preserve homicide as an American way of life, but – to quote the amendment again – 'a well regulated Militia, being necessary to the *security of a free State*'.[19] In 1789, the radical farmers had feared federal tyranny and sought refuge in the powers of the several states. In the 1950s, the states' rights tradition clung on tenaciously in the segregated South, which was to prove a testing ground for federal power.

By the end of the 1950s, two branches of the federal government had asserted their authority in the South: the Supreme Court and the President. On 17 May 1954, Chief Justice Earl Warren delivered the Court's unanimous decision in the case *Brown* v. *Board of Education of Topeka*. He overturned the 'separate but equal' legal rationale whereby state governments had distinguished between people on the basis of race, reversing, in effect, the *Plessy* v. *Ferguson* decision of 1896. According to the 1954 decision, separate provision for the public education of black children violated the Fourteenth Amendment's 'equal protection of the laws' clause, in that segregation meant, in practice, inferior treatment for the blacks.

In the 1960s, Congress took advantage of the new constitutional climate and passed civil rights legislation, notably the Civil Rights Act of 1964, and the Voting Rights Act of 1965. This action by the legislative branch of the federal government both reflected and encouraged victories being won through other means, namely, the courageous civil rights and voter registration activities of the southern blacks themselves. These activities, in turn, depended for their success on a prior diminution of the intimidation that had always been a harsh feature of southern race relations. Matters had come to a head at the Central High School, Little Rock, Arkansas, in the autumn of 1957. The teachers there had made careful plans to induct the first few blacks into their hitherto all-white school. But Governor Orval Faubus, an advocate of states' rights and segregation, sent in the National Guard. He instructed the soldiers to prevent integration, on the ground that it would provoke violence.[20]

Faubus's action was a direct military challenge to federal authority. There was no obvious constitutional or political solution to the problem, as President Eisenhower readily appreciated.[21] If there were acknowledged precedents for the use of federal force, they tended to be based on clearcut manifestations of disorder (such as the Whiskey Rebellion of 1794), or justified by explicit constitutional provisions (such as the interstate commerce clauses of the constitution in the case of railway strikes).[22] The use of federal troops against the wishes of local politicians, moreover, could generate immense controversy (as in the case of labour disputes in the

1890s), or contribute to a general decline in federal authority (one consequence of military rule in the South after the Civil War).[23]

In the event, Eisenhower authorised the first federal military intervention in the South since Reconstruction. His action led to the integration of Little Rock High School. It was clear that the President had been motivated by a desire to enforce the Supreme Court's ruling, rather than by any strong sympathy for the blacks.[24] Only incidentally did his action encourage the blacks and legitimise the civil rights crusade in the eyes of millions of white Americans. From Eisenhower's point of view, his chief vindication lay in the fact that the public respected his recourse to federal military power. In the South, it is true, only thirty-six per cent (according to a Gallup Poll) supported his action; indeed, in Arkansas, Governor Faubus won re-election on the basis of his stand for segregation and against federal tyranny. But, outside the South, seventy-four per cent of the people polled supported the President's use of federal military force.[25]

The American people continued to support, in the 1960s, the U.S. government's role in enforcing federal laws and preserving order. The Federal Bureau of Investigation (FBI) received some criticism because of its incompetence, its alleged failure to protect voting registration campaigners in the Deep South in 1962 and 1963, its disregard for civil liberties, and its fabrication of alarmist crime statistics purporting to show that there was an ever growing need for its services.[26] But the U.S. Army, more professional than the part-time state soldiers and less partisan, retained its effectiveness and prestige. The *Report of the National Advisory Commission on Civil Disorders* (1968) noted that 'within hours' after the arrival of U.S. paratroopers in Detroit on 24 July 1967, the 'riot-torn area occupied by them was the quietest in the city'.[27]

In the midst of racial trauma and controversy, affecting the South in the 1950s and then the industrial cities in the 1960s, the principle of federal police authority survived. Indeed, federal prestige may well have increased in this sphere.

In August 1968, Gallup pollsters asked a sample of Americans which of three stated factors they considered to be the 'biggest threat to the country in the future'. Twelve per cent said it would be big business, twenty-six per cent big labour, and fully forty-six per cent big government.[28] Clearly, the President's use of his police authority did not contribute to this widespread rejection of Washington's role. In contrast, a spate of attacks on C.I.A. activities did, on the whole, encourage a decline in respect for, and acceptance of, federal authority.

## IV

From the beginning, the Agency had had its critics. The *New York Times*'s Pulitzer-prize winning correspondent, Hanson Baldwin, at first an advocate of the C.I.A., expressed dismay as early as 1948 at its expansionist tendency.[29] Senate critics like Mike Mansfield made little headway in the 1950s. But the abortive C.I.A.-inspired 'Bay of Pigs' invasion of Cuba in 1961 changed the situation, not least because it created a rift between the President and the C.I.A., opening the way to future recrimination.

In 1964, the journalists David Wise and Thomas B. Ross published the first major systematic attack on the C.I.A. and the intelligence community: *The Invisible Government*. They conceded the necessity of intelligence work, but demanded a drastic curtailment of the C.I.A.'s freedom to launch covert operations.[30] Their book sold well, and made a significant if modest dent in the wall of self-confident secrecy that shrouded the C.I.A. until the 1970s.[31] In that decade, the agency suffered one blow after another. In 1974, the historian Arthur M. Schlesinger, Jr. published his influential work *The Imperial Presidency*. He described the C.I.A. as a dangerous arm of increasingly powerful Presidents.[32] It is generally held that the C.I.A. 'flap' or 'year of intelligence' started on 22 December 1974. On that day, Seymour M. Hersh revealed in an article in the *New York Times* that the Agency, legally charged only with foreign duties, nevertheless kept files on American citizens living in the United States.[33] Within weeks, the U.S. Senate had set up an investigating committee under Frank Church, and the House of Representatives an enquiry under Lucien N. Nedzi. Accused of tolerating C.I.A. infractions at a time of mounting public indignation, Nedzi soon had to make way for Otis G. Pike. The congressional committees, together with defectors from the intelligence community, informers in other parts of the federal bureaucracy, and enterprising journalists, 'blew the whistle' on the C.I.A.

The *Final Report of the Select Committee to Study Governmental Operations with Respect to Intelligence Activities* was published in 1976. Its deliberations had been accompanied by a deluge of leaks and by sensational press coverage, in spite of the moderate and responsible approach of its chairman, Senator Church. This was partly because of the entertainment value of an enquiry that brought forth stories about the alleged recruitment of call girls to undermine the French Communist Party, the existence of a C.I.A. Health Alteration Committee, and the plan to defoliate Fidel Castro's charismatic beard by secreting a poison in his sand shoes.[34]

There was, however, a more serious underlying concern. The Church Report questioned the constitutional and legal justification for some of the C.I.A.'s activities. While the Constitution made no specific provision for federal intelligence activities, the Report assumed that the foreign-policy provisions of the Constitution applied in this sphere. This meant that the President had considerable power to act through the C.I.A., an arm of the federal executive. But, equally, the C.I.A. was subject to the 'advice and consent' of the Senate, and to financial oversight by the House of Representatives.[35] The Report stated flatly that covert action undertaken without congressional consultation 'may be inconsistent with our constitutional system and its principle of checks and balances'.[36] Furthermore, the legislative foundations for covert action were infirm.[37] Wise, Ross and others had already challenged covert operations on the grounds that they were immoral, and, in the long term, ineffective, and there was a good deal of indignation about the C.I.A.'s attempts to destabilise or prop up governments around the world.[38] In the belief that legal and constitutional justification was at hand, Congress had in December 1974 adopted the Hughes–Ryan Amendment, which required prior congressional approval of any covert operation.

The struggle against C.I.A. powers represented a confluence of hitherto divergent streams of anti-governmental feeling. It was by no means a simple battle between interventionist or imperialist conservatives and their liberal critics. After all, President John F. Kennedy, a liberal by most people's standards, had authorised the ill-fated Bay of Pigs intervention, and supported the C.I.A.'s 'opening to the left' strategy: the secret subsidisation of foreign political parties to the right of Communism, but left of centre.[39] As we have seen, the C.I.A. owed its very existence to the liberal Truman. The mid-1970s struggle over the C.I.A. was essentially a constitutional one: if there were to be clandestine interventions, who should authorise them? If proper oversight were impractical, should clandestine operations be permitted at all?

One should take into account a wider aspect of the constitutional dimension of the intelligence controversy. For the controversy spilled over into the realm of diplomacy. In the 1790s, Congress had accepted the need for the President to use secret agents without congressional approval. Successive Presidents, however, took advantage of this privilege and, to the annoyance of Congress, used executive agents for diplomatic, not espionage purposes.[40] This sore was reopened by the use which President Nixon made of Henry Kissinger at a time when Kissinger was Presidential Special Advisor on National Security (1969–73). Without our recourse to congressional consultation, Kissinger became an exponent of 'shuttle diplomacy', travelling the world to ease tension with China and the Soviet Union, to reduce the possibility of Arab-Israeli conflict, and to negotiate peace terms with the North Vietnamese. Schlesinger complained that 'a *de facto* Secretary of State ran foreign policy in the basement of the White House'.[41]

A sure indication of resentment against secret, unaccountable methods was the spate of restrictive legislation in the mid 1970s. As we have noted, the Hughes–Ryan Amendment of 1974 restricted the C.I.A.'s covert operations. In the same year, Congress strengthened the Freedom of Information Act, to allow citizens to find out what files were being kept on them. In 1976, the Government in the Sunshine Act required congressional committees to conduct their business openly.[42]

The intelligence 'flap' of the mid 1970s clearly helped to undermine confidence not just in the federal government of the day, but in federal government generally. Yet, its duration, and, therefore, the duration of the particular kind of mistrust it generated, were relatively brief. Reluctantly, the American people came to accept that there was a continuing need for intelligence activities, and that these could not be the subject of open supervision and debate. As we have noted, Reagan's promise to 'unleash' the C.I.A. helped to secure his election to the presidency in 1980.[43]


V


We turn, then, to consider our third and final aspect of the exercise of federal power. If federal police and intelligence powers generated only short-term controversies, perhaps the 1970s revulsion against government was predominantly rooted in the problem of federal expenditure? Certainly, opposition to federal expenditure issued from several sources: the deregulators, the monetarists, the devolutionists and the anti-militarists. For this reason, it might be regarded as the most important point of confluence leading to the torrent of anti-federal feeling that it is possible to perceive in the political rhetoric of the late 1970s.

The deregulators' objections to federal expenditure were libertarian as much as economic. There was also the human factor. As Schlesinger put it in his discussion of New Deal regulatory agencies: 'Across the fingers of the business-man, it now seemed, fell not a statute but the intellectual pride of a Bright Young Man'.[44] The businessman felt that he, not some government official fresh from Harvard, should be in charge of his business.

Chronology is one element that needs to be considered in relation to regulation and the reaction against it. One might argue that the real boom in the proliferation of government agencies came in the 1930s.[45] But, in 1977, a special issue of the magazine *Business Week* played down the role of federal intervention in the 1930s, arguing that the significant expansion had occurred thirty years later. According to this argument, a host of new regulatory agencies appeared after 1960 – to further the employment opportunities of minorities and women, safeguard the environment, protect consumers from faulty products, and ensure safety at work. According to one estimate, the cost of administering these agencies was $2 billion in 1974, rising to $3.8 billion in 1978.[46] *Business Week* recorded the complaint of big corporation executives who said they had to spend twenty-five per cent to fifty per cent of their time dealing with the federal government and its agencies.[47] The implication of all this is that some deregulators, at least, desired to take one step back to 1960, not two steps back to 1932. In this case, therefore, it is necessary to qualify, once again, the strength of the reaction against federal government.

The monetarists, a school of economists led by Milton Friedman, viewed things from a different perspective. According to them, excessive government spending was a prime cause of the acute inflation of the 1970s. It followed that there should be a major cutback in Washington's expenditure. The other postulated antidote, government control of wages and prices, did not work. The monetarists said that such control merely bottled up inflation, which would later burst out with renewed vigour.

According to the view held by certain politicians, government spending was not only too great, but also entrusted to the wrong people. Federal officials were too far removed from the sovereigns of American politics, the people. This view has come to be associated predominantly with Ronald Reagan. Yet it would be a mistake to regard this mistrust of civil servants as a form of conservative Republicanism in the narrowest sense. During the liberal Democrats' 'War on Poverty' in the mid 1960s, one of the objectives had been to entrust to the poor themselves, within their own localities, the administration of federal funds allocated to them. Like the 'New Federalism' advocated by Reagan in 1982, such devolution was a concept less spontaneous than ideological in its provenance, and derived from intellectuals' perception of the Jeffersonian legacy. In both cases, freedom was thrust upon the localities from the centre. The New Federalism was different from the War on Poverty, on the other hand, in that cuts, as opposed to increments, in public expenditure were anticipated. It was assumed the local taxpayers would see to that. Consumers would back the cuts, in that reduced government expenditure was supposed to lead to lower prices.[48]

A final standpoint from which the iniquity of federal government was observed was that of anti-militarism. Anti-militarism was always a potent force in America, but reached a peak in the anti-Vietnam War protest of the 1960s. As in the 1930s (when suspicions of the arms manufacturers, the 'merchants of death', had resulted in dangerously isolationist arms embargoes), anti-militarism bordered on conspiracy phobia.[49] There was talk of a 'military-industrial complex' that governed the country undemocratically. The implication was that the complex influenced the lives of Americans irrespective of the wishes of their elected representatives in government. Ironically, the theory became an article of faith in radical circles largely because it had been invented by an innately conservative President, Eisenhower. In his farewell radio and television address to the American people, Eisenhower had warned of the technological implications of military-industrial advances: 'Research has become central . . . A steadily increasing share is conducted for, by, or at the direction of, the Federal government . . . . The free university, historically the fountainhead of free ideas and scientific discovery, has experienced a revolution in the conduct of research . . . . The prospect of domination of the nation's scholars by Federal employment . . . is gravely to be regarded'.[50] According to Eisenhower, the federal bureaucracy itself was implicated in a potentially undemocratic military-industrial-academic alliance.

Opinions on the government's role vis-à-vis the military-industrial-academic complex varied, perhaps because the motives of anti-militarists fell into three distinct categories. First, there were those who opposed the military because their chief concern was with peace. They included people

who wanted simply strategic arms discussions with the Russians, those who
desired unilateral nuclear disarmament, and, of course, outright pacifists.
Secondly, there were those who criticised the federal military budget
because the money was being spent on the wrong things. In the words of
one of the Christian opponents of military spending in Vietnam: 'The
ghettoes will continue to be rotten places to live in, Black and Mexican
farm workers will continue to get miserable wages. America's schools will
continue to cripple the hearts and minds of its pupils'.[51] Thirdly, however,
there were those who opposed government as such. They defied the military
activities of government *as government* in the spirit of Thoreau and (however
incongruous the partnership may seem) of Eisenhower and of Orwell. They
feared *Washington* might control the thoughts and consciences of individual
citizens.[52]

We have observed that the police function of federal government
generated controversy but never ceased to command respect, and that the
intelligence flap of the 1970s did not last long enough to impair confidence
in Washington permanently. Up to a point, the revolt against federal
expenditure also needs to be kept in perspective. Respected economists and
economic historians argued against the monetarist theory that cemented
together the various strands of economic anti-governmentalism. For
example, J. K. Galbraith insisted that big government was necessary in
order to control big business, and Douglass C. North suggested that
governmental institutions regulating commercial transactions might actually contribute to economic welfare.[53] It seems possible that such analysts
represented the majority view in their professions. Yet, it is perfectly
evident that they failed to persuade the majority of Americans. The public
reaction against federal 'overexpenditure' was real enough.

In spite of this, there was no remorseless logic about the economic case
against big government. As we have seen, the feeling behind it stemmed
from opposed, if not contradictory political sources. Additionally, the
economic case against large-scale federal expenditure was often a function
or even a by-product of highly varied ideological and other considerations.

This conclusion is inescapable if one examines a little more closely the
issue of *when* the supposedly elephantine expenditure expansion took place:
in the 1930s, or 1960s? The economist James M. Buchanan was not alone in
believing that the expansion occurred in neither decade. He thought the
real change was to be perceived at the beginning of the twentieth century.
He suggested that, in the nineteenth century, public expenditure was
expanding, but less rapidly than national income; federal expenditure was a
contracting fraction of local and state expenditure. But 'the twentieth
century is characterised by both an increasing governmental share in the
national economy and an increasing portion of this public-sector share
occupied by the federal government. Centralisation *and* growth have
occurred'.[54]

From the figures that are available, federal expenditure has increased from 2.4 per cent of Gross National Product in 1902 to 21.3 per cent of G.N.P. in 1970. In the 1930s, it is true, federal expenditure did increase at the expense of state spending. But otherwise, the Roosevelt years were unremarkable for any changes in the rate of government growth. In the reputedly expansionist 1960s, federal expenditure as a percentage of G.N.P. increased at a slower rate than usual; it actually declined as a proportion of total public expenditure, the states taking up the slack.[55] Whatever one's views on the long-term growth in federal expenditure, there seems to be little ground for singling out the 1930s or 1960s for particular monetarist opprobrium. Those decades were targeted for other reasons: for example, Republican partisan hostility to Democratic administration, ideological objections to the welfare state, and resentment at the enhanced status of the highly educated – the 'best and the brightest' who were so adept at making other people feel small.[56]

The nature of objections to overall military spending suggests that liberal critics of such expenditure were just as susceptible to ideological arguments as the conservatives hostile to social spending. If one looks at the problem in strictly economic terms, it has two interesting aspects. First, there is the hypothesis that military spending is wasteful by comparison with civilian spending on the industrial infrastructure: hydroelectric schemes, highways, airstrips, and so on. This is a promising line of argument, but was largely ignored.[57] There is a second, more popular line of reasoning. This is that excessive military expenditure is inflationary and destructive of the economy.

Whatever the truth in the premise, military expenditure does appear to have quickened the pace of government spending in the decades during which the United States became a world power. Government spending increased at the rate of 5.4 per cent per annum from 1902 to 1932, but 7 per cent per annum from 1932 to 1970. If defence spending is removed, one finds instead a slight decrease between the two periods, from 5.6 per cent to 5.3 per cent in the purely civilian rate of annual spending expansion. Many people, however, and not entirely without cause, place little faith in statistics.[58] There have been further, compelling reasons for criticism of defence spending. In understanding these, we comprehend one of the major sources of anti-governmental feeling.

Short-term fluctuation has contributed greatly to discontent about military spending. The fact that such spending was exceptionally low in the 1930s made it appear that military outlays had assumed frightening proportions since.[59] On top of this, there was the sudden escalation of the 1960s. Because of the Vietnam War, there was a substantial, if short-term bulge in military spending. An extra $20 billion per annum was spent at the height of the war. According to one estimate, total military spending soared to comprise 50 per cent of the federal budget in 1968.[60] It is conceivable that this did create an inflationary spiral, and that it weakened the United States' bargaining position in relation to the Organisation of Petroleum Exporting States. OPEC hoisted its prices accordingly, and inflation worsened. The American public, already disenchanted with the Vietnam War for other reasons, now blamed Washington – a more convenient target than Hanoi or Riyadh – for the state of the economy.

There is yet another political dimension to the size of the defence budget. Within ten years, military spending had dropped from 50 per cent to 30 per cent of total federal expenditure, and was still declining.[61] The Reaganite anti-governmentalists now declared the position had to be rectified – at the expense of *civilian* spending. Without question, short-term fluctuations in military expenditure fuelled anti-governmental feeling of more than one type.

The unpopularity of the Vietnam War was a circumstance that ensured liberal opposition to – and emasculation of – military expenditure. But one should not overlook two further considerations that encouraged conservatives, too, to take a hard look at defence spending. The first of these was the problem of 'burden-sharing'. There was a discrepancy between U.S. military spending and that of her allies. For example, in 1980, 0.9 per cent of Japan's G.N.P. went on defence, compared with 5.5 per cent of U.S. G.N.P. In 1981, 5 per cent of Japanese government spending was military, compared with 23.7 per cent (at a conservative estimate) in the case of America.[62] America's allies could plead that there were historical reasons for the discrepancy, that they accepted military risk and conceded leadership, and that the United States was a rich country that could well afford to pay more. But these arguments meant little to the American taxpayer and his champions in President Reagan's cabinet. Why should foreign countries, protected by the United States, be allowed to force the American government to levy punitive taxes that weakened her trade competitiveness with those very same countries? Foreigners should pay more, and Washington spend less.

The second factor encouraging conservatives to examine expenditure critically was the rise of the South and the West, especially the 'Sunbelt' regions of the United States. The broad band of states extending roughly from Florida on the Gulf to California on the Pacific increased in political importance largely because of the movement of people – workers and voters – out of the northeastern and middle western sections. The newly ascendant regions produced a string of Presidents after 1963: Johnson from Texas, Nixon and Reagan from California, and Carter from Georgia (Ford from the midwestern state of Michigan was an exception to prove the rule, as he was unelected). The Sunbelt conservatives – Goldwater (of Arizona), Nixon and Reagan – all favoured tax cuts. In addition, the Democratic Carter declared war on 'Big Government'. Several of the expanding states contained thriving new industries, and seemed to be able to do without the social expenditure needed to sustain the unemployed and other victims of commercial decline. The Sunbelt states were distant from Washington, and did not take kindly to strong federal government. In some regions, too, there was a sense of isolation from world affairs – in terms of American history, an old feeling that often seemed to affect new areas. Paradoxically, the West benefited from military expenditure in that region, yet shunned the executive-enhancing foreign entanglements that expenditure implied. The anti-expenditure conservative found much to encourage him in the rise of the Sunbelt regions.

## VI

Clearly, anti-governmental rhetoric enjoyed one of its heydays in the 1970s. We have just rehearsed the causes of resentment against both civilian and military expenditure by the federal government. Earlier in the chapter, we remarked on the deleterious if temporary effects that the Watergate affair and revelations about the C.I.A. had on the prestige of the federal government. Fear of '1984' was expressed in many ways, and for diverse reasons. But it should be stressed that the diversity threatened to divide the critics in the future, as it had done in the past. As for the fear, it was self-limiting. It bred a vigilance that kept dictatorship very obviously at bay. By that achievement, it kept alive an underlying trust in federal government.

Moreover, it is useful to distinguish between what was said, and what was done. Certainly, Congress placed restrictions on executive government in the 1970s. But the federal government still had the power to act vigorously in many areas that would have been untouchable in the nineteenth century. Its security and police work continued to be effective and acceptable. The C.I.A. (established in 1947) returned to its place in the sun. No-one suggested that the F.B.I. (1908) should be 'privatised', disbanded in favour of America's flourishing private detective agencies.[63] No-one suggested that the Peace Corps (1961) should be run by private philanthropists.[64] No-one suggested that there should be a return to 'voluntarism' in the field of foreign assistance.[65] Attempts to privatise the largest publicly owned corporation in the world, the Tennessee Valley Authority (1933), failed to win more than half-hearted support.[66] All these facts strongly suggest that many opponents of big government wanted to turn the clock back to the early 1960s, not to the early 1930s, when the federal government was neither a great power abroad nor a widely active ruler at home.

# Chapter 11

## The Federal Government's Harnessing of the Overseas Voluntary Spirit – The Peace Corps

### by Gerard T. Rice*

The idea of volunteering to go overseas and help others has deep roots in American history. Sensing this in the 1830s, Tocqueville suggested that a unique weakening of barriers of class and privilege in the United States engendered among Americans special feelings of compassion for all members of the human race. In his view, Americans were happiest when doing things for others.[1] In the twentieth century, secular voluntary assistance organisations proliferated, such as The Cooperative for American Remittances Everywhere (CARE), International Voluntary Services, the National 4-H Club, the Experiment in International Living and various college or foundation-sponsored overseas programmes.

Although the federal government increasingly accepted responsibility for the social and economic well-being of American citizens on the domestic front by the time of the New Deal, it was still quite content to leave assistance efforts in foreign countries largely to the private sector. In the post-1945 nuclear age, however, America became locked in a global struggle with the Soviet Union and White House strategists feared that Europe and the developing countries, in their dire need, might fall prey to communism. It was against this background that the United States government initiated a series of bilateral aid bureaucracies which began with the Point Four programme and culminated in the Agency for International Development (A.I.D.). Against this same background, in 1961, the Peace Corps was born. It was to become the largest non-military overseas operation in United States history and, in the process, the federal government finally harnessed the spirit of voluntary assistance overseas which was rooted in the American past.

I

Theodore Sorensen, John F. Kennedy's chief aide, liked to claim that the Peace Corps was 'the only important new idea to come out of the 1960 campaign'.[2] In reality, however, the idea of the federal government

* Staff officer and writer to the Vice-President and Secretary of the World Bank, Washington, D.C.

financing young Americans to work with poor peoples overseas had been around, under various guises, for a long time.[3] For example, Hubert Humphrey, the distinguished Democratic senator from Minnesota, had been an advocate of such an organisation for many years. Nevertheless, it was Kennedy who, during the last few weeks of the 1960 presidential campaign, breathed political life into a long-dormant idea.[4]

Why did Kennedy propose that the federal government should select, train, supervise and provide material support to young 'volunteers' in the developing countries? His critics – and his Republican opponent for the presidency, Richard Nixon, was vigorous among them – claimed that it was simply a Kennedy gimmick, a cheap shot to win votes at a crucial juncture in the campaign. It was true that, in such a close-run election (Kennedy's popular vote margin of victory over Nixon was a mere 112,881 out of 68,838,565 votes cast), the introduction of a fresh, exciting concept like the Peace Corps could well have had a significant impact on young voters, independents and even some liberal Republicans. Kennedy was well aware of the political benefits to be gleaned from the introduction of a distinctive new proposal. When he extemporaneously suggested the idea of a Peace Corps to students at the University of Michigan in October 1960, he sensed such a warm response that he made a formal proposal of it in San Francisco on 2 November – exactly one week before election day.

Purely political considerations notwithstanding, the Peace Corps was the kind of idea that would have personally appealed to Kennedy, for several reasons. First, the Peace Corps was fully consonant with his most famous bequest to the American people 'Ask not what your country can do for you, ask what you can do for your country'.[5] Secondly, Kennedy was determined to revamp the federal government's calcified and somewhat elitist foreign assistance bureaucracy. Throughout the 1950s, he persistently criticised the United States' failure to make the basic distinction between the type of aid needed for western Europe, where an expanding industrial process was already under way, and the Third World, where technical, grass-roots assistance was needed in addition to infusions of capital. Thirdly, as chairman of the Senate sub-committee on African Affairs and as a member of the Senate sub-committee on Latin America, Kennedy had consistently argued that America should pay more attention to the winds of change sweeping through the developing countries. In the 1950s, U.S. foreign policy was rigid in its East–West view of the world, and little consideration was given to the aspirations of the recently decolonised nations whose main concern was to initiate a North–South dialogue which would eventually lead to the restructuring of the international economic order.

There was another singular attraction for Kennedy in the idea of young Americans volunteering to go overseas to work in the Third World – it had the potential of contributing, at least a little, to the battle for the hearts and minds of the uncommitted nations. An avid Cold Warrior, Kennedy perceived the geopolitical significance of the Third World. Thus, when he first formally proposed the Peace Corps, he set it in the context of America's 'ambassadors of peace' competing in the developing countries against 'Castro-type or Communist exploitation'.[6]

The enthusiastic response to Kennedy's proposal owed a great deal to the widespread feeling among the American people in 1960 that the country needed to 'get moving again'. Despite the affluence of the Eisenhower era, it was generally felt to have been a time of political and moral stagnation, and many statesmen and intellectuals argued that the United States had lost its sense of national purpose. At home, self-critical books such as Galbraith's *The Affluent Society* and Riesman's *The Lonely Crowd* became national bestsellers; overseas, America seemed to be best known for its excessive wealth, Hollywood movies, and its destabilisation of governments which it deemed unfavourable. One foreign policy flap followed another: the Soviet launching of Sputnik, Castro's revolution in Cuba, demonstrations against Vice-President Nixon in Latin America, and the U-2 spy plane debacle.[7]

In this context, few books had more impact on the national consciousness than Eugene Burdick and William Lederer's popular novel, *The Ugly American*.[8] The villains of the piece were the professional American diplomats who, more often than not, confined their work overseas to moving from their air-conditioned offices to government-bought limousines, expatriate clubs and cocktail parties. The plot revealed the 'opportunism, incompetence and cynical deceit that have become imbedded in the fabric of our foreign relations', said the authors. Clearly, the message was that Americans were not liked overseas. In many ways, the Peace Corps was the federal government's attempt to counteract that image.

One other factor made 1960 the perfect moment for the institution of a programme like the Peace Corps. For the first time in some decades, fifty percent of the American population was under twenty-five years old. Having grown up surrounded by material prosperity, the 'baby boom' generation was ready for something adventurous and idealistic. Kennedy, with his inclinations geared towards inspiring the United States to renewed sacrifice, sensed this and challenged young Americans to join the government agency which he was about to create. 'I'd never done anything political, patriotic or unselfish because nobody ever asked me to', said one of the first Volunteers. 'Kennedy asked'.[9] Within a year, 12,644 Americans had volunteered to join the Peace Corps.

II

Shortly after the Peace Corps was launched by Executive Order on 1 March 1961, Sargent Shriver, Kennedy's brother-in-law and the first Director of the Peace Corps, sent a memorandum to Secretary of State Dean Rusk. 'The Peace Corps is a bold new idea requiring a bold new effort', he wrote, 'it should be and do, something different from all other kinds of organizations which the United States government has heretofore undertaken abroad'.[10] With this early declaration of intent, Shriver was emphasising his aim of making the Peace Corps a unique kind of agency which would not fall into the tried and routine ways of most government bureaucracies.

One way that Shriver guarded the Peace Corps against ossification was by establishing an internal self-evaluative unit which issued brutally frank and critical reports on all policies and personnel; these critiques were then acted upon. Shriver also had it written into the Peace Corps legislation that no American staff member could remain in the agency's employ longer than five years – thus guaranteeing a constant infusion of new talent and ideas. One political scientist claimed that this five-year-rule was 'the first time in the history of the American republic that a federal agency has deliberately moved to limit drastically the tenure of its own personnel for the specific purpose of avoiding bureaucratic arteriosclerosis'.[11]

Sharing Kennedy's abhorrence of bureaucratic arteriosclerosis, Shriver wanted to build an agency which would function in the fastest, most efficient manner possible. Within a month, an organisational structure had been erected in Washington, D.C.; within six months, the first fifty Volunteers had been assigned to Ghana and Tanzania; within two years, 7,000 Volunteers were working in forty-four Third World countries. By that time, the Peace Corps, in the words of *New Republic* journalist Andrew Kopkind, had earned itself the reputation of being 'one of the best inventions of the Kennedy years ... expectant, contradictory, optimistic, innovative and thoroughly frantic'.[12]

From the very beginning, Shriver was determined that the Peace Corps should not be seen as part of the traditional machinery of the American government. For this reason, he fought ferociously to ensure the Peace Corps' independence. There was a weighty body of opinion within government circles which, naturally, was sceptical of the abilities of young Americans to work in the Third World. Many ambassadors, foreign service officers and foreign assistance officials wanted to make the Peace Corps a part of The Agency for International Development (A.I.D.) – a huge government foreign aid organisation – so that they could keep their eye on the 'amateur' Volunteers.

Shriver disagreed. He argued that many young Americans would not volunteer for the Peace Corps if they thought it was going to be just a standard part of the federal bureaucracy. Abroad too, he said that independent-minded Third World leaders like Nehru, Nkrumah and Nyerere would be reluctant to accept the idea of a Peace Corps if it was tied to traditional United States efforts. In the end, with the support of Vice-President Johnson, Shriver was able to prevail upon Kennedy, and the Peace Corps was established as a semi-autonomous unit within the Department of State.

This decision had two major consequences. First, the Peace Corps came to be regarded as something of a 'renegade' agency by other parts of the federal government; second, the new organisation was free to develop outside the constricting boundaries of the official bureaucracy, with a life and identity of its own. In effect, the Peace Corps enjoyed the best of both worlds: while it was financed and supported by the federal government, it was generally perceived as being somewhat separate and definitely 'different' from traditional Washington bureaucracies.[13]

In many ways, the Peace Corps was moving into uncharted territory. It had to recruit, select and train thousands of young people to go to strange lands and perform services which the federal government had never attempted before. In 1961, many wondered whether these coddled youths, accustomed to air-conditioned houses, fast-food and gas-guzzling cars had the stamina to endure a more spartan existence in African villages or Latin American slums. 'We knew the Peace Corps would have only one chance to work', Shriver said in retrospect. 'As with the parachute jumper, the chute had to open first time'.[14]

The overall purpose of the Peace Corps, 'to promote world peace and friendship', was defined in the legislation passed by the U.S. Congress in 1961. The Peace Corps Act clearly stated the three major goals of Volunteers: to help the people of interested countries and areas meet their needs for trained manpower; to help promote a better understanding of Americans on the part of the peoples served; and to help promote a better understanding of other peoples on the part of Americans.

Successful applicants had to undergo a rigorous eight to twelve week training programme, mostly undertaken on the campuses of American colleges and universities. In many training courses, not enough attention was paid to thorough technical instruction, academic subjects were overemphasised, and an inordinate amount of time was spent on physical exercise and psychological tests. Congress insisted that Volunteers should receive some training in how to counteract possible communist attempts to subvert them and every trainee was furnished with a pamphlet entitled *What You Must Know About Communism*. No section of the Peace Corps' training programme was more disliked by the Volunteers – mostly because they found it boring and irrelevant. Yet, despite the various shortcomings of the early training courses, they performed an invaluable function in the sense that they gave Volunteers the basics of a foreign language and a practical, working skill – be it teaching or digging latrines.

From an organisational standpoint, the Peace Corps' relationship with the colleges and universities supervising the training function (and even some of the overseas programmes) was notable. By extending and sharing its responsibilities, the Peace Corps became more like a federation of different entities than one monolithic government institution. Of course, the Washington headquarters retained control over essential activities such as the budget, overseas programming, general policy-making and contacts with foreign governments. By contracting out other important tasks, however, a maximum number of people, from all walks of life, were given exposure to the Peace Corps at various levels. This established for the Peace Corps a strong domestic constituency which had its roots in the diversity of American life. Indeed, such was the extent of the public's exposure that, nearly twenty years later, a study published by the Aspen Institute for Humanistic Studies estimated that in virtually every American community, someone has had contact with the Peace Corps.[15]

## III

Although the Peace Corps had its headquarters in Washington, D.C., by far the largest part of the organisation functioned overseas – the Volunteers. While federal officials developed the programmes, set the policies and took care of logistical matters, the Volunteers in the field were essentially on their own. To the majority who served on the front lines of the Peace Corps, the Washington bureaucracy soon became somewhat irrelevant; indeed, to some, the Peace Corps' administrators were 'bumbling idiots who don't know what the heck they are talking about'.[16]

Whatever the Volunteers' thoughts on the subject, they were the responsibility of the federal government. In the early days especially, officials worried about the physical and psychological well-being of these vast numbers of young Americans being sent to live in relatively primitive environments. It was true that more Americans had been sent overseas during World War II, but the troops had been in organised units with safe food, clean water and medical care. These 'luxuries' were not always available to Volunteers working in the towns of El Salvador or the villages of Upper Volta. Shriver once wrote that he used to worry frantically about the health of the Volunteers: 'Could we go to the parents of this nation and say to them, yes, we want your sons and daughters, and admit at the same time that for two years they would be overseas ... with no medical assistance?'[17]

To some extent, this problem of providing adequate protection for the Volunteers was solved by assigning a small team of officials – including a doctor – to each country where there was a Peace Corps mission. However, the Volunteers' own common sense and resilience proved to be the greater solution. Most made the necessary effort to adapt to their new environment, listened to the advice of their host peoples and took whatever precautions were necessary. As a result, fewer than fifteen per cent of the first 7,000 Volunteers had to return home before the end of their two-year stint. No Volunteers died of malaria or beri-beri or were 'butchered' by 'natives', as had been predicted by some of the more ethnocentric American commentators. Indeed, that this had given such cause for concern shows the rather primitive view which many Americans had of the Third World in the early 1960s.

Overseas, 54.6 per cent of all Volunteers worked in education and 25.6 per cent were engaged in community development work – a somewhat nebulous label attached to virtually any type of project which helped improve local environments and societies. The remaining twenty per cent of programmes consisted of agricultural extension, health care, public works and public administration. Volunteers' living conditions varied greatly. Contrary to the popular image of the lone Volunteer working in the rough and remote back country, over half actually lived in towns or cities. All, however, lived on a 'subsistence wage' – commensurate to that of their host counterparts – and were assigned not as bosses or advisors, but as co-workers.

While Washington tried to develop programmes with enough scope to allow Volunteers to be relatively independent overseas, they also found it necessary to formulate a series of policies which would ensure that the federal government would not be seen as having no control over its newest strain of overseas representatives. In early councils, it had been debated as to whether Volunteers should wear a uniform, submit written summaries on their activities and report directly to the U.S. ambassador in their country of assignment. Although none of these particular ideas were implemented, there soon evolved a whole series of rules and regulations aimed at the Volunteer.

Some of these policies were relatively easily defined. It was decided that every Volunteer should receive $75 'termination allowance' for every month spent with the Peace Corps. This was paid to the Volunteers in a lump sum at the end of their service when they could use it to help re-establish themselves in the United States. Volunteers were given leave at the rate of two-and-a-half days for each month of service. Again, this could be accumulated and travel was permitted outside the Volunteers' host country (but no exotic vacations to Europe were allowed – travel was limited to the developing nations). Volunteers were also free to resign at any time. But to discourage them from just packing up and leaving when they felt like it, the Peace Corps ruled that the federal government would only pay for air fares home after two years of service had been completed.

In its ruling on the 'social' behaviour of Volunteers, the Peace Corps laid down guidelines on food, dress, language, alcohol and use of leisure time. On the matter of dress, Volunteers were warned that their personal appearance could reflect credit or discredit on the United States. The question of beards and their contemporary association with 'beatniks' was a particular problem. 'There seems little reason to tell a man who normally wears a neat, regular beard that he should shave it off', the Peace Corps said. 'However, a group of Volunteers who suddenly decide to grow shaggy, semi-ludicrous beards as a lark or as evidence of 'roughing it' will bring discredit on the Peace Corps'.[18]

The Peace Corps stressed that Volunteers were not U.S. diplomatic personnel and therefore should not seek the privileges and immunities customarily enjoyed by American officials overseas, especially 'PX' facilities (the right to buy in government-subsidised 'post exchange' shops).

Naturally, Volunteers were not allowed to own any kind of firearm or weapon. They were also forbidden to involve themselves with political parties overseas. On almost every issue concerning the Volunteer, it was necessary for the federal government – via Peace Corps headquarters – to formulate an opinion.

Many policy decisions were not open to specific or rigid guidelines. In these cases, flexibility was the key and each issue was judged according to its merits. Marriage during service (to either a fellow Volunteer or a host national) was one such issue; pregnancy was another. Here, the main criterion was the practical one – would the Volunteers concerned be as effective after marriage/pregnancy as they had been before?

Sexual behaviour in general was an extremely difficult issue on which to legislate. For example, in order to avoid 'Peace Corps babies' being born to Third World mothers, some officials argued that Volunteers should be issued with contraceptive devices, in the same manner as G.I.s had been supplied by the U.S. Army. In the end, the Peace Corps decided against this in the belief that contraception was a private matter and that Volunteers would behave responsibly. By and large, experience proved this belief to be justified.

There was some tension between Peace Corps officialdom in Washington and the Volunteers overseas. The Volunteers' attitude was similar to that of front-line soldiers towards the general staff – they felt that their 'bosses' had little sense of field realities. For example, when Shriver visited some Volunteers in Niger in 1963, a Peace Corps official reported that 'they accosted him like the English barons cornering King John at Runnymede'.[19]

For the majority of Volunteers, however, Peace Corps officials in Washington did not interfere in their lives enough to engender any deep-rooted feelings of antipathy. Once Volunteers were assigned to a small town or a rural area in a developing country, it was difficult for the federal government to exert any strict control over them – even had it wanted to. In fact, this was one of the great attractions for many Volunteers. Joining the Peace Corps did not seem at all like working in a government bureaucracy or being in the services. On the contrary, despite the various policies and guidelines, the Peace Corps represented to most Volunteers a chance to travel to exotic lands, immerse themselves in a different culture and have an adventure. It was a marvellous opportunity to be almost totally independent and – in the best American tradition – prove their rugged individualism. The fact that in the process they were also U.S. government servants, was almost irrelevant to their experience.

## IV

Despite the Volunteers' sense of independence overseas – and the Peace Corps' general claim that it was 'separate' from the rest of the federal government – the big question mark against the Peace Corps has always been the nature of its relationship with the American foreign policy establishment. Launched in the spring of 1961, the Peace Corps coincided with the United States' biggest armaments budget, the Bay of Pigs invasion, and President Kennedy's assertion that the struggle between communism and democracy was nearing its climax. Given this intense atmosphere, any foreign policy initiative was certain to have had Cold War connotations. The Peace Corps was no exception. Although its officials and Volunteers were always insistent that the Peace Corps should not be thought of, or used, as a means of achieving the short range political aims of the United States government, they could not deny that they were employees of that government and, therefore, they had responsibilities and obligations to it. The paradox at the heart of the Peace Corps was that despite its claim to be distinctly non-political, it was perceived – by foreign observers as well as by U.S. officials – as being representative of American foreign policy in its broadest sense.[20]

Many congressmen enthusiastically supported the Peace Corps because they believed that it would help combat the virus of 'atheistic communism' in the Third World. While Peace Corps officials never contradicted this view, they always argued that the Peace Corps was not simply an arm of America's anti-communist policy. 'A project must not be inconsistent with United States foreign policy', stated the Peace Corps' official policy paper on this issue; 'however, in order to make the maximum contribution to the foreign policy effort, a project should maintain the unique role and separate identity of the Peace Corps'.[21]

The difficulty was that the Peace Corps' claim to a 'separate identity' did not preclude all political calculations. In the early 1960s, in particular, Peace Corps officials were highly conscious of making special efforts to establish programmes in countries where the United States had not yet succeeded in making a significant social, economic or political impression. The aim in this, however, need not necessarily have been to win over 'neutralist' states to the American side. More simply, Peace Corps leaders realised that if the new agency was to gain any credibility as a force for peace in the Third World, it would have to prove its worth not only in friendly, pro-western countries, but also in the turbulent, non-aligned states. From the beginning, the Peace Corps was criticised by the Soviet Union as being a 'cover' for American espionage in the Third World. But in time, it became more prone to the general criticism that it was not contributing enough to the United States foreign policy effort – and this criticism came from American officials.

A number of American diplomats complained bitterly that the Peace Corps did not behave as part of the 'team' overseas. While the ambassador's formal approval of all Peace Corps programmes was required, Volunteers had little contact with the official American mission. Some American ambassadors deeply resented this 'aloofness' and were frustrated by the Volunteers' relatively independent status. Nevertheless, the Peace Corps stood firm on the principle that Volunteers should not be seen as part of the 'official' diplomatic effort and that they should not be used as its instruments. For example, when one ambassador in Liberia ordered Volunteers to make intelligence reports to him on field situations, the Volunteers refused. Moreover, when the matter was referred to Washington, the erring diplomat was severely reprimanded.[22]

Of course, the entire subject of the Peace Corps' relationship with the intelligence community – particularly the Central Intelligence Agency (C.I.A.) – was an extremely sensitive issue. Only a few days after being established, the Peace Corps was attacked by Radio Moscow as 'a plan...jointly prepared by the State Department, Pentagon and C.I.A.' Another propaganda piece appeared in a Polish newspaper. Alongside photographs of female Volunteers in training, the caption read: 'The Americans consider all means acceptable. Where other means do not succeed, sex may be very useful'. The Soviet news agency Tass likewise claimed that 'promiscuous' Volunteer teachers in Africa corrupted their pupils by demonstrating the 'indecent movements' of the American pop dance, the Twist.[23]

Despite Communist claims that the Peace Corps was nothing but a 'nest of spies', no case of C.I.A. infiltration of, or use of C.I.A. resources by, the Peace Corps has ever been substantiated. Officials knew that the mere hint of such an association would utterly destroy the Peace Corps' credibility. Thus, they took the strictest precautions. Most importantly, the Peace Corps received President Kennedy's assurance that the C.I.A. would not attempt to infiltrate its ranks and he personally imparted this message to Allen Dulles and John McCone, the two C.I.A. Directors of this period. In reply, on 28 February 1962, the C.I.A. informed the White House that the 'C.I.A. has nothing whatever to do and wants nothing whatever to do with the Peace Corps'.[24]

To a great extent, the full story of the C.I.A.'s interference in American overseas operations in the 1960s and 1970s remains to be told. Such was the clandestine nature of its work that almost any American working overseas could have been accused of spying. Furthermore, there might well have been some instances of over-zealousness by C.I.A. agents in the field in which Volunteers could conceivably have been recruited to perform a service for their government. The evidence so far, however, is negligible. The Peace Corps' own records have indicated only one incident, in 1963, when an agent of a U.S. military intelligence unit in Thailand attempted to influence a Volunteer. When the Volunteer reported this to Peace Corps officials, a message was sent directly from the White House to the intelligence unit involved, ordering it to desist from any attempts to gather information from the Peace Corps.[25] This incident aside, no investigation, including the thorough search of Senator Frank Church's Select Committee to Study Governmental Operations With Respect To Intelligence Activities in 1976, has turned up the slightest link between the Peace Corps and U.S. intelligence.

Although the American foreign policy establishment may well have liked to have used the Peace Corps as a policy instrument overseas, there was never any attempt to push the agency into political situations. Indeed, Volunteers were trained not to proselytise or to try to impose their political beliefs on their hosts. According to Kennedy, the Peace Corps would best serve American foreign policy by remaining separate from it, as a beacon of idealism in a sea of intrigue, self-interest and deceit. 'The Peace Corps . . . gives us an opportunity to emphasise a very different part of our American character', he said, 'and that which has really been the motivation for American foreign policy, or much of it, since Woodrow Wilson. That is, the idealistic sense of purpose'.[26]

Paradoxically, because the Peace Corps meticulously sought not to become a direct instrument of American foreign policy, it did in fact become a uniquely significant political asset to the U.S. government. By treating local host peoples according to their own needs and customs – without undue reference to their political alignments – the Peace Corps built up the kind of goodwill that did, ultimately, have considerable political effect. The more sophisticated American foreign policy-makers were well aware of this and realised that, as Secretary of State Dean Rusk put it, 'The Peace Corps is not an instrument of foreign policy because to make it so would rob it of its contribution to foreign policy'.[27]

## V

Over twenty years, some eighty thousand Americans have volunteered for the Peace Corps. In 1966 alone, a total of 15,336 Volunteers worked overseas, on a federal budget of $114 million. In 1981, there were about 5,000 Volunteers overseas and the budget was still around $100 million (although in terms of constant dollars, this was a substantial drop).[28] On Capitol Hill and in the country at large, the Peace Corps was one of the few federal agencies that received almost unqualified bipartisan support.

The Peace Corps was not free of problems in the 1960s and 1970s. The Vietnam experience made many young Americans question all aspects of their government's role overseas. To some, the Peace Corps was merely 'the smile on the devil's policy'.[29] The policies of the Nixon administration also had their impact. When Nixon placed the Peace Corps in a large new bureaucratic unit (ACTION, a federal agency which combined domestic and overseas voluntary organisations), many remembered his original distaste for Kennedy's idea and claimed he was trying to 'kill' the Peace Corps by stifling its independence.[30] The C.I.A. revelations of the 1970s also tended to foster a certain cynicism in the developing countries towards the much-vaunted 'idealism' of the United States. Some Third World states refused the offer of Peace Corps participation in their development and there was strong feeling among certain governments that American assistance was paternalistic and, ultimately, rooted in self-interest.

Despite these problems, the Peace Corps survived into the 1980s as America's official vehicle for voluntary assistance overseas. In the process, the federal government had a considerable impact in three broad areas. First, through the Peace Corps, it provided a significant amount of technical assistance and training to Third World peoples and helped to fight the many inhibitions to progress in the developing countries. In education alone, for example, it was conservatively figured that, from 1961 to 1981, the Peace Corps contributed some 62,951 classroom work-years to 4,721,400 Third World students. Former Volunteer Roger Landrum documented and described this achievement as 'one of the great revolutionary forces of the twentieth century: the more general diffusion of education to the masses of children and youth in the developing countries'.[31]

Secondly, through the Peace Corps, the U.S. government showed the world a 'different' kind of American. In 1960, Third World peoples had seen very few Americans who were not missionaries, G.I.s, businessmen or tourists. This seemingly new breed, who spoke the language, lived under local conditions, and were not afraid to get their hands dirty, had a tremendous impact on the developing world's perception of the United States. 'They came to live with our people not in hotels, not in sumptuous houses', exclaimed Thanat Khoman, foreign minister of Thailand in the 1960s, 'but in our farmers' huts, sharing their food and the roof'. Senator Robert Kennedy suggested that this dynamic was perhaps the Peace Corps' most enduring contribution. 'It shows what we stand for', he told a group of Volunteers in 1966, 'not a selfish society but a society that's interested in other people'.[32]

Thirdly, and perhaps most importantly for the longer term, the Peace Corps helped the federal government to give many Americans a more sensitive and sophisticated awareness of peoples in other countries. President Kennedy sent the first Volunteers overseas under the invocation to 'come back and educate us'. Tens of thousands of Volunteers have returned to work in education, social welfare, government and human resource development. One A.I.D. administrator said that he liked to remind Americans that 'We have an asset that no other country has. Instead of a bunch of retired colonial officers or international businessmen come home to settle, we've got almost 100,000 people (Volunteers and staff) who've been through the Peace Corps experience and who can share the experience with others'.[33] A 1979 survey revealed that approximately seventy-five per cent of returned Volunteers discussed their overseas experience with social, political and religious organisations back home and that 'most become actively involved in community groups'. It was also found that nearly fifty per cent go on to work with one type of voluntary organisation or another.[34] In these activities, returned Volunteers have passed on to their fellow Americans the lessons learned from living and working in another culture. This contribution to 'global' or 'development' education in America is often cited as one of the Peace Corps' greatest benefits.

Through the Peace Corps then, the federal government finally harnessed the overseas component of the traditional American spirit of helping peoples less fortunate than themselves. Moreover, through the vehicle created to carry that spirit, the government made its presence felt indirectly, in thousands of communities and millions of lives in America and overseas.

One final irony, however, might be mentioned. Recent studies have shown that a total of fifteen per cent of Volunteers have taken up positions with the United States government on their return to America (three per cent of the population as a whole enters federal employment). State Department statistics showed that ten per cent of each year's new Foreign Service officers were former Volunteers; 12.5 per cent of A.I.D. staff were also found to be returned Peace Corps people. In the 1980 Congress too, three representatives and two senators (one of whom, Paul Tsongas of Massachusetts, has been mentioned as a potential presidential candidate), had served with the Peace Corps.[35] In a way, this trend of returned Volunteers working for the government fulfilled Kennedy's initial hopes that the Peace Corps would provide a steady flow of personnel to the civil and foreign service. In another way, it indicated that former Volunteers were making their influence felt on the federal government and beginning to move it in the general directions which they and their ilk desired. After twenty years of the Peace Corps, it was not quite so clear whether the federal government had really harnessed the volunteer overseas movement or whether the converse might be true.

# Chapter 12

## Is American Federalism Still a Fundamental Value? Scholars' Views in Transition

### by Harold M. Hyman*

> In examining the Constitution of the United States . . . one is startled at the variety of information and the excellence of discretion which it presupposes in the people whom it is meant to govern. The government of the Union depends entirely upon legal fictions, the Union is an ideal nation which only exists in the mind, and whose limits and extent can only be discerned by the understanding.
> Alexis de Tocqueville, *Democracy in America* (Arlington House ed., 1970), p. 152.

'Federalism has been a central element of the American polity from its inception to the present day', wrote University of California-Berkeley law professor and dean Jessie H. Choper in 1977.[1] On its face, his statement would offend few students of law and history. In implicit harmony with Choper's view of federalism's seemingly fixed centrality in the American experience, William R. Brock, introducing his 1979 book *Parties and Political Conscience: American Dilemmas, 1840–1850,* asserted that the political party system in the United States 'existed within a federal, constitutional, and democratic framework'. Examining this interlocked trio, Brock suggested that constitutionalism involves a complex of attitudes towards the basic sources of decision-making and attendant procedures. This complex of attitudes, throughout American history, has been so tenacious and intense as to mystify foreign (and many native) commentators. Americans not only accepted constitutionalism as the core of their society, federalism as a treasured source of diverse laws and customs, and democracy (for most whites at least) as a key stitch in the social fabric: they revered them, and tried, through politics, to institutionalise them.[2]

But the essential if implicit agreements concerning federalism's past centrality and continuing importance, represented by Choper and Brock, prove, upon examination, to be by no means universal. Other scholars, especially certain historians and academic lawyers who have a strong social science background, and some political scientists, assert that federalism is no longer important, if it ever was, and that the Civil War and Reconstruction was a period in which centralisation replaced federalism's 'diffusion of power'.[3]

The present essay will attempt to suggest how and, however timidly, why

---

* William P. Hobby Professor of History, Rice University.

the denigration of federalism has attracted the interest of certain very able scholars and not of others. I assert at the outset my own judgement that greater plausibility goes to the Brock 'side' of the argument.

# I

The reverence Americans felt for the interrelationships of democracy, constitutionalism, and federalism, so often remarked upon, was nowhere more apparent than in the state-making procedures that Jacksonians evolved during the period to which Brock attended in his important book. The constitutional convention, an American invention, swiftly became a hallmark of the ante-bellum decades. In state constitutional conventions the voice of the people became, through political action, *vox dei*. Conventions were an essential early step in a political procedure by which majorities altered their basic policies on a host of the most intimately important market-place subjects in which ordinary people involved themselves on a daily basis.

Constitution-making excited Americans, and some post-Napoleonic Europeans also found inspiration and instruction in the ways that Americans transformed and modernised the forms of government, and of private or public law, both civil and criminal. As a result, Geoffrey Bruun suggested, a minor 'constitutional cult' developed in Europe, where it was remarked that the intensity of Americans' commitment to constitutionalism seemed to be almost a civil religion. Let savants here and abroad mock the recurring evidences in America of popular affection for formal constitutions as well as for constitutionalism. The affection persisted, and it centred in the 1787 Constitution as the mother-lode of union and of constitutionalism.[4]

Examining the national Constitution's role in the federal-constitutionalism-democracy triad, Brock agreed implicitly with numerous commentators that it allowed the better institutionalisation of, rather than the creation of, the federal system. This task of better institutionalising federalism was one that, in the 1770s, the British Empire's governors had failed to perceive, much less to achieve. In the 1780s, the Constitution's framers, ratifiers and critics envisaged their creation as one that, first, sketched the lineaments of a more perfect union. By so doing, the Constitution stabilised that union through alloting to the nation certain functions and duties that were both conformable and acceptable to the component state governments of the federal system. Secondly, the framers made their creation adaptable through both calendared and non-calendared opportunities for change (i.e. elections and amendments). Brock noted also the Constitution's sparse provisions on certain sensitive matters that were capable of touching the political conscience, such as the return of fugitive slaves. Later this sparseness impelled partisans on the subject, including high jurists, to evoke from the 1787 document 'higher law' principles favouring abolition or 'state sovereignty', the latter itself achieving mystical higher-law charm among its adherents.[5]

Democracy, like federalism itself, pre-existed the Constitution. The Constitution's framers understood their task to be one of creating a national government that could respond to state-based voting majorities that were as democratically representative as each state allowed. Out of these political procedures a sense of national will emerged, an emergence that in practice often proved to be very difficult 'because the national majority was the product of many local majorities', as Brock wrote. Even federal senators and representatives depended upon constituents in a single locality, although in the instances of senators that locality was an entire state. The political parties, once they came into being, organised themselves upwards from localities to state-wide coalitions. These state organisations assembled quadrennially to nominate and elect a President. Occasions were rare when states' men became statesmen. Therefore, both before and after the development of the political party systems, most politicians stressed particular, local issues that interested their constituents as well as national ones, so that the platforms of the national parties tended to resemble one another. Much political history, quantifying scholars have recently told us, represents the efforts of politicos to lure 'swing-voters' in their winner-take-all, single-member districts. In the decades before the Civil War, states and localities ventured into new arenas of public function or responsibility under the plenary umbrella of 'police power' constitutional and legal doctrines. Occasions were far rarer when majorities increased the duties or authority of the nation under the Constitution's taxing, war, commerce or other categories. Even so, by European measures America was little governed. Carlyle described the American way as anarchy plus a street constable.[6]

Now to federalism. As with newly-weds trying to define love, scholars and statesmen have found it difficult to define federalism satisfactorily. In his 1979 book Brock defined American federalism in terms that would have raised no eyebrows in a gathering of other eminent scholars such as William T. Hutchinson, Arthur McMahon, Charles Merriam, David Truman or Herbert Wechsler. America's 'federal framework' was and is a dynamic national union of states. In this union, complex interactions exist among all levels of government with both the federal and state governments exercising certain exclusive functional responsibilities but sharing many others. Federalism as depicted in Brock's *Parties and Political Conscience* is less a process of sharp divisions of power, functions and responsibilities between the central government and the states, than a process of sharing a changeable number of these powers and duties between the two authorities as well as between them and localities. This allocation necessarily changes in response to new public needs as majorities discern them. Nevertheless centralisation, whether desired or opposed, is as unlikely and excessive as state sovereignty.

Brock's approach would appear to be at least adequate.[7] His suggestion that federalism is usefully studied in terms of fluid tensions, and of mixtures of functions between nation and states, reflects ideas that were popular in historical, social science and legal scholarship in the 1950s and '60s. Brock implicitly accepts Morton Grodzins' and Daniel Elazar's simile of federalism as a fluid, intermixing, changing pudding rather than a static two-layered cake. Their federalism is cooperative, noncentralising, and dynamic: dual rather than duelling. As Grodzins described the recent past, 'No important activity of government in the United States is the exclusive province of one of the levels... There is no neat division of functions among ... [levels of government]'.[8]

## II

The Grodzins–Elazar view of cooperative, noncentralising federalism was far removed from earlier estimations going back to the 1840s and '50s. Then federalism was depicted as a neat, static, two-layered confection (or three-layered, if local governments are added to the recipe). This classic, layered view of dual federalism was one of strictly separated, mutually antagonistic and eternally combative national and state levels of government. Most fully developed by John Calhoun and Jefferson Davis, this classic view was, by the 1860s, to justify state secessions and civil war and, in the *E. C. Knight–Plessy–Lochner–Schechter* decades, the most egregious exaggerations of ideas on state right, police power, vested rights and liberty of contract.

Here is Jefferson Davis's pungent statement in 1848 on federalism. Since it presupposed a rigid, unchanging, layered federalism of adversary nature, in which a fixed store of power existed to be competed for by nation and states, the Davis view accepted also the existence of a constant threat of centralisation:

> The union of the States into one Confederacy gave no power to destroy local rights of property, or to change the condition of persons; but much to protect and preserve the existing rights of property and relative condition of persons, by extending the limits of their recognition, and enlarging the provisions for their security. Thus the Federal Government cannot take 'private property', except for 'public use', and by making 'just compensation' therefore; the States cannot pass laws on articles of commerce passing from the limits of one State to another; nor apprentices, indented servants, or slaves, by escaping into another State, be discharged from their obligations under the laws of that from which they fled. In these and similar instances; the Federal Government can do and has done much, which is beyond the power of a State, to protect and enlarge the value of property. To determine what shall be property what the condition of persons, are functions of sovereignty beyond its delegated authority, which can only be exercised by a sovereign State within its limits, and beyond that, by the majority of States required to amend the Constitution.[9]

Such hyperbole, it appears, was more for demagogues than scholars, at least for a long time after Appomattox. But during the 1960s and '70s, very able academics, especially among social scientists, concluded, in almost Davis-like terms, that the federal divisions of real power had long been dead; that centralisation was a fact. The United States 'had evolved into a highly centralised, integrated community', wrote political scientist Martin Landau. His co-disciplinarian William Riker judged that this centralisation was 'at the expense of the states'.[10]

How do we explain the sharp dichotomy between Brock's historical analysis and those of these eminent social scientists, some of whom are closely attuned to history and diligently probe the past in order to justify their dour estimations of the present and their predictions for the future?

A useful approach to an explanation of this dichotomy is to survey certain developments in the history of ideas about federalism and centralisation in the world of practising law and of campus-bound academic disciplines. This survey properly begins in the 1860s and early 1870s.

## III

Soon after Appomattox the lawyer John A. Campbell and Supreme Court Justices Joseph Bradley and Stephen Field managed to evoke pale but surprisingly tenacious echoes of Jefferson Davis's notions of rigid federalism. These echoes all but ignored the contrary 'abolitionist jurisprudence' accepted in the 1860s by Lincoln, Salmon Chase, and almost all Republicans and their constituents. Adherents of this briefly-dominant abolitionist jurisprudence concluded that vigorous federal action could and should co-exist and mix with states' functions in an evolutionary, organic, pragmatic manner, without detriment to state rights or to individual liberty; indeed, quite the reverse. To Republican legal commentators, state sovereignty had died, a casualty of Appomattox. Nevertheless Campbell, Field and Bradley, respectively, in the losing brief and dissents in the 1873 *Slaughterhouse* decision, signalled to lawyers and politicians that rigid state-versus-nation ideas of federalism were, unexpectedly, still viable modes of appeal in high courts, though not yet at the polls.

To be sure, the *Slaughterhouse* dissenters' idea of federalism was less catatonic than Jefferson Davis's destructive brand. But, like the defenders of slavery, the *Slaughterhouse* duo sought to blunt majority policies. First in *Slaughterhouse*, then in *Munn* v. *Illinois* (the 'Granger' cases, 1877), these Justices virtually redrafted the Thirteenth and Fourteenth Amendments into restraints primarily on official state action, thereby excluding the universe of intimate daily acts or non-acts by private persons. The Justices also restricted allowable restraints by states on economic activities and imposed in turn federal jurisprudential constraints on states if states' majorities went hog-wild and if state judges failed to rein in these runaway majorities. The triumph of these views occurred despite contrary evidence concerning the far-wider purposes of those Amendments' writers and ratifiers.[11]

Bradley's and Fields' views of two-layered adversary dual federalism found contemporary expression and support in several fundamentally important legal and constitutional treatises and commentaries. These volumes became standard textbooks and source compilations for briefs and opinions during many decades, in the new, paper-chasing Langdellian law schools that were spawning then in every state in imitation of the Harvard prototype. The legal commentaries included those by John Dillon on municipal corporations and bonds, by John Jameson on constitutional conventions, by Christopher Tiedemann on police power, and, above all, by Thomas McIntyre Cooley on the constitutional limitations states faced in the federal union (especially those limitations that Cooley hoped would be imposed by the national judiciary).[12]

Reinforcing the swiftly accumulating effects of this legal literature on classic, adversary federalism were German-style Ph.D. dissertations in history and its new, socially-scientific offshoot, political science. By the 1890s numbers of these dissertations were emerging from the graduate seminars of both the new privately-endowed institutions beginning with Hopkins, Chicago and Stanford, and the slightly less new Morrill Act state universities. When these dissertations treated federalism, they almost unanimously accepted classic, adversary, dual federalism assumptions.

One result of this acceptance was that this fine early work is heavily imbued with formalist approaches and Social Darwinian ideas about nation–state tensions leading to centralisation. The students of these pioneer Ph.D.s perpetuated these assumptions, which, in large measure, endure still.

But the assumptions had to adapt, no matter how partially, to the vastly differing conditions created in America by the decades dominated by Progressivism, World War I, the Depression and New Deal, and World War II. Some of these adaptations, as in ideas espoused by 'legal realists' and 'consensus historians', anticipated the Grodzins–Elazar conclusions in the 1970s about non-centralising, cooperative federalism; conclusions which in spirit and some details descend from the optimistic 'adequacy' positions of Civil War Republican-abolitionist constitutionalists such as Salmon Portland Chase and Timothy Farrar. Other adaptations were inspired by the notions of dual and duelling federalism expressed in the 1870s by Bradley and Field and revamped in the 1970s by such scholars as Landau and Riker. All these 'schools' were, as noted, profoundly affected in their development by the American experience in World Wars I and/or II and their aftermaths.[13]

## IV

World War I and its aftermath alienated – to use the modern word – many important American intellectuals. Until then the worlds of American letters and of higher education marched in close step and were overwhelmingly and warmly optimistic about progress. On American campuses, the talented first generation of Ph.D.s, including those in history and the burgeoning social sciences, were confidently applying their exciting new research methods to the advancement of 'Progressive' public policies.

With 1917, American scholars had plunged into war work. But many of these patriotic penmen emerged from the war- and from post-war revelations about its causes, conduct and results, deeply disillusioned, sceptical and frustated about the thwarted promise of American life. Some leaders in academic legal-social science-humanities scholarship, including the iconoclastic Charles Beard, Merrill Jensen, Karl Llewelyn and Thorstein Veblen, concluded that federalism itself had become obsolete and had long been an elusive and unusable illusion. These scholars were distressed by the 'real' life of capitalism disclosed both by their research and by contemporary events, by exposures of corruption in government on all levels of the federal system, by the racism of the post-*Plessy* decades, and especially by the home-front excesses during and after World War I.[14]

Leading scholars, having lost their innocence, read back into the American past the sense of federalism as a delusive fiction lacking reality or substance. Behaviourist social scientists and legal realists alike bequeathed a heritage of disinterest and cynicism about the importance of ideas and institutions long-embraced in the concept of federalism. Instead, these distinguished scholars preferred to concentrate on what they discerned as the real forces behind the quaint constitutional arrangements of the 18th century and the 19th century's allegedly hypocritical embellishments. These supposedly real forces were primarily economic and psychological in nature rather than constitutional. To many commentators, federalism, in so far as it lived at all, was moribund, inane, a formalistic charade, a symbol or myth, a Potemkin village behind which predatory economic robber barons attacked the body politic, then scurried back to the protective cave that adept lawyers and corrupted politicos created out of the doctrine of federalism on behalf of malefactors of great wealth.[15] Muckraking, in short, now had footnotes, and a corps of talented adherents whose own writings and teaching their students carry on to the present.


# V


Then the Depression, the New Deal, and what seemed to be the global successes of World War II and the Cold War as well as those of the several 'Great Society' reforms at home, especially in matters of race relations, impressed academics very differently from the ways World War I scholars reacted to the earlier events. Academic life itself was revolutionised after 1945, in part through the democratisation it enjoyed. Scholars celebrated the triumphs of the democratic dogma rather than its degradation. After 1945 dramatic reconsideration by scholars of almost every aspect of the American past got under way. The mid nineteenth-century, Brock's favoured exploration period, attracted a proud corps of co-researchers which re-evaluated political parties, constitutionalism and federalism, all of

which was vividly expressed in Samuel Eliot Morison's presidential address
to the American Historical Association in 1950.

Morison celebrated in part what he described as an end to the age of
'debunkers and dialectical materialists' among his co-practitioners. World
War II, Morison asserted, had made the difference. It improved the
attitudes of 'young intellectuals' toward America's past. Exposure to the
overweening evil of fascism suggested the appropriateness for renewed
study of earlier transcendent evils such as slavery. He estimated that young
scholars were commendably less cynical than their distinguished elders
about the merits of their nation's history in general and about its wars in
particular. Indeed, Morison suggested, many of the neophyte historians
then crowding into the profession in unprecedented numbers owing to the
effects of the G.I. Bill, the lowering of traditional barriers against the
admission of non-WASPS into academic historianship, and the enlargement
of tax-supported institutions of higher learning, were 'almost affectionate'
about American history.

By contrast, prominent senior scholars (Morison himself was a striking
exception) exhibited a tenacious scepticism about the motivations of
individuals, groups and nations. This dour heritage from World War I still
prevailed in the writings of leaders of the profession in 1950. Their stance,
Morison continued, had led to interpretations about other periods of
American history that 'ignored wars, belittled wars, [and] taught that no
war was necessary and no war did any good, even to the victor'. And so
Morison celebrated the impact of World War II on his audience. It had
taught that 'war does accomplish something, that war is better than
servitude, that war has been an inescapable part of human history', he
concluded.[16]


VI


'Admiral' Morison's 1950 navigation between the rocks of wars' causes and
the shoals of wars' results was especially relevant to re-estimations about
the Civil War and Reconstruction developed after 1950, both off and on
campuses. Off campuses, beginning in the 1950s, the validity of pre-World
War II histories of the Civil War and Reconstruction became a concern of
some prominent activists and government officials who participated in the
civil rights upsurge. For example, John Kennedy, according to Theodore
Sorensen,

> During his years as President...remarked more than once that history
> depends on who writes it. The consistent inaccuracy of contemporary press
> accounts caused him to wonder how much credence they would someday be
> given by those researching his era; and when the Mississippi legislature
> prepared an official report on the 1962 clash at its state university, placing all
> blame on the hapless Federal marshals directed by the Kennedys, the President
> remarked that this was the kind of local document that scholars a generation

from now would carefully weigh – and 'it makes me wonder', he said, 'whether everything I learned about the evils of Reconstruction was really true'.[17]

Attorney General Robert Kennedy also learned what the pre-war abolitonists and the reconstructing Radical Republicans that John Kennedy was reconsidering understood in the 1860s and '70s: that American federalism was state-centred and uncentralised, and that the quality of local justice and of individuals' legal rights depended on enforcements in fifty state capitals and in ten thousand towns and villages as well as on decisions in Washington. Again like Lincoln's Republicans, the Kennedy–Lyndon Johnson Democrats held fast to a constitutionalism of state-centred, dynamic, fluid, interacting federalism. So holding, in 1964 Thurgood Marshall, then of the NAACP and since become an Associate Justice of the U.S. Supreme Court, echoed Negro activist Frederick Douglass a century earlier. Marshall had heard a suggestion favouring the creation of a huge national civil rights police to overcome community resistance to school desegregation, resistance that state and local police were not punishing. To this proposal the black leader replied: 'The law is quite clear that the federal government is not the policing authority . . . which rests with the several states'.[18]

On campuses, civil rights and Cold War concerns parallelling those John Kennedy voiced about the reliability of long-accepted positions on the Civil War and Reconstruction helped to encourage an ongoing stream of new research on Lincoln's America, including its legal and constitutional histories. Unwearied even by the popular Civil War centennial observations, this research stream ran so strongly that it created, in effect, numerous scholarly Civil War and Reconstruction commemorations despite the disinclination of public officials to do so. This vigorous, compelling tide of fresh interpretations thrust itself into many areas of historians' interests. Such Civil War and Reconstruction topics included anti-disloyalty arrangements, civil–military and race relationships, the impacts of technology and communications on public policies and law, and the resiliency of democratic institutions. Lincoln biography, emancipation decisions and battle history also received significant attention. Perceptions sharpened by the civil rights emphases of our 'Second Reconstruction' and by some Black Studies and Womens' Studies programmes, generated additional inquiries into relevant aspects of the 'First Reconstruction'. Historians and associates from allied disciplines, including that of the law, employed methods such as quantification to which historians had not earlier devoted substantial attention. Some of these innovative researchers ignored W. H. Auden's advice: 'Thou shalt not sit/With statisticians nor commit/A social science', and so wearied syndicated columnist William Safire, that he coined the acronym 'MEGO' to describe his reaction – 'My Eyes Glaze Over'.

The results of this adventuring included highly controversial re-estimations of black family stability, of the quality of servitude itself, of women's legal rights, and of the economic effects of emancipation. Research into emancipations and race relations here and abroad also broadened our frames of reference, as did studies of Congress, states' legislatures, constitutional conventions, and other public policy-making institutions, legal (as mixed with constitutional) history, and wartime (as the base for post-Appomattox) Reconstruction. Nixon's impeachment accelerated revisions (re-revisions?) of Andrew Johnson's purposes and policies, revisions that so diminished Johnson's historical reputation as to evoke grumbles about the alleged growth of 'neo-Radical Republicanism' and to inspire unconvincing efforts to resurrect Johnson's still-sagging stature.[19] And federalism, constitutionalism, and democracy, one way or another, figured at least implicitly in all these re-evaluations as well as themselves being subjects for analysis. These ongoing re-estimations of the central periods and people of our past created a better, if more complex mirror for Americans than we had before.

But by the early 1980s scholars' expanding horizons were both widened by new methodologies and narrowed by Vietnam and Watergate. American historians lost the consensus about wars and morality in public policies that Morison anticipated in 1950. Instead, judgements about the fundamentally economic impulsions that move men and nations, of types that would not have surprised readers of histories written in the 1920–1950 decades, have revived. This revival of attitudes similar to those that infused earlier modes of interpretation, has, in part at least, regenerated the view of federalism as dual, antagonistic and centralising.[20]

## VII

Has the federal system given way, in fact, to a centralised one? Essentially negative replies have issued from Grodzins and Elazar among political scientists, and Brock, Allan Nevins, Oscar Handlin, Daniel Boorstin, Michael Les Benedict, Morton Keller and the present writer among historians. To them, American society through its history oscillated not between total centralisation or complete state independence in policies, but between greater local autonomy or stronger central authority. This oscillation occurred as new issues required not only new policies but, as in fugitive slave recaptures or enforcements of blacks' rights, actual implementations of policies. Controversies grew out of the intractability of a few public questions of this magnitude that engaged the nations's attention. All Americans accepted the principle of federalism, Brock judged, but 'its application generated heat that threatened to damage the whole structure'.[21]

By 1972, this view had seemingly become dominant. Old-fashioned, adversary, two-layered federalism was dead, and Michael Reagan wrote that year: 'Federalism – new style – is alive and well and living in the

United States. Its name is intergovernmental relations [hereafter, I.G.R.], . . . a political and pragmatic concept stressing the actual interdependence and sharing of functions between Washington and the states'.[22] The new I.G.R.-cooperative federalism idea gained quick respectability among historians mentioned earlier, as well as Patricia Allan Lucie, William Nelson, and William Wiecek among others. They found approaches to the phenomenon of federalism similar to the I.G.R.-Grodzins–Elazar inter- pretation to be both provocative and historically verifiable, and thus useful for certain periods and events at least. Derivative reinterpretations emerged of aspects of the legal and constitutional histories of the Civil War and Reconstruction decades and their aftermaths, reinterpretations that in significant measure reflect I.G.R.-cooperative federalism assumptions. One way or another, these reinterpretations depicted a non-duelling, non- centralising, non-adversary, non-static federalism.[23]

## VIII

Too many 'nons' existed in the newer views on federalism to sit well with a growing number of other significant scholars, especially, as noted earlier, for some involved in newer, methodological corners of political science and legal history. Their criticisms centre, not only on attitudes engendered by Vietnam, but on those inspired by some of the basic assumptions of social science, especially on the need for normative classifications. By such tests, a fundamental defect existed in scholarship on federalism leading to I.G.R.-type conclusions, a defect deriving from federalism's sheer varieties and diversities. For a very long time, ironically, the very idiosyncratic characteristics of federalism were thought by scholars, including leading social scientists and legalists, to be essential benefits of the federal system, or at least charming. I.G.R.-cooperative federalism, however, appeared to these critics to involve too sharp a wrench away from dual federalism and too few normative standards or empirical techniques to be reliable or even respectable. Indeed, I.G.R.-cooperative federalism encouraged the creation of too many federalisms, critics complained, so many as to result in a useless, formless cacophony. One wag suggested that every man could now 'invent your own federalism'. And one tabulation of 1978, by Diel Wright, was that forty-four variant federalisms could be counted under the too-loose I.G.R.-cooperative federalism umbrella.[24]

Valerie Earle's compendium on federalism, *Infinite Variety in Theory and Practice* (1968) provoked legal scholar Scheiber to assert that 'an analytic category susceptible to infinite [or even indefinite] variety whether of theory or application, is a category without coherent meaning'. Further, in the same able essay, Scheiber effectively exploited William H. Riker's dour article, 'Six Books in Search of a Subject – or Does Federalism Exist and Does it Matter?', to hammer the point of federalism's allegedly disreputable coat-of-too-many-colours.[25] Scheiber has systematically analysed the faults and virtues of I.G.R.-cooperative federalism. His prodigious, critical and sophisticated grasp of the scholarly literature and the methodologies of the law, constitutionalism, economics, political science and history, enabled him to deal in his essays with major elements of these disparate disciplines as they apply to the centralisation-federalism theme. Scheiber wholly rejects much of the scholarship on I.G.R.-cooperative federalism as insubstantial. Any notion of dual federalism as obsolete is 'utterly spurious', he wrote, as is the idea that 'historically the American system has always worked pragmatically, without serious regard to the tenets of constitutionalism that prescribes distinct coordinate governments'.

If Scheiber is correct, then the noncentralising analyses are seriously undercut and it is highly probable that Scheiber and like-thinking social science-minded historians will resurrect a new (or old) dual federalism redolent of Charles Beard if not of Jeff Davis. We will hear again (indeed, we hear already) dry, cynical, footnoted songs about individuals' and groups' motives and governments' goals, as, for example, from William Riker, respected social science specialist on federalism. In the 1970s Riker confessed to misdirected effort if not sin in continuing to study federalism. It was a legal fiction that made little difference in the way authorities really operated on any level of government. Therefore, in Scheiber's paraphrase of Riker, 'for purposes of social research we ought henceforth to regard it [federalism] as such [i.e. a mere fiction]'. Only political parties matter, Riker continued, not the governments they staff, goad and constrain. The study of the interactions of politics with government, long central in scholarship because, as Riker had believed earlier, that relationship 'reinforced the anticentralist functions of American federalism', was obsolete. Grudgingly, Riker admitted that for lawyers, who had actually to deal with diverse state laws and local customs, 'the most spectral kind of federalism' exists. But that's it, brethren; lawyers, and historians of contrary mind about federalism, grapple with ghosts.[26]

There are serious strains in this cacophonous dirge on federalism. One strain derives from the evidence of naivety about American history discernible in the surprise modern critics of federalism express on learning, as the respected legal scholar Sanford V. Levinson did when studying the chief justiceship of Salmon Portland Chase, that 'most of the so-called great debates of American constitutional law were based less on theory than on political or economic exigencies. Federalism was a value to be attacked or cherished depending on the ends of the debaters'. But Harvard law professor Nathan Dane had understood this in 1829, writing that 'States' rights and State sovereignty are expressions coined for party purposes, often by minorities, who happen to be dissatisfied with the measures of the General Government, and as they are . . . used, they produce only state delusion. In this business each large minority has had its turn'.[27]

Another strain results from the present popularity, especially among delightfully and usefully iconoclastic scholars, of slaying traditions, including disliked scholarly categories such as federalism. Of legal history, for example, Grant Gilmore of Yale Law School suggested recently that no reason exists to create it as a separate research–teaching area. Yet, like legal history, federalism lives, a robust complement to the curricula of graduate schools, of constitutional history and of constitutional law.[28]

## IX

To sum up, in the 1980s, two major streams of scholarship exist concerning federalism. The first is represented by history-focused scholars in both history and political science, including Brock, Grodzins and Elazar, who espouse variants on I.G.R.-noncentralising federalism. A second is typified by resurrectionists about dual federalism, chiefly political scientists or legal historians such as Scheiber, its major spear-carrier, who perceive evidence of gross centralisation in the past with more to come.

An increasingly minor third stream exists. In an effort to say more about federalism than to slay it, political scientist K. C. Wheare tried to redraw the contours of a modern, dual federalism. It was one in which the Constitution drew a vague line at best between the alloted spheres of function of nation and states. But once agreement existed that 'a government is acting within its allotted sphere, that government is not subordinate to any other . . . The principle of organisation upon which the American association [of governments] is based is that of the division of powers between distinct and co-ordinate governments'.[29]

The sources of this new criticism that, if it succeeds, might ultimately remake our conception of federalism into something like Wheare's two-layered static confection, are, in Scheiber's trenchant phrases, a result 'of the rediscovery [by scholars] of ideology forced upon the discipline by real-world events and expedited by the Vietnam disasters'.[30] But is a generation's reaction – even the reaction of a generation of scholars – to disillusionments, no matter how understandable these reactions might be, an adequate reason to accept or to reject any major verifiable scholarly interpretation? Is the historian 'whose ear is attuned to Madisonian rhetoric and logic', as Scheiber admitted was true of his own ear, responding to his inner-ear symphony in interpreting federalism, or is he attending to the way things actually were in the past? Is the sole or major purpose of the new, complementary constitutional and legal histories, to which wedding Scheiber himself is a major contributor, only to 'contribute profitably to an appraisal of the normative and empirical studies of contemporary federalism'? Many of the younger practitioners in the disciplines of economics, history, law and political science (in all of which Scheiber is expert) 'have a radical–critical orientation', Scheiber noted. They 'view constitutional and statutory principles as mere "rule formalism and proceduralism" that attempt to mask but cannot really hide an exploitative system's machinations'.[31]

Academics love ideological battlegrounds. But even successful generals should not mistake any or every-scholars'-lands for fully-conquered provinces. Federalism of whatever variety must be better understood than is presently the case before it is convincingly pronounced dead, alive, or in between; before its centralised or non-centralised characteristics appear to be generally and verifiably apparent. Understanding about federalism is unlikely to emerge from conclusions of the sort offered by political scientist Riker: 'Almost no ordinary citizens of the United States . . . concern themselves often or seriously about federalism'.[32] Of course Riker is correct if by 'concern' he means attention to federalism as academics view it. But both academics and those mythical 'ordinary citizens' worry a great deal about federalism when their particular oxen are being ignored or fattened. Transformed into 'anti-centralisation' or 'local defenses of constitutional rights', or 'New Federalism', as examples, federalism has never failed to engage the interests of voting John Does.

In this sense of involvements with the rhythms of political procedures and constitutionalism, federalism, considered historically, remains what Brock described: one leg of the tripod which stabilises American society and permits it to operate. Its removal, attenuation, or exaggeration for reasons of ideological repugnance to wars or to the draft or to any public policies, imperils the fragile burden that, now as for two centuries past, rests on those three linked bases.

# A Summing Up

## by Rhodri Jeffreys-Jones

A wide spectrum of ideas and information about the growth of federal power has been encountered in this volume. The contributions suggest that there should be an awareness, on several levels, of the problem of definition. On the semantic level, there would appear to be little difficulty in comprehending the meaning of Confederation, as applied to the 1770s, or Confederacy, as applied to the breakaway states in the 1860s. As Professor Pole points out, Madison preferred a more national style of government. Confusion immediately enters the picture, however, for that national style came to be referred to as federal, and Madison himself as one of the authors of Federalist Papers. To cap it all, President Reagan called, in 1982, for a New Federalism, by which he clearly did not mean a stronger national government. In the light of such semantic disparity, it is less astonishing that Diel Wright managed to identify 'forty-four variant federalisms'.[1] If only in the interest of sanity, it is necessary to keep reminding oneself that the term 'federal government' should usually be used synonymously with 'national government', in discussions about the United States.

On the conceptual level, it is necessary to distinguish between the growth of unity, making for the existence of a national federal government that is strong in relation to the individual states, and the growth in the scope of federal governmental activities. Of course, the growth of unity is a necessary precondition for the later growth of federal governmental functions. Furthermore, the unity movement's history is not confined to the events of 1787, the War of 1812 and the Civil War. As Dr Rice and Professor Hyman demonstrate, centralisation is still a vibrant political issue in the twentieth century. But one can still distinguish between the growth of unity and the growth of federal government in other respects.

Those other respects are themselves open to definitional subdivision. Various contributors have written about the three branches of federal government, the Executive, Congress and Supreme Court. Dr Spackman shows how George F. Hoar pressed the powers of the U.S. Congress over those of the states in 1870: an apparently straightforward assertion of federal authority. But in the 1890s, the same senator was sharply assertive of Congress's right to curb presidential foreign-policy-making powers.[2] One might define his attitude as an expression of localism against the most dangerously expansive branch of federal government, the Executive. As Dr

Harrison remarks of Hoar's contemporaries in Congress: 'Their standing at home mattered more to them than their standing on the Hill'. On the other hand, Hoar's strictures against the Executive in the 1890s are usually seen as part of an intra-federal governmental struggle, having little bearing upon national authority as a whole, except in so far as internal conflict weakens any institution.

Then, there are further problems of definition *associated* with, and inseparable from an analysis of, the growth of federal power. Dr Harrison, in his treatment of the late nineteenth century, illustrates the way in which the government regulation issue cut across party lines. Elsewhere, it is shown that one must beware of making too lightly the twentieth-century assumption that liberals stand for expanded federal government, conservatives for minimal government. Dr Turley suggests that the ante-bellum radicals' attitude to government was 'paradigmatic': they were often against it in principle, but in many cases accepted it as a means to an end. As for the post-New Deal conservatives, it may be pointed out that they have not been against federal expenditure on defence, and have urged, as Dr Collins shows, government enforcement of morality.

Several chapters, then, serve as a useful warning against facile labelling and rigid generalisation. At the same time, their very diversity and attention to conceptual detail make it possible to discuss with greater confidence the growth of federal power in American history – bearing in mind that it means national power, embraces both the consideration of unity and the growth of all three sources of national authority (the Executive, Congress and Supreme Court), and is, by virtue of common parlance, a cause espoused by the twentieth-century liberal, regardless of party affiliation.

The authors of this book are historians, and the book's distinctive utility is that it treats the nature and growth of federal power over time. The past and myths about it have been exploited, on the one hand, by believers in progress, whom one might describe as Whigs, Progressives, or liberals. Their object has often been to tame the beast of federal power by massaging the beholder, to show that the allegedly overweening statism decried by conservatives has a respectable pedigree, is not at threatening levels in the present, and is part of the American political tradition that conservatives purport to revere. Conservatives, on the other hand, speak fondly of a golden past of minimal government, with which the present-day monster in Washington presents an alarming contrast. Dr Collins locates Milton Friedman's golden age in the late nineteenth century, and Henry Carey's in the age before Jackson. One is therefore introduced to the idea of a movable past, conforming to the ideological requirements of an historically illiterate present.

Whether one's aim is to rid the present generation of policy-makers of encumbering myths about the past, or to purge from historical writing past preconceptions based on contemporary prejudice, there is a case for examining anew the timing of government growth. Various previous writers have placed the critical expansion of federal power in the 1960s, 1930s, late nineteenth century and earlier.[3] The perspective of most speculators on the subject of timing has hitherto been economic, and to that extent narrow. This volume has gone some way towards meeting the need for a more catholic, as well as a more objective approach to the problem of timing and its causation.

The chapters in this book have opened several windows on the timing of federal governmental growth, and on its nature and causes. Professor Pole's essay on the preconditions of unity introduces the notion that while certain long-term factors (some of them repeated later, notably religion and war) prepared the way for the original union, union was entertained as a means to an immediate end, not as a long-term end in itself. 'Union' was the North's slogan in the Civil War, but it should not be too lightly assumed that the pragmatic priorities of the Founding Fathers, as identified by Pole, had withered away. Dr Spackman shows that, for the Radical Reconstructionists, the power of the union was a means to the end of protecting the liberties of all citizens, regardless of race. Dr Thompson's treatment of the Progressive publicists raises anew the question of whether twentieth-century reformers were sure about their ends: social release, or social control? But they accepted implicitly the view that federal government was a means to an end.

If Pole discusses the very genesis of federal government power, Dr MacLeod is concerned with one of the first great reactions against it. In this context, it is worth dwelling on the powers conferred upon central government by war, and the rhetorical reactions against them. The French and Indian War nurtured the concept of unity. The Revolutionary, 1812 and Civil Wars encouraged it, and, like ensuing wars, led to an increase in the scope, as well as authority, of federal government. For example, Dr Collins observes that the greatest single increase in the number of federal jobs occurred in World War II, not during some period of domestic reform. But if wars increased the powers of government on the ratchet principle, the ratchet had missing teeth. Dr MacLeod demonstrates that the nationalism engendered by the War of 1812 may have sustained the mood behind the rechartering of the Bank of the United States and the Republican Tariff of 1816, but it soon crumbled under the impact of the slavery crisis. Dr Thompson describes the disillusionment with Washington one hundred years later, in the aftermath of World War I. Perhaps the Watergate affair was a natural sequel to the Vietnam War. There were, indeed, reactions against federal power after most wars.

One of the points illuminated in this book is the way in which the post-war anti-governmental reactions varied in nature, intensity and permanence. It may be true that there was always some kind of post-war attack on the powers which national government had assumed in the name of patriotism. But the federal union was enshrined in the Constitution just

half a decade after the Peace of Paris; after Dr Turley's anti-authoritarian
Garrisonians had supported the use of federal power during the Civil War,
Dr Spackman's Reconstruction radicals advanced their 'doctrine of national
power'; federal police powers continued unabated in 1919 as Dr Cook
demonstrates, while federal foreign-policy powers did not perceptibly
wither in the aftermath of World War II. So long as crises persisted in
particular spheres, the habit of looking to Washington for solutions
endured, even in times of general revulsion against war and the augmented
powers of war cabinets. A second point to be made about the
war-and-reaction hypothesis is that it does not cover every circumstance
completely. Anger about the Vietnam War and apparent overspending on
defense was a significant, but not necessarily overriding cause of objection
to big government in the 1970s and 1980s. In their different ways, Dr
Collins and Professor Hyman provide plenty of evidence for that.

Peering through the welter of qualifications and exceptions, one might
suggest that very often pragmatism and war have been at the root of union
and the expanding scope of federal government. But the chapters in this
book have made it clear that a rich profusion of other factors needs to be
considered. Dr Harrison conjures up a bit of railroad determinism: since
railroads were necessarily inter-state, their expansion necessarily invited a
growth in federal government. Dr Badger firmly rejects New Left arguments in explaining the political momentum behind the federally-organised
welfare state of the 1930s. Dr Rice invokes a combination of short-term
social factors and long-term anti-Communism in explaining the birth of that
most charismatic of federal agencies, the Peace Corps. The picture is full of
refutations and contradictions over time. The descendents of the Westerners whose nationalism had been so unacceptable to the consolidationism of
Henry Carey were to lead the attack on national power in the 1970s.
According to Professor Pole, the religious revivalists of the eighteenth
century helped to create a national consciousness; according to Dr Turley,
those of the nineteenth were perfectionist and hostile to the federal government as its authority became increasingly linked to the maintenance and
extension of slavery; by common consent, those of the 1960s and 1970s
believed in federal restraint in everything except defense and the
enforcement of morality.

If one examines factors other than the economic, the impression gained is
that federal power increased in different ways at different times for different
reasons. No single-factor explanation applied to a particular period is
satisfactory. This generalisation may be extended to economic activities as
such. Certainly, governmental regulatory powers and expenditure have
increased in the twentieth century. But one might adapt Wiebe's
incapsulation of Progressive dualism to suggest that the result may have
been economic release, as much as economic control.[4] The quality of one's
interpretation of the data concerning federal government's economic
expansion depends upon the sophistication of one's premises: the degree of

federal economic oppression is no more a foregone conclusion than it is for any other aspect of federal expansion.

Yet, E. H. Carr cautioned historians against holding back from general interpretation: 'History properly so-called can be written only by those who find and accept a sense of direction in history itself'.[5] The contributors to this volume have advanced the ideas that the growth of federal power owes much to pragmatism and war. Have they contributed any further general explanations? It is most unusual for a team of British writers with several ideas in common to write collectively on a theme in American history. It would be satisfying to be able to say that this book reflects in some places a distinctly British approach, perhaps even more specifically an Anglo-Scottish approach in that it springs from the scholarship of historians who exchanged views with William Brock before and after his departure from Cambridge to a chair in Glasgow. Of course, it might be objected that British historians as a whole are too similar to their American counterparts for their nationality to matter. For example, there is little to differentiate G. K. Fry's economic history treatise *The Growth of Government* (1979) from its American counterparts.[6] Conversely, one might resurrect the hoary myth that if British Americanists do not manifest the same point of view as native American historians, they are prejudiced.[7] But there is really no need to feel hidebound by convention, or to be paralysed by fear of Transatlantic criticism.

The Norwegian scholar Sigmund Skard noted some years ago the special interest that Scotsmen had shown in America: Adam Smith, William Robertson, James Bryce, and D. W. Brogan comprise just a short list of some of Scotland's more distinguished writers on American affairs.[8] As Dr Collins observes, Bryce was fully aware of the 'two spheres' of American government. The dual nature of the Anglo-Scottish monarchy since 1603, and the history of conflict and federation between Scotland and her powerful neighbour, England, meant that the Scots were always aware of the problems inherent in plans for federation, whether they involved Ireland, more distant parts of the Empire, or the United States.[9] It meant, too, that they rarely underestimated the need in America for authority, or 'played down the importance of federal government and its components in favour of the states and the townships', Tocqueville's 'blunder' according to Hugh Brogan.[10]

The Scots took an early lead, in the Anglophone world, in the writing of American history.[11] Their perspective has continued to be influential in England, perhaps because Englishmen profess more faith than Americans (if less than the Germans and French) in central government. For example, the Conservative government in the early 1980s pursued spending cuts by concentrating in London some of the taxation powers hitherto vested in local authorities. As Dr Badger observes, spending cuts were sought on the *local* level in 1930s America; in the 1980s, President Reagan expected similar local stringency in calling, in stark contrast to his British counterpart, Prime Minister Thatcher, for a devolution of authority. Without doubt, the contributors to this volume reflect a Scottish intellectual and English political tradition: they are 'biased' in favour of federal unity and assertive federal government. Unlike many American citizens, they are not innately distrustful of 'Big Government', nor of its more controversial functions, such as the furtherance of economic and social welfare. To say that many American academics share this view is to miss the point: the perspective is British in origin, and carries especial conviction, still, on the point of a British pen.

What has been said in this volume seems to lend support to a distinction between the British and American approaches to union. Various British plans for federation and unity, whether in the British Isles, Europe, the Empire and Commonwealth, or within South Africa, have flowed from theoretical formulations designed to improve political efficiency, encourage economic harmony, and prevent the outbreak of military conflicts in the future.[12] In contrast, the American union has been progressively tightened as an ad hoc, pragmatic measure to cope with immediate crises – and to fight wars, as much as to prevent them.

It is ironic that Americans, conceiving of themselves as pragmatists in peace as in war, should have adopted a written Constitution, whereas the British, by inference sometimes portrayed as the prisoners of ideological preconceptions, should be free of such a document.[13] But there is a perverse logic in the irony. The Constitution may be said to have enshrined the idea of union because that union was so fragile. In the United States, unity had to be bolstered by the symbol of a written document, for the theoretical and popular consensus that upheld the unity of the United Kingdom could not, in America, be taken for granted.

Reflecting the importance which British writers would naturally attach to intellectual and popular support for a unified system of government, the contributors to this volume have paid attention to expectations. Professor Pole's colonists 'had to learn to think of themselves as British in order to think of themselves as American'. Drs MacLeod, Turley, and Collins write of both low *and* inflated expectations of federal government by politicians, reformers and economists in the ante-bellum decades. The issue is prominent again in Dr Spackman's 1860s, as it is for Dr Thompson's Progressive publicists and the millions of pro-New Deal voters whose faith in Washington had to be treated with respect by local politicians all over America (Dr Badger's chapter). Dr Harrison injects a refinement in arguing that Ostrogorski was taken in by Americans' low expectations of government in the late nineteenth century. The British contributors to this volume give substance to Professor Hyman's contention that American federalism, in so far as it mattered historically, was a set of attitudes.

Pragmatism and war have encouraged the strengthening of the federal union and increases in the scope of its activities. Economic and social factors, too, helped to account for the strengthening of the union, as well as for the growth of federal regulatory activities and expenditure. But perceptions of these economic and social factors, as well as the factors themselves, were important. Equally, a knowledge of intellectual trends and political thought in general helps to promote understanding of the growth of federal government in American history. Without a comprehension of the myths and expectations that governed Americans' behaviour, moreover, it is difficult, if not impossible, to explain the apparently cyclical reactions *against* federal power. Failure to understand these reactions in turn impedes one's comprehension of the cycle as a whole. For the expansions of the future are to be understood, as well as measured, against the contractions and stagnations of the past. Historians should heed Pieter Geyl's warning.[14] Failure to understand myths and expectations leads to a slavish dependence on past prejudices and current belief.

# Notes

## INTRODUCTORY

1. Peter Steinfels, *The Neoconservatives* (New York, 1980 edn.). A prediction that a long period of growing federal power might be followed by a period of greater decentralisation is offered in William R. Brock, *The Evolution of American Democracy* (New York, 1970), pp. 248–9. On the paucity of Republican intellectuals in the 1960s and early 1970s, see Theodore H. White, *American in Search of Itself: The Making of the President, 1956–1980* (New York, 1982) p. 232.
2. The latter view is put most forcibly in Milton Friedman and Rose Friedman, *Free to Choose. A Personal Statement* (Harmondsworth, Middx., 1980).
3. Robert Nozick, *Anarchy, State and Utopia* (Oxford, 1974).
4. Alan Crawford, *Thunder on the Right. The "New Right" and the Politics of Resentment* (New York, 1980) is especially strong on the organisation of 'New Right' groups and the articulation of their feelings.
5. For various observations related to this issue, see J. R. Pole, *The Pursuit of Equality in American History* (Berkeley, 1978), pp. 333–5, 348–51.
6. Lance E. Davis *et al.*, *American Economic Growth. An Economist's History of the United States* (New York, 1972) p. 657.
7. Friedmans, *Free to Choose*, chs. 9–10.
8. Samuel Smiles, *Self-Help* (London, 1968).
9. Friedmans, *Free to Choose*, p. 164.
10. The rhetoric of liberty endangered by extending central power is most tellingly analysed in Bernard Bailyn, *The Ideological Origins of the American Revolution* (Cambridge, Mass. 1967).
11. Steinfels, *The Neoconservatives*, ch. 7; Morris Janowitz, *The Last Half-Century: Societal Change and Politics in America* (Chicago, 1978), pp. 3, 9–10, 163, 214–17, 395; J. K. Galbraith, *The New Industrial State* (London, 1967).
12. One conservative economist concluded in 1978: 'We now live with an absence of public confidence in politicians and bureaucrats along with the absence of belief that political–bureaucratic institutions can accomplish results that are either desired or intended. This loss of public confidence in government is solidly grounded'. James M. Buchanan, 'The Economic Constitution and the New Deal: Lessons for Late Learners' in Gary M. Walton (ed.), *Regulatory Change in an Atmosphere of Crisis* (New York, 1979), pp. 13–26 (quotation, p. 20). The Friedmans (in *Free To Choose)* see America in the grip of a wider moral crisis; for example, in chs 2, 6–8.
13. Gardner Ackley's elegant textbook is one example of an elaboration upon Keynesian theory which gives little space to refutations of that central theory. Gardner Ackley, *Macroeconomic Theory*, (New York, 1961). And there is an engaging blandness in Professor Winch's respectfully neo-Keynesian reflections upon developments in the 1960s; Donald Winch, *Economics and Policy: A Historical Study* (London, 1969), ch. 14.
14. I am thinking here of William F. Buckley's journalistic writings, and Russell Kirk's *The Conservative Mind* (London, 1954). There is a very detailed account in George H. Nash, *The Conservative Intellectual Movement in America Since 1945* (New York, 1976).
15. Owen Fiss and Charles Krauthammer, 'The Rehnquist Court', *The New Republic*, 10 March 1982, pp. 14–21.
16. Michael Barone and Grant Ujifusa, *The Almanac of American Politics 1982* (Washington, D.C., 1981), pp. xxviii–xxix.
17. Bernard Schwartz, *American Constitutional Law* (Cambridge, 1955), pp. 44–8, 208–16.
18. U.S. Bureau of the Census, *Historical Statistics of the United States, Colonial Times to 1957* (Washington, D.C., 1960), pp. 709–10.
19. James T. Patterson, *The Welfare State in America, 1930–1980*, BAAS Pamphlets in American Studies 7 (Durham, 1981), p. 28.

20. Those who believe that the complexities of inter-governmental relations disappear within a federal system where the federal government is extremely powerful would be disabused of their mistaken beliefs by George F. Break, *Financing Government in a Federal System* (Washington D. C., 1980).

21. Friedmans, *Free to Choose*, pp. 149–55; Carter Goodrich, *Government Promotion of American Canals and Railroads, 1800–1890* (New York, 1960).

22. Patterson, *Welfare State in America*, pp. 18–20; J. Wreford Watson, *Social Geography of the United States* (London and New York, 1979), pp. 213, 215–16.

23. Patterson, *Welfare State in America*, pp. 22–7. The more ample and systematic provision of welfare payments in the 1960s altered attitudes of recipients and administrators towards welfare. One reason for rapidly rising expenditure upon various welfare programmes was that the proportion of those eligible applying for assistance rose markedly, as did the proportion of those actually granted aid. In this respect, the 1960s helped remove the Victorian stigma attached to poverty, be it merely short-term or more structural. *Idem*, pp. 31–2.

24. Break, *Financing Government in a Federal System*, p. 2.

25. Peter Temin in Gary M. Walton (ed.), *Regulatory Change in an Atmosphere of Crisis* (New York, 1979), pp. 59–60.

26. Charles L. Schultze in Henry Owen and Charles L. Schultze (eds.), *Setting National Priorities: The Next Ten Years* (Washington, D.C. 1976), p. 345.

27. Friedmans, *Free to Choose*, p. 158.

28. Richard A. Easterlin, *Birth and Fortune. The Impact of Numbers on Personal Welfare* (London, 1980), p. 17. On economists' use of non-recession G.N.P., see Charles L. Schultze 'Federal Spending: Past, Present, and Future' in Owen and Schultze, *Setting National Priorities*, pp. 323–69.

29. Janowitz, *The Last Half-Century*, pp. 126–7.

30. James Bryce, *The American Commonwealth* (3 vols. London and New York, 1888), vol. I, p. 432.

31. For an intelligent discussion of federal planning, which distinguishes carefully between comprehensive national plans and the sort of planning undertaken by American governments, see Otis L. Graham, Jr., *Toward a Planned Society: From Roosevelt to Nixon* (London, 1976).

CHAPTER 1

1. Lawrence H. Gipson, *The Great War for the Empire* (New York, 1949).

2. Gary M. Nash, *The Urban Crucible: Social Change, Political Consciousness and the Origins of the American Revolution* (Cambridge, Mass., 1979), esp. ch. 7.

3. Alan Rogers, *Empire and Liberty: American Resistance to British Authority, 1755–1763* (Berkeley, 1974), pp. 84–6, 133.

4. Alan Heimert, *Religion and the American Mind from the Great Awakening to the Revolution* (Cambridge, Mass., 1966), esp. ch. vii.

5. Paul Langford, 'British Correspondence in the Colonial Press, 1763–1775: a Study in Anglo-American Misunderstanding before the American Revolution' in Bernard Bailyn and John B. Hench (eds.), *The Press and the American Revolution* (Worcester, Mass., 1980), pp. 290–309.

6. Pauline Maier, *From Resistance to Revolution: Colonial Radicals and the Development of Opposition to Britain, 1765–1776* (New York, 1972), pp. 235–6.

7. John Adams to H. Niles, 13 February 1818 in Charles Francis Adams (ed.), *Works of John Adams* (Boston, 1856), vol. x, p. 282.

8. See above, vol. x, p. 87.

9. J. R. Western, *Monarchy and Revolution: The English State in the 1680s* (London, 1972), p. 379.

10. This theme has emerged from recent scholarship on the period from the Glorious Revolution into the eighteenth century, but its significance for colonial history has not been appreciated. See Geoffrey Holmes, *British Politics in the Age of Anne* (London, 1967); P. G. M. Dickson, *The Financial Revolution in England* (Oxford, 1967).

11. The argument suggested here is developed at greater length in J. R. Pole, *The Gift of Government: an Essay on Political Responsibility from the English Restoration to American Independence* (Athens, Ga., 1983), ch. 3.

12. Jack P. Greene, 'Political Mimesis: a Consideration of the Political and Cultural Roots of Legislative Behavior in the British Colonies in the Eighteenth Century', *American Historical Review*, lxxv (1969–70), 337–60.
13. Mary P. Clarke, *Parliamentary Privilege in the American Colonies* (New Haven, 1943).
14. Lyman H. Butterfield, *et al.* (eds.), *The Diary and Autobiography of John Adams* (Cambridge, Mass., 1961), vol. ii, pp. 122–6.
15. Bernard Bailyn, *The Ideological Origins of the American Revolution* (Cambridge, Mass., 1967).
16. James Abercromby, 'Magna Charta for America: an Examination of the Acts of Parliament Relative to the Trade and Government of Our American Colonies' (1752). There are copies in the Huntington Library, the Clements Library and the Pennsylvania State Archive. A forthcoming edition has been edited by Jack P. Greene, Charles F. Mullett and Edward C. Papenfuse, together with Abercromby's 'De Jure et Gubernatione Coloniarum' (1774). I am most grateful to Professor Greene for allowing me to read the typescript. See also, Leland J. Bellot, *William Knox: the Life and Thought of an Eighteenth Century Imperialist* (Austin, Texas, 1977).
17. Butterfield *et al.*, *Diary and Autobiography of John Adams*, vol. ii, pp. 195–9.
18. J. Bigelow (ed.), *The Works of Benjamin Franklin* (10 vols., New York, 1887), vol. v, pp. 548–54.
19. Philip S. Foner (ed.), *The Complete Writings of Thomas Paine* (2 vols., New York, 1945), vol. i, pp. 28–9.
20. *Journals of the Continental Congress*, (Washington, 1823), vol. i, pp. 72–4.
21. Jack N. Rakove, *The Beginnings of National Politics: an Interpretive History of the Continental Congress* (New York, 1979), pp. 195–6. This book gives an excellent account of the ways in which the practical life and work of the Congress affected its making of policy.
22. Jacob E. Cooke (ed.), *The Federalist* (Middletown, Conn., 1961), pp. 3–50.
23. The leading work is Merrill Jensen, *The New Nation* (New York, 1948).
24. Max Farrand, ed., *The Records of the Federal Convention of 1787*, revised edn., (4 vols., New Haven, 1937), vol. i, pp. 437–8; 444–5.
25. *ibid.*, pp. 492–3; 501; 502.
26. *ibid.*, pp. 323; 36; 37; 49; 52.
27. *ibid.*, p. 449.
28. *The Federalist*, no. 39 in *op. cit.*, p. 257.
29. Farrand, *The Records of the Federal Convention*, pp. 486–7, 566.
30. Worthington Chauncy Ford, ed., *Writings of George Washington*, (14 vols. New York, 1892), vol. 13, pp. 277–325.

## CHAPTER 2

1. John Taylor of Caroline, *A Letter on the Necessity of Defending the Rights and Interests of Agriculture* (Petersburg, 1821), p. 4.
2. *ibid.*, p. 5.
3. *ibid.*, p. 6.
4. Joyce Appleby, 'Commercial Farming and the "Agrarian Myth" in the Early Republic', *The Journal of American History*, 68 (1982), 833–49.
5. *Richmond Enquirer*, 21 March 1820; see also John Taylor, *An Inquiry into the Principles and Policy of the Government of the United States* (Fredericksburg, 1814), p. 352.
6. *Fletcher* v. *Peck*, 6 Cranch 87; *Dartmouth College* v. *Woodward*, 4 Wheaton 624; *Stuges* v. *Crowninshield*, 4 Wheaton 122.
7. *Martin* v. *Hunter's Lessee*, 1 Wheaton 304.
8. *McCulloch* v. *Maryland*, 4 Wheaton 400; *Annals of Congress*, 15 Cong., 2 sess., vol. II, pp. 1240–71, 1283–1328, 1330–93, 1394–1402, 1411–15.
9. Gerald Gunther (ed.), *John Marshall's Defense of McCulloch* v. *Maryland* (Stanford, 1969) contains the court decision, Marshall's newspaper defence of it, and two attacks on the decision which appeared in the *Richmond Enquirer;* one, written over the pseudonym 'Amphictyon', was probably penned by Judge William Brockenbrough and the other by Judge Spencer Roane, writing as 'Hampden'.
10. Gunther, *John Marshall's Defense* p. 112.
11. *Annals of Congress*, 15 Cong., 1 sess., p. 234; the reference to the Treaty of Ghent (see below) is on p. 235.

12. Spencer Roane to James Monroe, 16 February 1820, in New York Public Library, *Bulletin*, X, 175.

13. Don E. Fehrenbacher, *The Dred Scott Case: Its Significance in American Law and Politics* (New York, 1978), pp. 102–6, and more generally, pp. 100–13. See also the standard history, Glover Moore, *The Missouri Controversy, 1819–1821* (Lexington, Ky., 1953) and the account in Donald L. Robinson, *Slavery in the Structure of American Politics 1765–1820* (New York, 1971), ch. 10.

14. Betty Fladeland, *Men and Brothers: Anglo-American Antislavery Cooperation* (Urbana, Chicago, London, 1972), pp. 150–51.

15. *Annals of Congress*, 16 Cong., 1 sess., pp. 1074, 1154–5, 1384, 104, 348–9. See also Philip F. Detweiler, 'Congressional Debate on Slavery and the Declaration of Independence, 1819–1821', *American Historical Review*, 63 (1958), 598–616.

16. See above, no 8.

17. Robinson, *Slavery in the Structure of American Politics* p. 410; cf. Plumer of New Hampshire, *Annals of Congress*, 16 Cong., 1 sess., pp. 1412–40.

18. Duncan J. MacLeod, *Slavery, Race and the American Revolution* (Cambridge, 1974), pp. 40–4.

19. See above, no 11; the 'Horrors of Slavery' was the title of a contemporary anti-slavery tract by John Kenrick.

20. MacLeod, *Slavery, Race and the American Revolution*, pp. 57–8.

21. Daniel Raymond, *The Missouri Question* (Baltimore, 1819).

22. The substance of King's senate speeches is in Charles R. King (ed.), *The Life and Correspondence of Rufus King* (6 vols., New York, 1899), vol. VI, pp. 690–703; see also vol. VI, pp. 235–7. King's 1825 resolution is recorded in *Register of Debates in Congress*, 18 Cong., 1 sess., vol. I, p. 623.

23. I shall argue in a forthcoming article that the strength and militancy of early anti-slavery were greater than is normally considered to be the case; and that, as a consequence, we shall need to re-think the transition in the 1820s from 'gradualism' to 'immediatism'.

24. One work which charts the continued high temperature is William W. Freehling, *Prelude to Civil War. The Nullification Controversy in South Carolina, 1816–1836* (New York, 1965); for evidence that these passions were widespread and penetrated all ranks of society, see Duncan MacLeod, 'Racing to War: Antebellum Match Races between the North and the South' in *Southern Exposure*, VII (1979), 7–10.

25. For the benevolent reform movement see Carroll Smith-Rosenberg, *Religion and the Rise of the American City: The New York City Mission Movement, 1812–1870* (Ithaca, London, 1971); Charles I. Foster, *An Errand of Mercy: The Evangelical United Front, 1790–1837* (Chapel Hill, 1960).

26. See Moore, Fehrenbacher and Robinson cited in no 13.

27. *Annals of Congress*, 15 Cong., 2 sess., pp. 1437, 1205; *ibid.*, 16 Cong., 1 sess., pp. 1203–5, 1437.

28. Paul E. Johnson, *A Shopkeeper's Millenium: Society and Revivals in Rochester, New York, 1815–1837* (New York, 1978), pp. 8, 115, 136–41; Paul Boyer, *Urban masses and Moral Order in America, 1820–1920*, part I (Cambridge, Mass., 1978).

29. Fehrenbacher, *The Dred Scott Case*, p. 110. The most important and influential contemporary attempt to construct an integrated account and philosophy was John Taylor of Caroline's *Construction Construed and Constitutions Vindicated* (Richmond, 1820 – Da Capo Reprint, New York, 1970).

30. Richard H. Brown, 'The Missouri Crisis, Slavery, and the Politics of Jacksonianism', *South Atlantic Quarterly*, LXV, (1966), 55–72.

31. See John Ashworth, '"Agrarians" and "Aristocrats": Party Political Ideology in the United States, 1837–1846', Unpublished D. Phil. thesis, University of Oxford, 1978: some of the themes of this work, including reference to Taylor's influence appear in John Ashworth, 'The Jacksonian as Leveller', *Journal of American Studies*, 14 (1980), 407–21.

## CHAPTER 3

1. Stanley Elkins, *Slavery: A Problem in American Institutional and Intellectual Life* 3rd edn (Chicago, 1976); John L. Thomas, *The Liberator: William Lloyd Garrison, A Biography*, (Boston and Toronto, 1963); John L. Thomas, 'Romantic Reform in America, 1815–1865'

reprinted in David Brion Davis (ed.), *Ante-Bellum Reform* (New York; 1967), pp. 153–176; George M. Fredrickson, *The Inner Civil War: Northern Intellectuals and the Crisis of the Union* (New York, 1965).

2. Elkins, *Slavery*, p. 160.
3. Salmon P. Chase to Thaddeus Stevens, 8 Apr. 1842 quoted in Eric Foner, *Free Soil, Free Labor, Free Men: The Ideology of the Republican Party before the Civil War* (New York, 1970), p. 80.
4. William R. Brock, *Parties and Political Conscience: American Dilemmas, 1840–1850* (Millwood, New York, 1979), pp. 24–6.
5. William M. Wiecek, *The Sources of Antislavery Constitutionalism in America, 1760–1848* (Ithaca and London, 1977), pp. 15–16.
6. J. R. Pole, *Paths to the American Past* (New York, 1979), p. 157.
7. Brock, *Parties and Political Conscience*, pp. 140–43.
8. *Liberator*, 30 July 1831.
9. W. L. Garrison to Samuel J. May, 17 Jan. 1836; to George W. Benson, 14 June 1837, Garrison Papers, Boston Public Library (hereafter BPL); to J. H. Kimball, 16 Aug. 1837 in *Liberator*, 1 Sept. 1837.
10. W. L. Garrison to Samuel J. May, 23 Sept. 1836, Garrison Papers, BPL. Wendell Phillips did not accept Garrison's perfectionist doctrines but he did believe the progressive enlightenment of opinion possible.
11. *Liberator*, 15 Dec. 1837. For a more general discussion of the intellectual sources of anti-government attitudes see Lewis Perry, *Radical Abolitionism: Anarchy and the Government of God in Anti-slavery Thought* (Ithaca and London, 1973), pp. 33–54.
12. *Liberator*, 28 June 1839.
13. W. L. Garrison to Isaac Knapp, 23 Aug. 1836, Garrison Papers, BPL.
14. Wiecek, *Antislavery Constitutionalism*, pp. 228–48.
15. *Liberator*, 31 May 1844.
16. Wendell Phillips, *Can Abolitionists Vote or Take Office under the United States Constitution?* (1845), reprinted in William H. Pease and Jane H. Pease (eds.), *The Antislavery Argument* (Indianapolis, 1965), p. 473.
17. William G. McLoughlin (ed.), *Lectures on the Revivals of Religion by Charles Grandison Finney* (Cambridge, Mass., 1960), pp. 452, 403.
18. Theodore Weld to C. G. Finney, 22 April 1828 in Gilbert H. Barnes and Dwight L. Dumond (eds.), *Letters of Theodore Dwight Weld, Angelina Grimke Weld and Sarah Grimke 1822–1844* (2 vols., Gloucester, Mass, 1965), vol. 1, pp. 14–17.
19. Resolution of a Convention of Friends of Abolition, Warsaw, New York, 13 Nov. 1839; Benjamin Fenn to James G. Birney 17 Feb. 1840 (mailed 14 Apr.) in Dwight L. Dumond (ed.), *Letters of James Gillespie Birney 1831–1857*, (2 vols., Gloucester Mass., 1966), vol. 1, pp. 512 note 2, 530.
20. Joshua R. Giddings [Pacificus], *The Rights and Privileges of the Several States in Regard to Slavery* (1842); Arnold Buffum, *Lecture Showing the Necessity of a Liberty Party* (1844) reprinted in Pease and Pease, *Antislavery Argument*, pp. 411–27.
21. Wiecek, *Antislavery Constitutionalism*, pp. 249–75.
22. Foner, *Free Soil*, pp. 73–102.
23. Leonard L. Richards, *'Gentlemen of Property and Standing' Anti-Abolition Mobs in Jacksonian America* (New York, 1971), pp. 14–16, 37–40, 75–81, 92–100.
24. Robert Price, 'Further Notes on Granville's Anti-Abolition Disturbances of 1836', *Ohio Archaeological and Historical Quarterly*, 45 (1936), 365–8; Mary P. Ryan, *Cradle of the Middle Class: The Family in Oneida County, New York, 1790–1865* (London, New York, 1981) pp. 94–5; Bertram Wyatt-Brown, 'Proslavery and Antislavery Intellectuals: Class Concepts and Polemical Struggle' in Lewis Perry and Michael Fellman (eds.), *Antislavery Reconsidered: New Perspectives on the Abolitionists*, (Baton Rouge and London 1979), pp. 314–15; Don Harrison Doyle, *The Social Order of a Frontier Community Jacksonville, Illinois 1825–70* (Urbana, Chicago, London, 1978) pp. 51–7.
25. Donald G. Mathews, 'The Abolitionists on Slavery: The Critique behind the Social Movement', *Journal of Southern History*, 33 (1967), 175.
26. Note particularly the language of the correspondence of the 'Lane rebels' to each other in 1835 and 1836 in Barnes and Dumond, *Letters*, vol. 1.
27. Alan M. Kraut, 'The Forgotten Reformers: A Profile of Third Party Abolitionists in Antebellum New York', in Perry and Fellman, *Antislavery Reconsidered*, pp. 141–4.

28. John L. Hammond, *The Politics of Benevolence, Revival Religion and American Voting Behaviour* (Norwood, New Jersey, 1979), pp. 1–2, 116–17; Doyle, *Frontier Community*, pp. 58–9.

29. 'Declaration of The Radical Political Abolitionists assembled in Syracuse in the State of New York on the 26th, 27th and 28th days of June A.D. 1855', *British and Foreign Anti-Slavery Reporter*, 1 Oct. 1855.

30. Foner, *Free Soil*, p. 57.

31. Foner, *Free Soil*, pp. 116–17.

32. Wendell Phillips, *Speeches, Lectures and Letters* (Boston, 1863), pp. 74–81; Michael Fellman, 'Theodore Parker and the Abolitionist Role in the 1850's', *Journal of American History*, 61 (1974), 674.

33. Phillips (1863), *Speeches*, p. 71; *Liberator*, 13 Feb. 1857.

34. Wendell Phillips, *Speeches, Lectures and Letters. Second Series* (Boston, 1894), pp. 303, 308.

35. Phillips (1863), *Speeches*, pp. 387, 375.

36. *Ibid.*, p. 399; George M. Fredrickson (ed.), *William Lloyd Garrison* (Englewood Cliffs, N.J.; 1968), pp. 63–6.

37. Eric Foner, *Politics and Ideology in The Age of the Civil War* (New York, 1980), pp. 57–76; Joseph G. Rayback, 'The American Workingman and the Antislavery Crusade', *Journal of Economic History*, 3 (1943), 152–63; Jonathan A. Glickstein, '"Poverty is Not Slavery": American Abolitionists and the Competitive Labour Market', in Perry and Fellman, *Antislavery Reconsidered*, pp. 195–218.

38. Foner, *Free Soil*, pp. 9–10. This essay has deliberately excluded discussion of black abolitionists. Their importance was undoubted, but they are not primarily to be understood in the terms developed here.

CHAPTER 4

1. For economists' frustrations with political expediency, see F. W. Taussig, *The Tariff History of the United States* (4th edn. revised New York, 1961), pp. 454–5, 474, Milton and Rose Friedman, *Free to Choose: A Personal Statement* (Harmondsworth, Middx. 1980), pp. 155–8, 338–47, 350–3. For a central banker's frustration with the opponents of the Bank of the United States in the 1830s, see Bray Hammond, *Banks and Politics in America from the Revolution to the Civil War* (Princeton, 1957), pp. 323–5, 358–68, 438–50.

2. U.S. Bureau of the Census, *Historical Statistics of the United States, Colonial Times to 1957* (Washington, D.C., 1960), pp. 718–19, 726.

3. The clearest statement of this view is Steven A. Channing, *Crisis of Fear: Secession in South Carolina* (New York, 1970). See also Allan Nevins, *The Emergence of Lincoln* (2 vols., New York, 1950), vol. II, p. 331.

4. Friedmans, *Free to Choose*, pp. 25–6, 88–94, 145–55, 158, 347–59. Paul K. Conkin, *Prophets of Prosperity: America's First Political Economists* (Bloomington, Ind., 1980), pp. 313–4, sees the history of economic theory as part of the history of moral philosophy.

5. Daniel W. Howe, *The Political Culture of the American Whigs* (Chicago, 1979), p. 113; Eric Foner, *Free Soil, Free Labor, Free Men: The Ideology of the Republican Party Before the Civil War* (London, 1970), p. 37; Arnold W. Green, *Henry Charles Carey, Nineteenth Century Sociologist* (Philadelphia, 1951), pp. 50, 73, 82–4; Vernon L. Parrington, *Main Currents in American Thought* (3 vols., New York, 1930), vol. III, pp. 105–11. Parrington (p. 106) refers to *The Harmony of Interests*, a densely packed work of over 200 pages, as a pamphlet and says that it was written in 1852. In fact, its precise time of composition (the winter of 1849–50) was of considerable relevance to its contents. Joseph Dorfman, *The Economic Mind in American Civilisation, 1606–1865* (2 vols., New York, 1946), vol. II, pp. 789–805 is not very subtle on Carey's public role. Rodney J. Morrison, 'Henry C. Carey and American Economic Development', *Explorations in Entrepreneurial History*, 2nd Series, 5 (1967–68), 132–144, emphasises technical theory.

6. Howe, *Political Culture*, pp. 108–22, rightly stresses Carey's role as a moral philosopher (p. 110); Foner, *Free Soil, Free Labor, Free Men*, pp. 36–8.

7. Henry C. Carey, *The Harmony of Interests. Agricultural, Manufacturing, and Commercial* (2nd ed., New York, 1852); Carey, *Letters to the President, on the Foreign and Domestic Policy of the Union, and Its Effects, as exhibited in the Condition of the People and the State* (Philadelphia, 1858).

8. Carey, *Harmony of Interests*, pp. iii, 154–60, 205.

9. Carey, *Harmony of Interests*, pp. 201, 204, 220; *Letters to the President*, p. 96.
10. Carey, *Harmony of Interests*, p. 140; Conkin, *Prophets of Prosperity*, pp. 285–6.
11. Carey, *Ibid.*, p. 79; also pp. 9–16.
12. Carey, *Letters to the President*, p. 158.
13. Hammond, *Banks and Politics in America*, chs. 18, 19, 21, 22; James R. Sharp, *The Jacksonians versus the Banks: Politics in the States after the Panic of 1837* (New York, 1970); William G. Shade, *Banks or No Banks: The Money Issue in Western Politics 1832–1865* (Detroit, 1972).
14. Carey, *Harmony of Interests*, p. 161. Conkin briefly mentions Carey's frequent abuse of historical data; *Prophets of Prosperity*, p. 261.
15. Carey, *Ibid.*, pp. 145, 199.
16. Carey, *Ibid.*, pp. 136, 201; *Letters to the President*, pp. 50–6.
17. Howe, *Political Culture*, pp. 116–17 stresses the importance of nostalgia for rural life to Whig as well as Jacksonian Democratic thought; Carey, *Harmony of Interests*, p. 209.
18. Carey, *Harmony of Interests*, pp. 141, 149; *Letters to the President*, pp. 31–4, 60.
19. Green, *Henry Charles Carey*, p. 37; Carey, *Harmony of Interests*, pp. 161–64.
20. Carey's political commitments are well known to historians. He was, for instance, a leading economic contributor to the Whig, and subsequently Republican, *New York Tribune* from 1849 to 1857. He served as a Republican fund-raiser and as president of the Republican clubs of Philadelphia in 1856. (Green, *Henry Charles Carey*, pp. 25, 34.) But his writings are not properly placed in their *specific* and *immediate* political context. For the lengths to which Carey was prepared to go to mollify southern feelings on slavery, see Carey, *Harmony of Interests*, p. 169: 'Of all the chapters in the history of the people of this Union, the most honourable to them . . . is that in which is recorded the history of the negro race. The three hundred thousand barbarians imported into this country are now represented by almost four millions of people, far advanced towards civilisation and freedom, and to that number they have grown because they have been well fed, well clothed, well sheltered, and reasonably worked. It is a case totally without parallel in the world'. There was a sting in the tail of this flattery, in the mention of the slaves' progress towards freedom.
21. Carey, *Harmony of Interests*, pp. 200–1.
22. Carey, *Letters to the President*, pp. 21, 24–30.
23. Carey, *Ibid.*, p. 30.
24. See, for example, B. W. Collins, 'Economic Issues in Ohio's Politics During the Recession of 1857–1858', *Ohio History*, 89 (1980), 46–64, esp. 62–3.
25. *Historical Statistics of the United States*, p. 710. Of the 31 million Americans of 1860, only 7 millions were adult white males.
26. *Historical Statistics of the United States*, pp. 7, 710.
27. *Ibid.*, p. 711.
28. On the economy, see Douglass C. North, *Economic Growth of the United States, 1790–1860* (Englewood Cliffs, N.J., 1961), pp. 204–15. On southern interest in expansion into the Caribbean, see Foner, *Free Soil, Free Labor, Free Men*, p. 98; Robert E. May, *The Southern Dream of a Caribbean Empire, 1854–1861* (Baton Rouge, 1973), pp. 75–6, 159–61, 169–78.
29. The totals are provided in 'Report of the Secretary of the Interior' *House Executive Documents* 39th Congress (Washington, D.C. 1866), pp. 165–8.
30. Robert R. Russell, *Critical Studies in Antebellum Sectionalism: Essays in American Political and Economic History* (Westport, Conn., 1972), ch. 6; Robert W. Johannsen, *Stephen A. Douglas* (New York, 1973), pp. 304–6, 391–5, 436–7, 691–2.
31. *National Intelligencer*, January 24, 1859, quoted in Philip S. Klein, *President James Buchanan. A Biography* (University Park, Penn., 1962), p. 327.
32. Foner, *Free Soil, Free Labor, Free Men*, pp. 173–6.
33. The idea that Republicans were challenging the Slave Power for control of the national government and for possession of federal power is well described in Foner, *Free Soil, Free Labor, Free Men*, pp. 99–102. For historians' recent stress on the importance of state and local issues, see, for example, Michael F. Holt, *Forging A Majority: The Formation of the Republican Party in Pittsburgh, 1848–1860* (New Haven, 1969); Ronald P. Formisano, *The Birth of Mass Political Parties: Michigan 1827–1861* (Princeton, 1971); Michael F. Holt, *The Political Crisis of the 1850s* (New York, 1978), J. Mills Thornton, III, *Politics and Power in a Slave Society. Alabama 1800–1860* (Baton Rouge, 1978).
34. The tension between nationalism and sectionalism and state rights thinking is well discussed in David M. Potter (completed and edited by Don E. Fehrenbacher), *The*

*Impending Crisis, 1848–1861* (New York, 1976), ch. 17.
35. Friedmans, *Free to Choose*, p. 158.


CHAPTER 5

1. W. R. Brock, *An American Crisis: Congress and Reconstruction 1865–1867* (London, 1963), pp. 264, 298–301.
2. William Gillette, *Retreat from Reconstruction 1869–1879* (Baton Rouge, 1979), p. xii; Morton Keller, *Affairs of State: Public Life in Late Nineteenth Century America* (Cambridge, Mass., 1977), pp. 108–10.
3. David Donald, *Charles Sumner and the Rights of Man* (New York, 1970), pp. 421–7, 433, quotations at 423 and 426. (Hereafter referred to as *Sumner II.)*
4. I have derived this formulation of the federal consensus from William M. Wiecek, *The Sources of Antislavery Constitutionalism in America, 1760–1848* (Ithaca, 1977), pp. 15–16; Harold Hyman, *A More Perfect Union: The Impact of the Civil War and Reconstruction on the Constitution* (Boston, 1973), p. 298.
5. On the 'Force Acts' see Everette Swinney, 'Enforcing the Fifteenth Amendment 1870–1877', *Journal of Southern History*, 28 (1962), 202–18; and Gillette, *Retreat*, pp. 25–55. On the educational plans see S. G. F. Spackman, 'National Authority in the United States', Unpublished Ph.D. dissertation, Cambridge University, 1971, pp. 63–90. On the Civil Rights measure see Alfred H. Kelly, 'The Congressional Controversy over School Segregation 1867–1875', *American Historical Review*, 64 (1959), 537–63; James McPherson, 'Abolitionists and the Civil Rights Act of 1875', *Journal of American History*, 52 (1965), 493–510; Donald, *Sumner II*, pp. 531–40, 544–7; S. G. F. Spackman, 'American Federalism and the Civil Rights Act of 1875', *Journal of American Studies*, 10 (1976), 313–28.
6. Wiecek, *Antislavery Constitutionalism*, pp. 106–25, 168–9; David Donald, *Charles Sumner and the Coming of the Civil War* (New York, 1965), pp. 227–35, quotation at 230.
7. Wiecek, *Antislavery Constitutionalism*, pp. 228–75; Jacobus ten Broek, *Equal Under Law* (new edn. rev. New York, 1965), p. 85, n. 20.
8. *Congressional Globe*, 42nd. Congress, 2nd. Session, p. 728 (31 Jan. 1872). (Hereafter referred to as C.G. 42.2.728 etc., and the *Congressional Record* as C.R. 43.1.000 etc.)
9. E. Rockwood Hoar, C.R. 43.2.979 (4 Feb. 1875); Bingham, C.G. 42. 1. Apdx. 85 (3 Mar. 1871); George Hoar, C.G. 42.1.332 (29 Mar. 1871).
10. Timothy Dwight Farrar, *Manual of the Constitution of the United States of America* (2nd edn. Boston, 1868), p. 127.
11. Harold M. Hyman (ed.), *New Frontiers of the American Reconstruction* (Urbana, 1966), pp. 28–32.
12. Hoar, C.G. 41.2. Apdx. 478 (6 June 1870) and C.G. 42.1.333 (29 Mar. 1871); Perce, C.G. 42.2.862 (6 Feb. 1872).
13. Joel Tiffany, *A Treatise on Government* (Albany, 1867), pp. 50, 84, 86.
14. C.G.42.1.487 (5 April 1871); C.R. 43.1.425 (6 Jan. 1874).
15. Bingham, C.G. 42.1. Apdx. 85 (31 Mar. 1871); Monroe, C.G. 42.1.370 (31 Mar 1871).
16. Wiecek, *Antislavery Constitutionalism*, pp. 63, 119–20, 269–70.
17. Donald, *Sumner II*, pp. 199–205, 245–47, quotation at 246; Michael Les Benedict, *A Compromise of Principle: Congressional Republicans and Reconstruction 1863–1869* (New York, 1974), p. 413, n. 29.
18. Rush Welter, *Popular Education and Democratic Thought in America* (New York, 1962), p. 3; Hoar, C.G. 41.2. Apdx. 479 (6 June 1870); Perce, C.G. 42.2.862 (6 Feb 1872); Boutwell, C.R. 43.1.4116 (21 May 1874).
19. Hyman, *New Frontiers*, pp. 30–31; Charles O. Lerche, Jr., 'Congressional Interpretations of the Guarantee of a Republican Form of Government during Reconstruction', *Journal of Southern History*, 15 (1949), 192–211; Gillette, *Retreat from Reconstruction*, pp. 104–35.
20. Butler, C.G. 42.3.542 (13 Jan. 1873); Schurz, C.G. 42.3.1874 (27 Feb. 1873); Carpenter, C.G. 42.3. Apdx. 199 (27 Feb. 1873) and C.R. 43.1. Apdx. 86–89 (4 Mar. 1874).
21. C.G. 42.3.542 (13 Jan. 1873).
22. C.R. 43.2.490 (15 Jan. 1875).
23. C.G. 41.2.3607 (19 May 1870).
24. C.G. 42.1.577 (11 April 1871).
25. Alcorn, C.R. 43.1. Apdx. 304 (22 May 1874).

26. The most useful discussion of the problems raised by this issue is James H. Kettner, *The Development of American Citizenship, 1608–1870* (Chapel Hill, 1978), pp. 248–333. See also ten Broek, *Equal Under Law*, pp. 94–115.
27. *Scott* v. *Sandford*, 19 How. 406 (U.S. 1857).
28. *U.S.* v. *Hall*, 26 Fed. Cases 81 (No. 15,282) C.C.E.D.Ala. (1871); Loren Miller, *The Petitioners: The Story of the Supreme Court of the United States and the Negro* (New York, 1966), p. 138; C. Peter Magrath, *Morrison R. Waite: The Triumph of Character* (New York, 1963), p. 121.
29. C.R. 43.1.3454 (29 April 1874).
30. For a concise survey of the legal controversies see Henry J. Abraham, *Freedom and the Court: Civil Rights and Liberties in the United States* (New York, 1967), pp. 32–40. Joseph B. James, *The Framing of the Fourteenth Amendment* (Urbana, 1956) is the standard monograph, but in my view should be read in conjunction with ten Broek, *Equal Under Law*.
31. C.G. 39.1.2459 (8 May 1866).
32. ten Broek, pp. 116–22.
33. C.G. 42.1. Apdx. 84 (31 Mar. 1871).
34. 21 L. Ed. 394–426 (1873). The case arose when a butchers' monopoly in New Orleans was challenged on the grounds that the state legislature's grant infringed the privileges and immunities as U.S. citizens of the butchers put out of business, depriving them of liberty and property without due process of law and denying them the equal protection of the laws, thus giving the Court an opportunity to rule on the scope of the Fourteenth Amendment. The Court upheld the legality of the monopoly grant and defined fundamental privileges and immunities as coming under state rather than national protection.
35. S. S. Cox, resolution defining the powers of the Federal Government (written by Parke Godwin of the N.Y. *Evening Post*), C.G. 42.3.1235 (10 Feb. 1873); Samuel Shellabarger, 'The Domestic Commerce of the United States', *International Review*, 1 (1874), 828.
36. Henry Wilson, 'New Departure of the Republican Party', *Atlantic Monthly*, 27 (1871), 110.
37. John C. Gooden to Senator Thomas Bayard of Delaware, 12 Oct. 1872, Bayard papers, Library of Congress.

CHAPTER 6

1. Moisei Ostrogorski, *Democracy and the Organisation of Political Parties* (2 vols., London and New York, 1902), vol. II, 550. Cf. Matthew Josephson, *The Politicos, 1865–1896* (New York, 1938); Richard Hofstadter, *The American Political Tradition* (New York, 1948), pp. 162–82.
2. Wallace D. Farnham, 'The "Weakened Spring of Government": A Study in Nineteenth-Century History' *American Historical Review*, 68 (April 1963), 662–80; Ostrogorski, *Democracy*, vol. II, p. 577.
3. Morton Keller, *Affairs of State: Public Life in Late Nineteenth-Century America* (Cambridge, Mass., 1977), p. 409. Keller's book offers the most complete description of the pattern of both state and federal legislation during this period.
4. Robert Lively, 'The American System: A Review Article', *Business History Review*, 29 (1955), 94; James Willard Hurst, *Law and the Conditions of Freedom in the Nineteenth-Century United States* (Madison, Wis., 1956), pp. 6 and 3–70; Harry N. Scheiber, 'Government and the Economy; Studies of the "Commonwealth" Policy in Nineteenth-Century America', *Journal of Interdisciplinary History*, 3 (Summer 1972), 135–51. Some of the more important studies are Carter Goodrich, *Government Promotion of American Canals and Railroads, 1800–1890* (New York, 1960); Oscar and Mary Handlin, *Commonwealth: A Study of the Role of Government in the American Economy: Massachusetts, 1774–1861* (New York, 1947); Louis Hartz, *Economic Policy and Democratic Thought: Pennsylvania, 1776–1860* (Cambridge, Mass., 1948).
5. The distinction between 'distributive' and 'regulatory' policies is formulated by Theodore J. Lowi in 'American Business, Public Policy, Case Studies, and Political Theory', *World Politics*, 16 (1964), 677–715. It is developed further in Richard L. McCormick, 'The Party Period and Public Policy: An Exploratory Hypothesis', *Journal of American History*, 66 (Sept. 1979), 279–98.
6. Goodrich, *American Canals and Railroads*, pp. 162–262; Keller, *Affairs of State*, pp. 164–8, 185–9, 381–2; Farnham, *Weakened Spring of Government*, pp. 662–76; Lewis H. Haney, *A*

*Congressional History of Railways in the United States* (2 vols., Madison, Wis., 1908–1910), vol. II, pp. 13–54.

7. Frederick W. Taussig, *A Tariff History of the United States* (New York, 1931), pp. 230–360; Tom E. Terrill, *The Tariff, Politics and American Foreign Policy, 1874–1901* (Westport, Conn., 1973); H. Wayne Morgan, *From Hayes to McKinley: National Party Politics, 1877–1896* (Syracuse, N.Y., 1969), pp. 166–70, 519–20; Lewis L. Gould, 'The Republican Search for a National Majority', in H. Wayne Morgan (ed.), *The Gilded Age* (revised edn., Syracuse, N.Y., 1970), pp. 176–84; Richard S. Edwards, 'Economic Sophistication in Nineteenth-Century Congressional Tariff Debates', *Journal of Economic History*, 30 (Dec. 1970), 821–38; S. Walter Poulshock, 'Pennsylvania and the Politics of the Tariff, 1880–1888', *Pennsylvania History*, 29 (1962), 291–304.

8. Gould, 'Republican Search', p. 187. See also Morgan, *From Hayes to McKinley*, especially pp. 526–7; R. Hal Williams, *Years of Decision: American Politics in the 1890s* (New York, 1978), pp. 10–11.

9. A. Hunter Dupree, *Science in the Federal Government: A History of Policies and Actions to 1940* (Cambridge, Mass., 1957), pp. 151–73; Leonard D. White, *The Republican Era: A Study in Administrative History, 1869–1901* (New York, 1958), pp. 232–56; Alfred C. True, *A History of Agricultural Experimentation and Research in the United States, 1607–1925* (Washington, 1937), pp. 41–66, 118–164; John A. Garraty, *The New Commonwealth, 1877–1890* (New York, 1968), pp. 57–66; Margaret W. Rossiter, 'The Organisation of the Agricultural Sciences', in Alexandra Oleson and John Voss (eds.), *The Organisation of Knowledge in Modern America, 1860–1920* (Baltimore and London, 1979), pp. 211–48.

10. Dupree, *Science in the Federal Government*, pp. 195–214, 258–63.

11. Charles S. Rosenberg, 'Science, Technology and Economic Growth: The Case of the Agricultural Station Scientist, 1875–1914', *Agricultural History*, 45 (1971), 1–20 (the quotation is at p. 2); Dupree, *Science in the Federal Government*, p. 161 and *passim;* Rossiter, *Organisation of the Agricultural Sciences*, pp. 211–20; White, *Republican Era*, pp. 251–2.

12. Samuel P. Hays, *American History as Social Analysis* (Knoxville, Tenn., 1980), pp. 250–5, 308–24; Hays, *The Response to Industrialism, 1885–1914* (Chicago, 1957), pp. 48–70; Robert H. Wiebe, *The Search for Order, 1877–1920* (New York and London, 1967); Hurst, *Law and the Conditions of Freedom*, pp. 71–108.

13. Richard L. McCormick, *From Realignment to Reform: Political Change in New York State, 1893–1910* (Ithaca, N.Y., 1981), p. 255; Hurst, *Law and the Conditions of Freedom*, p. 73; Lowi, 'American Business', pp. 290–1.

14. George H. Miller, *Railroads and the Granger Laws* (Madison, Wis., 1971), pp. 24–58; Lee Benson, *Merchants, Farmers and Railroads: Railroad Regulation and New York Politics, 1850–1887* (Cambridge, Mass., 1957), pp. 1–9: Harry H. Pierce, *Railroads of New York: A Study of Government Aid, 1826–1875* (Cambridge, Mass., 1953).

15. Miller, *Railroads and the Granger Laws*, pp. 97–116 and *passim;* Gerald D. Nash, 'Origins of the Interstate Commerce Act of 1887', *Pennsylvania History*, 24 (July 1957), 181–90; Benson, *Merchants, Farmers and Railroads*, p. 212 and *passim;* Edward A. Purcell Jr., 'Ideas and Interests: Businessmen and the Interstate Commerce Act', *Journal of American History*, 54 (1967), 561–78; Gabriel Kolko, *Railroads and Regulation, 1877–1916* (Princeton, 1965), pp. 20–6; Ben H. Procter; *Not Without Honor: The Life of John H. Reagan* (Austin, Tex., 1962), pp. 241–2. Ari and Olive Hoogenboom, *A History of the ICC: From Palliative to Panacea* (New York, 1976), pp. 8–13, is a useful summary. On the pattern of railway rates see William Z. Ripley, *Railroads: Rates and Regulation* (New York, 1912), pp. 101–296; Miller, *Railroads and the Granger Laws*, ch. 1. The differences between shippers are noted in Benson, *Merchants, Farmers and Railroads*, pp. 221–31; Kolko, *Railroads and Regulation*, pp. 31–4.

16. Kolko, *Railroads and Regulation*, pp. 3, 26–44. But cf. Thomas C. Cochran, *Railroad Leaders, 1845–1890: The Business Mind in Action* (Cambridge, Mass., 1953), pp. 189–98; Benson, *Merchants, Farmers and Railroads*, pp. 221–3, 232–8; Hoogenboom, *History of the ICC*, p. 17; Purcell, 'Ideas and Interests', pp. 575–8; James W. Nielson, *Shelby Cullom: Prairie State Republican* (Urbana, Ill., 1962), pp. 114–16.

17. Benson, *Merchants, Farmers and Railroads*, pp. 62–75, 150–5, 160–2, 174–82; Procter, *Not Without Honor*, pp. 218–60; Gerald Nash, 'The Reformer Reformed: John H. Reagan and Railroad Regulation', *Business History Review*, 29 (June 1955), 190–3; Hoogenboom, *History of the ICC*, pp. 13–15.

18. For a summary see Ripley, *Railroads: Rates and Regulation*, pp. 452–3. See also Albro Martin, 'The Troubled Subject of Railroad Regulation in the Gilded Age – A

Reappraisal', *Journal of American History*, 61 (1974), 339–71; Hoogenboom, *History of the ICC*, p. 18; Nielson, pp. 108–17.

19. Paul W. Macavoy, *The Economic Effects of Regulation: The Trunk-Line Railroad Cartels and the Interstate Commerce Commission Before 1900* (Cambridge, Mass., 1965), pp. 110–53; Hoogenboom, *History of the ICC*, pp. 21–31; Cochran, *Railroad Leaders*, pp. 198–9; Alan M. Jones, 'Thomas M. Cooley and the ICC: Continuity and Change in the Doctrine of Equal Rights', *Political Science Quarterly*, 81 (1966), pp. 609–27; Kolko, *Railroads and Regulation*, pp. 45–71.

20. Hoogenboom, *History of the ICC*, pp. 32–8; Ripley, *Railroads: Rates and Regulation*, pp. 456–86; Kolko, *Railroads and Regulation*, pp. 80–3.

21. Procter, *Not Without Honor*, pp. 236–7; Edward C. Kirkland, *Industry Comes of Age: Business, Labor and Public Policy, 1860–1897* (New York, 1961), p. 125. On the view of the role of the ICC held by its first chairman, Thomas M. Cooley, see Jones, 'Thomas M. Cooley and the ICC', pp. 609–16.

22. William Letwin, *Law and Economic Policy in America: The Evolution of the Sherman Antitrust Act* (New York, 1965), pp. 95–6, 53–99 *passim;* Hans B. Thorelli, *The Federal Antitrust Policy* (Baltimore, 1955), pp. 214–32; John D. Clark, *The Federal Trust Policy* (London, 1931), pp. 35–51; Garraty, *New Commonwealth*, pp. 123–7.

23. Letwin, *Law and Economic Policy*, pp. 100–81; Thorelli, *Federal Antitrust Policy*, pp. 369–410, 595–609; Gerald G. Eggert, *Richard Olney: Evolution of a Statesman* (University Park, Pa., 1974), pp. 87–100; Bruce Bringhurst, *Antitrust and the Oil Monopoly: The Standard Oil Cases, 1890–1911* (Westport, Conn., 1979), pp. 1–9, 108–21; Alfred S. Eichner, *The Emergence of Oligopoly: Sugar Refining as a Test Case* (Baltimore and London, 1969), pp. 173–87.

24. Keller, *Affairs of State*, pp. 171–2, 413, 418–22; R. Alton Lee, *A History of Regulatory Taxation* (Lexington, Ky., 1973), pp. 3–27; Thomas A. Bailey, 'Congressional Opposition to Pure Food Legislation, 1879–1906', *American Journal of Sociology*, 36 (July 1930), 52–64; Haney, *Congressional History of Railways*, vol. II, pp. 260–9; James E. Anderson, *The Emergence of the Modern Regulatory State* (Washington, D.C., 1962), pp. 59–61.

25. Gerald G. Eggert, *Railroad Labor Disputes: The Beginnings of a Federal Strike Policy* (Ann Arbor, Mich., 1967), pp. 201, 178 and *passim;* Felix Frankfurter and Nathan Greene, *The Labor Injunction* (New York, 1930), p. 20; Eggert, *Olney*, pp. 115–69; Almont Lindsey, *The Pullman Strike* (Chicago, 1942); Robert V. Bruce, *1877: Year of Violence* (Indianapolis, 1959). On the move towards arbitration see Olney, *Railroad Labor Disputes*, pp. 212–25; James Leiby, *Carroll D. Wright and Labor Reform* (Cambridge, Mass., 1960), pp. 164–71; Lindsey, *Pullman Strike*, pp. 350–8. On the development of labour injunctions see Frankfurter and Greene, *Labor Injunction*, pp. 2–24; Donald L. McMurry, 'The Legal Ancestry of the Pullman Strike Injunctions', *Industrial and Labor Relations Review*, 14 (1961), 235–56. The use of the Army in these and other disputes is discussed in Jerry M. Cooper, *The Army and Civil Disorders: Federal Military Intervention in Labor Disputes, 1877–1900* (Westport, Conn., 1979); B. C. Hacker, 'The United States Army as a Federal Police Force: The Federal Policing of Labor Disputes', *Military Affairs*, 33 (April 1969), 255–64.

26. Keller, *Affairs of State* offers the fullest account.

27. Ibid., pp. 176–80, 423–5; Kirkland, *Industry Comes of Age*, pp. 112–26. For examples see Edward C. Kirkland, *Charles Francis Adams, Jr., 1835–1915: The Patrician at Bay* (Cambridge, Mass., 1965), pp. 34–64; Miller, *Railroads and the Granger Laws*, pp. 59–171; Benson, *Merchants, Farmers and Railroads*, pp. 141–94.

28. Thorelli, *Federal Antitrust Policy*, pp. 155–6, 259–61; Bringhurst, *Antitrust and the Oil Monopoly*, pp. 10–67.

29. Lee, *History of Regulatory Taxation*, pp. 15–23; Keller, *Affairs of State*, pp. 418 and 509–10. See also the general discussion of federal-state cooperation in Loren Beth, *The development of the American Constitution, 1877–1917* (New York, 1971), pp. 48–60.

30. Kolko, *Railroads and Regulation*, pp. 89–90; Doezema, 'Railroad Management', pp. 155–62. On the attractions of the federal courts see Miller, *Railroads and the Granger Laws*, pp. 177–80; Bringhurst, *Antitrust and the Oil Monopoly*, pp. 45–8; Frankfurter and Greene, *Labor Injunction*, pp. 5–17. Cf. Harry N. Scheiber, 'Federalism and the American Economic Order', *Law and Society Review*, 10 (Fall 1975), 116–17.

31. Beth, *Development of the American Constitution*, pp. 138–60; Anderson, *Emergence of the Modern Regulatory State*, pp. 55–70; Lee, *History of Regulatory Taxation*, pp. 3–8, 25–7.

32. Beth, *Development of the American Constitution*, pp. 143–7; Hurst, *Law and the Conditions of Freedom*, pp. 44–8; Scheiber, 'Federalism', pp. 100–2; Tony Allen Freyer, *Forums of Order:*

*The Federal Courts and Business in American History* (Greenwich, Conn., 1979), pp. 102–12.

33. Scheiber, 'Federalism', 104 and 102–7 *passim*; Beth, *Development of the American Constitution*, pp. 41–6, 166–83; Robert G. McCloskey, *American Conservatism in the Age of Enterprise* (Cambridge, Mass., 1951), pp. 72–126; Arthur S. Miller, *The Supreme Court and American Capitalism* (New York, 1968), pp. 50–62; Charles W. McCurdy, 'Justice Field and the Jurisprudence of Government-Business Relations: Some Parameters of Laissez-Faire Constitutionalism', *Journal of American History*, 61 (1975), 970–1005. The number of laws allowed and disallowed is tabulated in Keller, *Affairs of State*, pp. 368–9.

34. Anderson, *Emergence of the Modern Regulatory State*, p. 150. There is an excellent section on judicial activism in Keller, *Affairs of State*, pp. 358–70.

35. *Ibid.*, p. 162. See also Sidney Fine, *Laissez-faire and the General Welfare State: A Study of Conflict in American Thought, 1865–1901* (Ann Arbor, Mich., 1956), pp. 1–125; Richard Hofstadter, *Social Darwinism in American Life* (New York, 1943); Henry F. May, *Protestant Churches and Industrial America* (New York, 1941), pp. 39–81.

36. John A. Garraty, *Henry Cabot Lodge: A Biography* (New York, 1953), p. 138. For discussion of business attitudes see Cochran, *Railroad Leaders*, pp. 198–201; Purcell, 'Ideas and Interests', pp. 568–75; Kolko, *Railroads and Regulation*, pp. 4–5. The pragmatism of businessmen disturbed the orthodox. John G. Sproat, *The 'Best Men': Liberal Reformers in the Gilded Age* (New York, 1968), pp. 143–7. See also James Bryce, *The American Commonwealth*, (2 vols., New York, 1910), vol. II, pp. 587–99.

37. David Rothman, *Politics and Power: The United States Senate, 1869–1901* (Cambridge, Mass., 1966), p. 81; W. R. Brock, *An American Crisis: Congress and Reconstruction* (London, 1963), p. 50; Dorothy G. Fowler, *John Coit Spooner: Defender of Presidents* (New York, 1961), p. 102; Robert Harrison, 'The Structure of Pennsylvania Politics, 1876–1880' (Unpublished Ph.D. dissertation, University of Cambridge, 1971), pp. 304–16, 392–4, 448–60. On turnover see Nelson Polsby *et al.*, 'The Institutionalisation of the United States House of Representatives', *American Political Science Review*, 62 (1968), 146.

38. Allan Nevins, *Abram S. Hewitt: With Some Account of Peter Cooper* (New York, 1935), p. 401; William A. Robinson, *Thomas B. Reed. Parliamentarian* (New York, 1930), p. 65; Kirkland, *Adams*, p. 111. See also Bryce, *American Commonwealth*, vol. I, pp. 191–208; Garraty, *New Commonwealth*, pp. 231–6; White, *Republican Era*, pp. 45–92. On the Senate see Rothman, *Politics and Power*, pp. 11–42, 73–90.

39. Robert M. La Follette, *La Follette's Autobiography: A Personal Narrative of Political Experiences* (Madison, Wis., 1913), p. 38; Lowi, 'Public Policy', p. 690; White, *Republican Era*, pp. 68–84.

40. Quoted in Josephson, *Politicos*, p. 35.

41. Carl Degler, 'Political Parties and the Rise of the City: An Interpretation', *Journal of American History*, 51 (1964), 45. See also Keller, *Affairs of State*, pp. 251–5, 552–64; Morgan, *From Hayes to McKinley*, pp. 69–70, 267–70; Gould, 'Republican Search for a National Majority'; R. Hal Williams, '"Dry Bones and Dead Language": The Democratic Party', in Morgan (ed.), *Gilded Age*, pp. 129–48; Williams, *Years of Decision*, pp. 5–8.

42. Keller, *Affairs of State*, p. 379. See also Terrill, *Tariff, Politics, and American Foreign Policy*, pp. 7–36; Morgan, *From Hayes to McKinley*, pp. 120–1, 166–70; Gould, 'Republican Search', pp. 176–82; Williams, '"Dry Bones and Dead Language"', pp. 134–8.

43. See, for example, Morgan, *From Hayes to McKinley*, p. vi. For an analysis of voting on the Interstate Commerce Act see Hoogenboom, *History of the ICC*, pp. 16–17. Almost nobody voted against the Sherman Act. For a summary of contemporary criticism of the parties' neglect of important issues see Bryce, *American Commonwealth*, vol. II, pp. 21–30.

44. Williams, '"Dry Bones and Dead Language"', p. 130; Robert Marcus, *Grand Old Party: Political Structure in the Gilded Age* (New York, 1971). On the grass-roots strength of nineteenth-century parties see Hays, *American Political History*, pp. 298–308. Some of the more important voting studies are Paul Kleppner, *The Cross of Culture: A Social Analysis of Midwestern Politics, 1850–1900* (New York, 1970); Kleppner, *The Third Electoral System, 1853–1892* (Chapel Hill, N.C., 1979); Richard Jensen, *The Winning of the Midwest: Social and Political Conflict, 1888–1896* (Chicago, 1971).

45. Degler, 'Political Parties and the Rise of the City', pp. 41–9; Keller, *Affairs of State*, pp. 565–87; Kleppner, *Cross of Culture*, pp. 269–368; Jensen, *Winning of the Midwest;* Williams, *Years of Decision*, pp. 77–90, 115–25. Two of the more recent discussions of electoral realignments are W. Dean Burnham, *Critical Elections and the Mainsprings of American Politics* (New york, 1970), especially chs. 1–2; Jerome Clubb *et al.*, *Partisan Realignment: Voters,*

*Parties and Government in American History* (Beverley Hills, 1980). Clubb and his co-authors believe that realignments are made fundamentally by policy innovations that win new support, turning a temporary into a permanent majority, but they have difficulty in demonstrating any such transformation for the Republican party in the 1890s. McCormick finds Republican strategy in New York almost completely unchanged. *From Realignment to Reform*, pp. 61–8, 98–103.

46. Robinson, *Thomas B. Reed*, pp. 182–239; Williams, *Years of Decision*, pp. 19–25; Randall B. Ripley, *Party Leadership in the House of Representatives* (Washington, D.C., 1967), pp. 18–22, 51–3; DeAlva S. Alexander, *History and Procedures of the United States House of Representatives* (Boston, 1916), chs. 9–11; George B. Galloway, *History of the House of Representatives* (New York, 1961), pp. 49–53; 131–6. On the Senate see Rothman, *Politics and Power*, pp. 43–72; Fowler, *John Coit Spooner*, pp. 200–16; Nathaniel W. Stephenson, *Nelson W. Aldrich: A Leader in American Politics* (New York, 1930), pp. 132–7. See also Horace S. and Marion G. Merrill, *The Republican Command, 1897–1913* (Lexington, Ky., 1971).

47. Hays, *American Political History as Social Analysis*, pp. 293–8, 318–24; Lowi, 'American Business', pp. 690–715; McCormick, *From Realignment to Reform*, pp. 251–72; Marcus, *Grand Old Party*, pp. 251–65; Robert H. Wiebe, *Businessmen and Reform: A Study of the Progressive Movement* (Cambridge, Mass., 1962), ch. 2. On the decline in party regularity see W. Dean Burnham, 'The Changing Shape of the American Political Universe', *American Political Science Review*, 57 (1963), 7–28; Burnham, *Critical Elections*, pp. 71–118; Clubb, *Partisan Realignment*, pp. 278–86. On the strength of anti-party traditions and the political importance of independent movements see Kleppner, *Third Electoral System, passim;* McCormick, *From Realignment to Reform*, pp. 40–52, 98–137; Sproat, *The 'Best Men'*, pp. 46–141, 244–71; Gerald W. McFarland, *Mugwumps, Morals and Politics, 1884–1920* (Amherst, Mass., 1975).

48. Henry Adams, *The Education of Henry Adams: An Autobiography* (Cambridge, Mass., 1919), p. 294; Keller, *Affairs of State*, p. 289.

## CHAPTER 7

1. John D. Buenker, 'The Progressive Era: The Search for a Synthesis', *Mid-America*, 51 (July 1969), 193; Otis L. Graham, Jr., *An Encore for Reform: The Old Progressives and the New Deal* (New York, 1967), p. 3.

2. Otis Graham, *An Encore for Reform*, and *The Great Campaigns: Reform and War in America, 1900–1928* (Englewood Cliffs, New Jersey, 1971).

3. Arthur M. Schlesinger, Jr., *The Age of Jackson* (Boston, 1945), p. 505.

4. Arthur Link, 'What Happened to the Progressive Movement in the 1920s?', *American Historical Review*, LVIV (July 1959), p. 836.

5. Robert H. Wiebe, 'The Progressive Years, 1900–1917' in William H. Cartwright and Richard L. Watson, Jr. (eds.), *The Reinterpretation of American History and Culture* (Washington, D.C., 1973), pp. 427, 425.

6. Samuel P. Hays, "The New Organisational Society" in Jerry Israel (ed.), *Building the Organisational Society: Essays on Associational Activities in Modern America* (New York, 1972), pp. 2–5.

7. Wiebe, "The Progressive Years", p. 437.

8. See, for example, Robert H. Wiebe, *Businessmen and Reform: A Study of the Progressive Movement* (Cambridge, Mass., 1962); Gabriel Kolko, *The Triumph of Conservatism: A Reinterpretation of American History, 1900–1916* (New York, 1963), *Railroads and Regulation, 1877–1916* (Princeton, 1965); K. Austin Kerr, *American Railroad Politics, 1914–1920: Rates, Wages and Efficiency* (Pittsburgh, 1968).

9. Samuel P. Hays, 'Political Parties and the Community-Society Continuum' in William N. Chambers and Walter Dean Burnham (eds.), *The American Party Systems* (New York, 1967), pp. 168, 171.

10. Louis Galambos, 'The Emerging Organisational Synthesis in Modern American History', *Business History Review*, XLIV (Autumn, 1970), 282.

11. Ellis W. Hawley, 'The Discovery and Study of a 'Corporate Liberalism'', *Business History Review*, LII (Autumn 1978), 309, 314, 313.

12. 'If the literature on the F.T.C. agrees on one point, it is that the F.T.C. has seldom governed and served a larger public interest'. See Douglas Walter Jaenicke, 'Herbert Croly, Progressive Ideology, and the F.T.C. Act', *Political Science Quarterly*, 93, No. 3 (Fall 1978), 489–90. Nonetheless, this is surely too simple a view. See Robert D. Cuff, *The War Industries Board: Business-Government Relations during World War I* (Baltimore, 1973), pp. 275–6.

13. Samuel P. Hays, 'The Politics of Reform in Municipal Government in the Progressive Era', *Pacific Northwest Quarterly*, LX, (October 1964), 167. See also James Weinstein, 'Organised Business and the City Commission and Manager Movements', *Journal of Southern History*, 28 (May 1962), 166–82.

14. Samuel P. Hays, 'Preface to the Atheneum Edition', *Conservation and the Gospel of Efficiency: The Progressive Conservation Movement, 1890–1920* (New York, 1969); Hayes, 'The New Organisational Society', pp. 2–3.

15. Ellis W. Hawley, 'The Discovery and Study of a 'Corporate Liberalism''', p. 311.

16. Samuel Hays, 'Political Parties and the Community-Society Continuum', pp. 173–81.

17. See, for example, some of the essays in Israel (ed.), *Building the Organisational Society*.

18. 'Modernity is thus not all of a piece. The American experience demonstrates conclusively that some institutions and some aspects of a society may become highly modern while other institutions and other aspects retain much of their traditional form and substance'. See Samuel P. Huntington, 'Political Modernisation: America vs. Europe' in *Political Order in Changing Societies* (New Haven, 1968), pp. 93–139. Quotation at p. 132.

19. Cuff, *The War Industries Board*, p. 9.

20. Robert H. Wiebe, *The Search for Order, 1877–1920* (London, 1967) p. 223.

21. *Ibid*, p. 21.

22. *Ibid*, pp. 302, 154.

23. This essay is based upon a study of the writings of Ray Stannard Baker, George Creel, Herbert Croly, Norman Hapgood, Frederic C. Howe, Walter Lippmann, Amos Pinchot, Gifford Pinchot, Chester Rowell, Charles Edward Russell, John Spargo, Lincoln Steffens, William English Walling, Walter E. Weyl and William Allen White, and of the journals, *The New Republic, The Survey, Harper's Weekly, The Independent* and *The Public*.

24. e.g. Kolko, *The Triumph of Conservatism*.

25. Wiebe, *The Search for Order*, pp. 293–6; Paul A. C. Koistinen, 'The Industrial-Military Complex in Historical Perspective: World War I', *Business History Review*, 41 (Winter 1967), 378–403; Melvin I. Urofsky, *Big Steel and the Wilson Administration* (Columbus, 1918).

26. The Keating-Owen Act of 1916 was declared unconstitutional by the Supreme Court in *Hammer* v. *Dagenhart* (1918).

27. e.g. Henry R. Seagar, 'Outline of a Program of Social Reform', *Charities and the Commons*, 17 (April 1907), 828–32; Walter E. Weyl, *The New Democracy: An Essay on Certain Political and Economic Tendencies in the United States*. (New York, 1912), pp. 323–4; F. C. Howe, 'Unemployment: A Problem and a Program', *The Century Magazine*, 89 (April 1915), 845–8; *The Survey*, 34 (May 22, 1915), 183–4; Edward T. Devine, 'Preparedness', *The Survey*, 35 (18 March 1916), 732–34; W. A. White to Charles F. Scott, 27 Nov. 1916 (W. A. White papers, Library of Congress); Chester Rowell to Alexander McCabe, 10 Sept. 1917 (Chester Rowell papers, University of California, Berkeley). For more evidence on the campaign for health insurance, see Forrest A. Walker, 'Compulsory Health Insurance: "The Next Great Step in Social Legislation"', *Journal of American History*, 56 (1969), 290–304. On the very limited nature of advances in social welfare before 1930, see James T. Patterson, *America's Struggle Against Poverty, 1900–1980* (Cambridge, Mass., 1981), pp. 28–30.

28. Weyl, *The New Democracy*, p. 278.

29. F. C. Howe, *The City: the Hope of Democracy* (New York, 1905), Chapters VIII–IX.

30. F. C. Howe, *Privilege and Democracy* (New York, 1910), pp. 283–92; Amos Pinchot, 'The Cost of Private Monopoly', *The Annals (of the American Academy of Political and Social Science)*, (July 1913), 185; White to Hiram Johnson, 23 Nov. 1914 (White papers); George Creel, 'Can a Democratic Government Control Prices?', *The Century Magazine*, 93 (Feb. 1917), 610; Rowell to E. B. Osborne, 31 July 1915 (Rowell papers); *New Republic*, I (19 Dec. 1914), 8–9; *The Independent*, 89 (5 Feb. 1917), 204.

31. Gifford Pinchot to W. A. White, 16 June 1916 (Gifford Pinchot papers, Library of Congress).

32. e.g. Howe, *The City: the Hope of Democracy*, p. 119; Norman Hapgood, *Industry and Progress* (New Haven, 1911), p. 84; Amos Pinchot to George F. Porter, 25 Feb. 1915 (Amos Pinchot papers, Library of Congress).
33. Amos Pinchot to Gilson Gardner, 15 July 1914 (Amos Pinchot papers).
34. *New Republic*, I (14 Nov. 1914), 9.
35. See Lincoln Steffens to Theodore Roosevelt, 6 May 1908; Scrapbook No. 3 (1916), quotation at p. 73. (Lincoln Steffens papers, Columbia University).
36. Amos Pinchot to Henry J. Whigham, 1 Sept. 1915 (Amos Pinchot papers).
37. Walter Lippmann, *Drift and Mastery: An Attempt to Diagnose the Current Unrest* (Englewood Cliffs, 1961), p. 99. See also Weyl, *The New Democracy*, pp. 282, 287.
38. 'The industrial goal of the democracy', explained Weyl, 'is the attainment of the largest possible industrial control and of the largest possible industrial dividend'. (*The New Democracy*, p. 276).
39. Press release, Nov. 1906 (Steffens papers).
40. Pamphlct, 'What's the Matter with America' (Box 225, Amos Pinchot papers); A. P. to E. W. Scripps, 11 Sept. 1914.
41. Howe, *Privilege and Democracy*, p. 273.
42. George Creel, 'What the Industrial Commission Discovered', *Pearson's Magazine*, 35 (March 1916), 194–5.
43. Herbert Croly, *The Promise of American Life* (New York, 1909), p. 22.
44. W. A. White, *The Autobiography of William Allen White* (New York, 1946), pp. 487–8.
45. Amos Pinchot, 'The Cost of Private Monopoly', p. 184; William English Walling, *Socialism as it is: A Survey of the World-Wide Revolutionary Movement* (New York, 1912) pp. 17–18; Charles Edward Russell, 'The Farmers' Fight for Industrial Freedom – the Example of Ireland', *Pearson's Magazine*, 34 (Sept. 1915), 262.
46. Chester Rowell, 'The State', Address delivered to the City Club of Los Angeles, 13 Jan. 1912. See also Rowell to Dr Jerome B. Thomas, 3 March, 7 April 1913 (Rowell papers).
47. Howe, *The City: The Hope of Democracy*, p. 303.
48. Walter Lippmann, *A Preface to Politics* (Ann Arbor, 1962), p. 201. See also *Drift and Mastery*, p. 171.
49. Lippmann, *A Preface to Politics*, p. 200.
50. Weyl, *The New Democracy*, pp. 353–4.
51. William Allen White, 'The Kansas Conscience', *Reader Magazine*, Oct. 1905, 488–93.
52. Walling, *Socialism As It Is, passim*.
53. *New Republic*, III (29 May 1915), 95–8.
54. William English Walling, *Progressivism – and After* (New York, 1914), p. 126.
55. Herbert Croly, *The Promise of American Life*, pp. 230–9. See also Howe, *The British City: The Beginnings of Democracy* (New York, 1907), pp. 300, 303,; Lincoln Steffens, *The Autobiography of Lincoln Steffens*, (New York, 1931), pp. 703–8.
56. *New Republic*, III (3 July 1915), 215–16. See also Charles Edward Russell, 'Why England Falls Down', *Pearson's Magazine*, 34 (Aug. 1915), 201–19; *Harper's Weekly*, LXI (25 Sept. 1915), 289; *The Independent*, 84 (13 December 1915), 419–20.
57. 'Eighteen months ago Germany was to the American state socialist what America had been to the European liberal in the early nineteenth century – a country where the heart's desire had been enacted into law, a country where labor won comfort and security, where privileges and obligations were held in true correlation'. *New Republic*, IV (30 Oct. 1915), 343.
58. F. C. Howe, *Socialized Germany* (New York, 1915), p. 1.
59. Howe to House, 20 Sept. 1915. (E. M. House papers, Yale University).
60. *Emporia Gazette*, 8 April 1915. See also *The Survey*, 33 (7 Nov. 1914), 143–4; *The Independent*, 80 (30 Nov. 1914), 305–6; Walter E. Weyl, *American World Policies* (New York, 1917), p. 143.
61. *New Republic*, II (10 April 1915), 249–50.
62. *The Survey*, 32 (12 Sept. 1914), 587–9; *New Republic*, II (27 March 1915), 205–7; *Harper's Weekly*, LXI (3 July 1915), 3; *The Independent*, 82 (28 June 1915), 525–6; *Baker Notebook* VII (Aug. 1915), 55–7 (R. S. Baker papers, Library of Congress).
63. *The Survey*, 35 (18 Dec. 1915), 337.
64. *New Republic*, X (3 March 1917), 124.
65. *The Survey*, 35 (18 Dec. 1915), 337. See also *The Independent*, 82 (10 April 1915), 249–50.
66. Howe, *Socialized Germany*, p. 1. See also *The Survey*, 33 (7 Nov. 1914), p. 144; *Harper's*

*Weekly*, LXI (28 Aug. 1915), 193; *The Survey*, 35 (26 Feb. 1916), 643–4.

67. White to Theodore Roosevelt, 15 Jan. 1915 (White papers).
68. Amos Pinchot, Howe, Steffens and Weyl were among those who took part in a conference on real preparedness in Washington, D.C., June 1916. (*The Survey*, 36 (15 July 1916), pp. 420–1). For more evidence for these publicists' views on the domestic implications of preparedness, see J. A. Thompson, 'American Progressive Publicists and the First World War, 1914–17', *Journal of American History*, LVIII (September 1971), 376–8.
69. *New Republic*, V (6 Nov. 1915), 6–7.
70. 'Preparedness', *The Public*, XIX (4 Feb. 1916), 110–13.
71. *The Public*, XX (16 Feb. 1917), 149; Amos Pinchot to Samuel Gompers, 10 March 1917 (Amos Pinchot papers).
72. Paul U. Kellogg, 'The Fighting Issues', *The Survey*, 37 (17 Feb. 1917), 577; *The Public*, XX (2 March 1917), 195.
73. Pinchot to Gompers, 10 March 1917.
74. *New Republic*, X (14 April 1917), 307.
75. *New Republic*, X (21 April 1917), 336, 335.
76. *New Republic*, XIII (19 Jan. 1918), 331.
77. *The Independent*, 93 (5 Jan. 1918), 8.
78. e.g. *The Independent*, 95 (21 Sept. 1918), 374–5; *New Republic*, XI (2 June 1917), 129–31.
79. 'The Future of the State', *New Republic*, XII (15 Sept. 1917), 179–83.
80. G. Pinchot to White, 1 Aug. 1917 (Gifford Pinchot papers).
81. A. Pinchot to Alfred Bishop Mason, 28 Aug. 1918 (Amos Pinchot papers).
82. Weyl Diary, 19 May 1918. (With the permission of Professor Charles B. Forcey).
83. F. C. Howe, *The Land and the Soldier* (New York, 1919), p. 3.
84. F. C. Howe, *The Confessions of a Reformer* (New York, 1925), p. 282.
85. F. C. Howe, *Revolution and Democracy* (New York, 1921), pp. 98–9, 118.
86. *The Freeman*, I (7 July 1920), 394–6.
87. *New Republic*, XXI (31 Dec. 1919), 136–9.
88. e.g. Russell 'Compulsory Arbitration: The Next Battle Prize: Why It Failed in New Zealand', *Reconstruction*, April 1920, 150–3; Creel, "Where Do We Go From Here?" *Colliers*, (9 July 1921) 22–3.
89. Howe, *Confessions of a Reformer*, p. 324.
90. *New Republic*, XXIV (27 Oct. 1920), 210–16 at 215–16.
91. White to Baker, 28 Dec. 1920 (White papers).
92. Samuel Haber, *Efficiency and Uplift: Scientific Management in the Progressive Era* (Chicago, 1964).
93. Richard L. McCormick, 'The Discovery that "Business Corrupts Politics": A Reappraisal of the Origins of Progressivism', *American Historical Review*, LXXXVI (April 1981), 274. See also William L. O'Neill, *The Progressive Years: America Comes of Age* (New York, 1975), pp. x, 157–8; Richard H. K. Vietor, 'Businessmen and the Political Economy: The Railroad Rate Controversy of 1905', *Journal of American History*, LXIV (June 1977), 48, 66.
94. J. R. Pole, *Paths to the American Past* (Oxford, 1979), p. 251.

CHAPTER 8

This is a preliminary version of a chapter in a larger work now in progress, a full study of the Red Summer and the Red Scare. My research has been supported by grants from the U.S. International Communications Agency and the Albert J. Beveridge Grants for Research in American History of the American Historical Association, and I would like to express my thanks for their help.

1. Robert K. Murray, *Red Scare: A Study in National Hysteria, 1919–1920* (Minneapolis, 1955), though inadequate, is the only general study of America's Great Leap Backwards. I have also used Stanley Coben, *A. Mitchell Palmer, Politician* (New York, 1963), and Burl Noggle, *Into the Twenties: The United States from Armistice to Normalcy* (Urbana, 1974) to supplement my own research in contemporary U.S. newspapers and magazines.
2. Stanley Coben, 'A Study of Nativism: The American Red Scare of 1919–20', *Political Science Quarterly*, LXXIX (March 1964), 52–75.
3. A variety of interpretations has been offered to explain the decline of socialism in the

United States after World War I. The most convincing explanation is the simplest: American socialism was frightened out of existence by the Red Scare.

4. Arthur E. Shipley, *The Voyage of a Vice-Chancellor* (Cambridge, 1919), pp. 42–46. Mark Sullivan, *Our Times, The United States, 1900–1925.* V *Over Here, 1914–1918* (New York, 1933), pp. 652–654. Alfred W. Crosby, Jr., *Epidemic and Peace, 1918* (Westport, Conn., 1976), *passim.*

5. Coben, 'A Study of Nativism', pp. 66–68.

6. *Washington Post,* Tuesday 22 April 1919.

7. Discharged soldiers were supposed to wear a red chevron on the left sleeve of their shirt, coat and overcoat, but this regulation was not always obeyed. Major-General Henry Jervey to J. O. Lucas, 24 July 1919; Newton D. Baker to S. M. Kendricks, 25 July 1919, Papers of the Chief of Staff, 1917–1921, 1470 Uniforms 195, R.G. 165, National Archives, Washington, D.C. [Hereafter N.A.].

8. *Washington Post,* Saturday 2 August 1919.

9. Helen Hayes, with Sandford Dody, *On Reflection. An Autobiography* (London, 1969), p. 37. W. P. Livingstone, *The Race Conflict. A Study of Conditions in America* (London, 1911), p. 149.

10. Constance McLaughlin Green, *Washington. Capital City, 1879–1950* (Princeton, N.J., 1963), pp. 4–6, 35–60, 101–131, 171–186, 200, 207–233, 260–272.

11. Kathleen L. Wolgemuth, 'Woodrow Wilson and Federal Segregation', *Journal of Negro History*, XLIV (April 1979), 158–173; George C. Osborn, 'The Problem of the Negro in Government, 1913', *The Historian*, XXIII (May 1961) 330–347. Henry Blumenthal, 'Woodrow Wilson and the Race Question', *Journal of Negro History*, XLVIII (January 1963) 5–10.

12. Helen Nicolay, *Our Capital on the Potomac* (New York, 1924), p. 515. *New York Times Magazine*, 30 March 1919. *Washington Post*, Sunday 20 April 1919.

13. See James Borchet, *Alley Life in Washington, D.C. Family; Community, Religion and Folklife in the City, 1850–1970* (Urbana, 1979).

14. William Henry Jones, *The Housing of Negroes in Washington, D.C. A Study in Human Ecology* (Washington, D.C., 1929), p. 61.

15. *Washington Post*, Wednesday 25 December 1918.

16. *Washington Post*, Friday 17 January 1919. Lloyd M. Abernethy, 'The Washington Race War of July, 1919', *Maryland Historical Magazine*, 58: 4, (December 1963) 310–314. *Nashville Banner*, Saturday 19 July 1919.

17. *Washington Post.* Monday 27 January; Thursday, 30 January; Sunday 16 March; and Thursday 24 April 1919. Major Raymond W. Pullman to Mary White Ovington, 22 August 1919, enclosing a completed questionnaire on coloured policemen, Records of the National Association for the Advancement of Colored People, Box C-4, Manuscripts Division, Library of Congress, Washington, D.C. [Hereafter L.C]. Washington *Bee*, Saturday 13 October 1917; Saturday 21 December 1918; Saturday 8 February 1919; and Saturday 12 July 1919.

18. Abernethy, 'The Washington Race War', p. 314. *Washington Post*, Sunday 20 July 1919.

19. *Washington Post*, Saturday 19 July 1919. Apparently Mrs. Stephnick had only recently been married, and first reports of the incident gave her name as Miss Elaine Williams.

20. This hut was a social centre for servicemen in Washington, D.C., run by the Catholic fraternal organisation, but open to all.

21. *Washington Post*, Sunday 20 July 1919. *New York Tribune*, Sunday 20 July 1919. *New York Times*, Monday 21 July 1919. *Atlanta Journal*, Sunday 20 July 1919.

22. *Washington Post.* Monday 21 July 1919. *New York Tribune*, Monday 21 July 1919. *New York Times,* Monday 21 July 1919.

23. Two memoranda from Major-General Henry Jervey, Assistant Chief of Staff, Director of Operations, to the Adjutant-General, 21 July 1919, Papers of the Chief of Staff, 1917–1921, 1503, Washington D.C. War Exhibits, 201, R.G. 165, N.A. *The Leatherneck* (Quantico, Va.), Friday 25 July 1919. U.S. Marine Corps' Recruiters' Bulletin, August 1919. Muster Rolls of Officers and Enlisted Men of the U.S. Marine Corps, Quantico, 1–31 July 1919, U.S.M.C. Headquarters, Arlington, Va.

24. *Washington Post*, Tuesday 22 July 1919. *New York Times*, Tuesday 22 July 1919. *New York Herald*, Tuesday 22 July 1919. *New York Tribune*, Tuesday 22 July 1919. Diary of Josephus Daniels, Monday 21 July 1919, Daniels Papers, L.C.

25. Major-General Henry Jervey to the Adjutant-General, 22 July 1919; Major-General Jervey to the Director of Purchase, Storage and Traffic, 22 July 1919; Brigadier-General

E. D. Anderson to the Adjutant-General, 25 July 1919, Papers of the Chief of Staff, 1917–1921, 1503, Washington, D.C. War Exhibits, 201, R.G. 165, N.A. General G. C. Barnhardt, Adjutant General, to the Commanding General, Camp Humphries, Va., 24 July 1919; General Barnhardt to the Commanding General, Camp Meade, Md., 24 July 1919; The Secretary of War to the Secretary of the Navy, 29 July 1919, Records of the Department of Justice, Glasser File, Racial Riot, Washington, D.C., R.G. 60, N.A. Major-General W.G. Haan to the Chief of Staff, 1 August 1919, War Department Papers, Office of the Chief of Staff, War College Division, A.W.C. 9744, R.G. 165, N.A. Log Book, U.S.S. 'Mayflower' and Log Book U.S.S. 'Sylph', 21–27 July 1919. Records of the Bureau of Naval Personnel, R.G. 24, N.A.

26. Newton D. Baker to Woodrow Wilson, 23 July 1919, Newton D. Baker Papers, L.C. *Washington Post*, Wednesday 23 July 1919. Pittsburgh *Gazette-Times*, Wednesday 23 July 1919. *Boston Post*, Wednesday 23 July 1919. *New York Tribune*, Wednesday 23 July 1919. *New York Herald*, Wednesday 23 July 1919. *New York Times*, Wednesday 23 July 1919.

27. Not six, as many accounts have it.

28. *Washington Post*, Tuesday 22 July; Wednesday 23 July, Thursday 24 July and Wednesday 30 July 1919. Muster Rolls of Officers and Enlisted Men of the U.S. Marine Corps, Quantico, Va., 1–31 July 1919, U.S.M.C. Headquarters, Arlington, Va.

29. *Washington Post*, Sunday 20 July; Monday 21 July; Tuesday 22 July, Wednesday 23 July; Saturday 2 August 1919. *New York Times*, Tuesday 22 July 1919. Muster Rolls of Officers and Enlisted Men of the U.S. Marine Corps, Quantico, 1–31 July 1919, U.S.M.C. Headquarters, Arlington, Va.

30. See Charles Crowe, 'Racial Massacre in Atlanta. September 22, 1906', *Journal of Negro History*, LIV (April 1969), 150–173.

31. John R. Shillady, Secretary, N.A.A.C.P., to A. Mitchell Palmer, 25 July 1919; Assistant Attorney – General Robert P. Stewart to Shillady, 29 July 1919, Records of the Department of Justice, File No. 203477, Box 3090, R.G.60, N.A.

32. Chalmers M. Roberts, *The Washington Post: The First Hundred Years* (Boston, 1977), pp. 142–9, 158–9.

33. Even though the newspapers made frantic efforts to increase the speed of their reporting, which led to such classic bloomers as the famous *Chicago Tribune* headline of Election Night, 1948, 'Dewey Defeats Truman'.

34. Major-General W. G. Haan to the Chief of Staff, 1 August 1919, War Department Papers, Office of the Chief of Staff, War College Division, A.W.C. 9744, R.G. 165, N.A. *Washington Post*, Thursday 24 July; Friday 25 July; and Saturday 26 July 1919. *New York Herald*, Thursday 24 July 1919. *New York Times*, Thursday 24 July 1919.

35. Adrian Cook, *The Armies of the Streets: The New York City Draft Riots of 1863* (Lexington, Ky., 1974), p. 133. Crowe, 'Racial Massacre in Atlanta'.

36. W. E. B. Du Bois in *The Crisis*, August 1919.

37. Letter signed 'E.G.M.' in *The Nation*, 9 August 1919.

38. *Boston Post*, Thursday 24 July 1919.

39. George Foster Peabody to Newton D. Baker, 24 July 1919, Baker Papers, L.C.

## CHAPTER 9

An earlier version of this essay was delivered to the Research Seminar of the Department of American Studies, University of Manchester, June 1982. I am grateful for the helpful comments of the seminar participants.

1. Arthur M. Schlesinger, Jr., *The Age of Roosevelt* (3 vols. Boston, 1957–60). Frank Freidel, *Franklin D. Roosevelt* (4 vols. Boston, 1952–73).

2. James T. Patterson, *The New Deal and the States: Federalism in Transition* (Princeton, 1969), pp. 3–49.

3. *Ibid.*, pp. 50–101. Patterson, *America's Struggle against Poverty, 1900–1980* (Cambridge, Mass. and London, 1981), pp. 76–77.

4. Patterson, *New Deal and the States*, pp. 129–167.

5. *Ibid.*, pp. 168–193.

6. *Ibid.*, pp. 206–7.

7. One measure of the improvement in analytical content is to compare the recent studies with those dissertations on Tennessee, Vermont, Michigan, Pennsylvania and Colorado

which were written before the publication of Patterson's book and which have been recently published by Garland Publishing Company, New York, in *Modern American History: A Garland Series*, edited by Frank Freidel.

8. Francis Schruben, *Kansas in Turmoil, 1930–1936* (Columbia, Mo., 1969), p. 105. Charles H. Trout, *Boston, The Great Depression and the New Deal* (New York, 1977), pp. 79–80. Jack Irby Hayes, Jr., 'South Carolina and the New Deal, 1932–1938' (Unpublished Ph.D. thesis, Univ. of South Carolina, 1972), p. 15. James F. Wickens, 'Depression and the New Deal in Colorado', in John Braeman, Robert Bremner and David Brody (eds.), *The New Deal*, 2 vols, Vol. 2, *The State and Local Levels* (Columbus, Ohio, 1975), p. 273.

9. Robert E. Burton, 'The New Deal in Oregon', in Braeman, Bremner and Brody, vol. 2, p. 357.

10. Keith L. Bryant, Jr., 'Oklahoma and the New Deal', in *ibid.*, vol. 2, p. 169.

11. Trout, *Boston, The Great Depression* pp. 50–64.

12. Anthony J. Badger, *North Carolina and the New Deal* (Raleigh, N.C., 1981), pp. 11–12.

13. William Anderson, *The Wild Man From Sugar Creek: The Political Career of Eugene Talmadge* (Baton Rouge, 1975), pp. 62–81. Talmadge wore red suspenders or gallusses to appeal to his rural audiences.

14. Michael P. Malone, *C. Ben Ross and the New Deal in Idaho* (Seattle, 1970), p. 28.

15. Roger D. Tate, Jr., 'Easing the Burden: The Era of Depression and New Deal in Mississippi' (Unpublished Ph.D. thesis, Univ. of Tennessee, 1978), pp. 57–8.

16. Barbara Blumberg, *The New Deal and the Unemployed: The View from New York City* (Lewisburg, Pa., 1979), pp. 19–31; Robert P. Ingalls, *Herbert H. Lehman and New York's Little New Deal* (New York, 1975), p. 41.

17. Michael S. Holmes, *The New Deal in Georgia: An Administrative History* (Westport, Conn., 1975), pp. 34–8.

18. Hayes, 'South Carolina and the New Deal', pp. 199–203.

19. Tate, 'Easing the Burden', p. 118.

20. Blumberg, *The New Deal and the Unemployed*, pp. 184–217, 287. Holmes, *The New Deal in Georgia*, pp. 125–166.

21. Tate, 'Easing the Burden', p. 143.

22. Joseph J. Veredicchio, 'New Deal Work Relief and New York City, 1933–1938' (Unpublished Ph.D. thesis, New York University, 1980), p. 179.

23. Blumberg, *The New Deal and the Unemployed*, pp. 46–7, 286–7. William W. Bremer, '"Along the American Way": The New Deal's Work Relief Programs for the Unemployed', *Journal of American History*, 42 (1975), 636–52.

24. Blumberg, *The New Deal and the Unemployed*, pp. 117–118. Lawrence Lashbrook, 'Work Relief in Maine: the administration and progress of the WPA' (Unpublished Ph.D. thesis, Univ. of Maine, 1978), pp. 242–6.

25. Raymond E. Marcello, 'The North Carolina Works Progress Administration and the Politics of Relief' (Unpublished Ph.D. thesis, Duke Univ., 1969), pp. 116–18, 122–6, 138–63.

26. Bruce Stave, *The New Deal and the Last Hurrah: Pittsburgh Machine Politics* (Pittsburgh, 1970), pp. 142–7. Lyle Dorsett, *Franklin D. Roosevelt and the City Bosses* (Port Washington, N.Y., 1977), pp. 46, 76, 88.

27. Frances Fox Piven and Richard A. Cloward, *Regulating the Poor: The Functions of Public Welfare* (London, 1972), pp. 61–117.

28. Frances Fox Piven and Richard A. Cloward, *Poor People's Movements: Why they succeed, How they fail* (New York, 1977), pp. 68–76. Roy Rosenweig, 'Radicals and the Jobless: The Musteites and the Unemployed Leagues, 1932–1936', *Labor History* 16 (1975), 52–77 and '"Socialism in Our Time": The Socialist Party and the Unemployed', *Labor History* 20 (1979), 486–509. Musteites were radical followers of A. J. Muste's American Workers Party. They attempted to organise the unemployed in support of striking workers.

29. Blumberg, *The New Deal and the Unemployed*, pp. 39, 52–7, 86–95, 101–3, 107–110, 286–7. Veredicchio, 'New Deal Work Relief', pp. 1–11.

30. Hayes, 'South Carolina and the New Deal', pp. 198–202.

31. Wickens, 'Depression and the New Deal in Colorado', p. 275.

32. Richard Lowitt and Maurine Beasley, *One Third of a Nation: Lorena Hickok's Reports on the Great Depression* (Urbana, Chicago and London, 1981), pp. 12–13, 79, 85. For a judicious summary of the attitudes of the poor and the unemployed in the 1930s see Patterson, *America's Struggle against Poverty*, pp. 37–55.

33. Burton, 'The New Deal in Oregon', p. 365; quotation from Anderson, *The Wild Man from Sugar Creek*, p. 168.

34. Ingalls, *Herbert H. Lehman*, pp. 73–122, 251. When George Earle and Frank Murphy tried to provide decisive leadership in Pennsylvania and Michigan they were ultimately stymied by Democratic factionalism and conservative reaction, see Richard Keller, 'Pennsylvania and the New Deal', in Braeman, Bremner and Brody, *The New Deal*, vol. 2, pp. 58–72, Sidney Fine, *Frank Murphy: The New Deal Years* (Chicago and London, 1979), pp. 481–528.

35. David Maurer, 'Relief Problems and Politics in Ohio', in Braeman, Bremner and Brody, vol. 2, pp. 91–9.

36. Ronald L. Feinman, *Twilight of Progressivism: The Western Republican Senators and the New Deal* (Baltimore and London, 1981), pp. 117–56, 203–9.

37. Fine, *Frank Murphy*, pp. 225–9.

38. A. Cash Koeniger, 'The New Deal and the States: Roosevelt versus the Byrd Organisation in Virginia', *Journal of American History* 68 (1982), 876–896.

39. Dorsett, *Franklin D. Roosevelt and the City Bosses*, pp. 51–60. T. Harry Williams, *Huey Long* (New York, 1969), pp. 636–40, 793–814. Long, who had achieved dictatorial power in Louisiana, had originally supported Roosevelt but had broken with the New Deal in 1933, both over patronage and the failure of the New Deal to redistribute wealth. His 'Share our Wealth' scheme appeared to offer a radical challenge to Roosevelt in 1934 and 1935 and his possible third-party candidacy clearly alarmed Roosevelt's advisers. He was assassinated in September 1935 and his successors soon came to an amicable understanding with the national administration.

40. Dorsett, *Franklin D. Roosevelt*, pp. 79–81, 107–111.

41. Marvin L. Cann, 'Burnet Maybank and the New Deal in South Carolina, 1931–1941' (Unpublished Ph.D. thesis, Univ. of North Carolina, 1967), p. 191.

42. Koeniger, 'The New Deal and the States', pp. 887–96.

43. Williams, *Huey Long*, pp. 689–92.

44. Dorsett, *Franklin D. Roosevelt*, pp. 83–97. Stave, *New Deal and the Last Hurrah*, pp. 162–82, and "Pittsburgh and the New Deal" in Braeman, Bremner and Brody, vol. 2, pp. 398–99. John W. Jeffries, *Testing the Roosevelt Coalition: Connecticut Society in the Era of World War II* (Knoxville, Tenn., 1979) pp. 3–50. Fine, *Frank Murphy*, pp. 490–92, 524. John M. Allswang, *The New Deal and American Politics: A Study in Political Change* (New York, 1978), pp. 85–8. James L. Sundquist, *Dynamics of the Party System: Alignment and Realignment of Political Parties in the United States* (Washington D.C., 1973), pp. 211–12. Even in the northern industrial states the success of the New Deal realignment was not immediate and complete. Democratic hegemony did not necessarily replace Republican hegemony; the New Deal years often heralded a period of two-party competition between the Democrats and a liberalised Republican party. Nor did conservative old-style Democrats disappear overnight. In many states it was the 1940s before 'issue-oriented' liberals took over from 'patronage-oriented' Democrats.

45. Allswang, *New Deal and American Politics*, pp. 48–9.

46. Richard Lowitt, *George Norris: The Triumph of a Progressive, 1933–1944* (Urbana, Chicago and London, 1978), pp. 305, 454. See also Schruben, *Kansas in Turmoil*, pp. 134, 164, 212, 220.

47. For an extended analysis of the distribution of New Deal spending see Don C. Reading, 'A Statistical Analysis of the New Deal's Economic Programs in the Forty-Eight States, 1933–1939' (Unpublished Ph.D. thesis, Utah State University, 1972).

48. Tate, 'Easing the Burden', p. 204.

49. F. Alan Combs, 'The Impact of the New Deal on Wyoming Politics', Michael P. Malone, 'The Montana New Dealers', and James F. Wickens, 'Depression and the New Deal in Colorado' in Braeman, Bremner and Brody, vol. 2, pp. 222–25, 234, 257, 263. See also James T. Patterson, 'The New Deal and the West', *Pacific Historical Review* 38 (1969). Utah was one possible exception to the picture of continuity. The election and re-election of Elbert Thomas gave the Democrats a permanent foothold in that centre of Mormon Republicanism, Allswang, *New Deal and American Politics*, pp. 107–8.

50. Harvard Sitkoff, *A New Deal for Blacks: The Emergence of Civil Rights as a National Issue*, vol. 1, *The Depression Decade* (New York, 1978), pp. 102–138.

51. For the tentative southern liberal revival of the 1940s see Numan V. Bartley and Hugh D. Graham, *Southern Politics and the Second Reconstruction* (Baltimore and London, 1975), pp. 24–50.

52. For the fate of the S.C.H.W see Thomas A. Kreuger, *And Promises to Keep: The Southern Conference for Human Welfare, 1938–1948* (Nashville, 1967).

53. Fine, *Frank Murphy*, pp. 445–6. Douglas Carl Abrams, 'North Carolina and the New Deal, 1932–1940' (Unpublished Ph.D. thesis, Univ. of Maryland, 1981), pp. 268–75. Hayes, 'South Carolina and the New Deal', p. 451.

54. Trout, *Boston*, pp. 152–4. Badger, *North Carolina and the New Deal*, pp. 52–3. Hayes, 'South Carolina and the New Deal', pp. 279–284.

55. James P. Johnson, *The Politics of Soft Coal: The Bituminous Industry from World War 1 through the New Deal* (Urbana, 1979), pp. 122, 124, 131, 151–64. Louis Galambos, *Competition and Cooperation: The Emergence of a National Trade Association* (Baltimore, 1966), pp. 158–65.

56. Johnson, *Politics of Soft Coal*, p. 216. Galambos, *Competition and Cooperation*, pp. 269–70. Gerald D. Nash, *United States Oil Policy, 1890–1964: Business and Government in Twentieth-Century America* (Pittsburgh, 1968), pp. 131–3, 136, 168. James E. Fickle, *The New South and the 'New Competition': Trade Association Development in the Southern Pine Industry* (Urbana, 1980), p. 138. Thomas R. Winpenny, 'Henning Webb Prentiss and the Challenge of the New Deal', *Journal of the Lancaster Historical Society* 81 (1977), 1–24.

57. F. J. Harper, 'The Small Retailer and the New Deal', Paper delivered at the FDR Centennial Colloquium, David Bruce Centre for American Studies, University of Keele, 23 April 1982.

58. The literature on the southern tenant farmers is extensive: the most important works are Donald H. Grubbs, *Cry from the Cotton: The Southern Tenant Farmers' Union and the New Deal* (Chapel Hill, 1971); Donald Holley, *Uncle Sam's Farmers: The New Deal Communities in the Lower Mississippi Valley* (Urbana, 1975) and Paul E. Mertz, *New Deal Policy and Southern Rural Poverty* (Baton Rouge, 1978). For migrant farm workers see Cletus Daniel, *Bitter Harvest: A History of California Farmworkers, 1870–1941* (Ithaca and London, 1981), pp. 105–285.

59. Donald Worster, *Dust Bowl: The Southern Plains in the 1930s* (Oxford and New York, 1980), part 5.

60. Daniel, *Bitter Harvest*, p. 256.

61. Mertz, *New Deal Policy*, p. 171.

62. James Green, 'Working-Class Militancy in the Depression', *Radical America* 6 (1972), 1–36. Alice and Staughton Lynd (eds.), *Rank and File: Personal Histories by Working Class Organisers* (Boston, 1973). Piven and Cloward, *Poor People's Movements*, pp. 96–175.

63. Johnson, *Politics of Soft Coal*, pp. 166–71. Hayes, 'South Carolina and the New Deal', pp. 340–63. Sidney Fine, *Sit-Down: The General Motors Strike of 1936–1937* (Ann Arbor, 1969), pp. 54–99, 133–148.

64. David Brody, *Workers in Industrial America: Essays on the Twentieth-Century Struggle* (New York, 1980), p. 106.

65. Howell J. Harris, *The right to manage: Industrial Relations Policies of American Business in the 1940s* (Madison, 1982), ch. 1.

66. Another example of the difficulties of sustaining rank-and-file militancy prior to the Wagner Act is provided in Robert H. Zieger, 'The Limits of Militancy: Organising Paper Workers, 1933–35', *Journal of American History* 63 (1976–77), 638–57.

67. Brody, *Workers in Industrial America*, pp. 104–6.

68. Robert H. Zieger, *Madison's Battery Workers, 1934–1952: A History of Federal Labor Union 19587* (Ithaca, 1977), pp. 3–5, 47–53. Contrast with Peter Friedlander, *The Emergence of a UAW Local, 1936–1937: A Study in Class and Culture* (Pittsburgh, 1975).

69. Brody, *Workers in Industrial America*, pp. 132–3, 152–7. Robert S. McElvaine, 'Thunder Without Lightning: Working-Class Discontent in the United States, 1929–1937' (Unpublished Ph.D. thesis, State Univ. of New York, Binghamton, 1974), pp. 147–52.

70. John Dollard, *Caste and Class in a Southern Town* (New York, 1937). Robert and Helen Lynd, *Middletown in Transition: A Study in Cultural Conflicts* (New York, 1937). E. Wight Bakke, *The Unemployed Worker: A Study of the Task of Making a Living without a Job* (New Haven, 1940) and *Citizens without Work: A Study of the Effects of Unemployment upon the Workers' Social Relations and Practices* (New Haven, 1940). Note the recent studies of ethnic tensions and of women in the 1930s, Ronald H. Bayor, *Neighbors in Conflict: The Irish, Germans, Jews, and Italians of New York City, 1929–1941* (Baltimore and London, 1978) and Lois Scharf, *To Work and to Wed; Female Employment, Feminism and the Great Depression* (Westport and London, 1980).

CHAPTER 10

1. A. M. Schlesinger, Jr., *The Coming of the New Deal* (Boston, 1959), pp. 455–62; George Wolfskill, *The Revolt of the Conservatives: A History of the American Liberty League 1934–1940* (Boston, 1962), pp. 108–110. On the growing opposition to FDR's use of presidential power towards the end of World War II, see Richard Polenberg, *War and Society: The United States, 1941–1945* (Philadelphia, 1972), pp. 174–5, 182–3.

2. Harold J. Laski, *The American Presidency: An Interpretation* (London, 1940), p. 277; Richard E. Neustadt, *Presidential Power: The Politics of Leadership* (New York, 1960), p. 157; James T. Patterson, *The New Deal and the States: Federalism in Transition* (Princeton, 1969), p. 207; Alonzo L. Hamby, *Beyond the New Deal: Harry S. Truman and American Liberalism* (New York, 1973), pp. xiii, xvii.

3. R. Harris Smith, *OSS: The Secret History of America's First Central Intelligence Agency* (New York, 1972), p. 364.

4. Daniel Bell in the *New Leader*, 25 June 1949, p. 8, rept. in Jeffrey Meyers (ed.), *George Orwell, the Critical Heritage* (London, 1975), pp. 262–6.

5. Richard Hofstadter, *The Paranoid Style in American Politics and Other Essays* (London, 1966), p. 97.

6. Barry Goldwater, *The Conscience of a Conservative* (New York, 1960), pp. 4, 15.

7. Barry Goldwater, *The Conscience of a Majority* (Englewood Cliffs, 1970), pp. 99–100.

8. David L. Barnett, 'Time to Rein in Federal Government?' *U.S. News & World Report*, 11 May 1981, p. 50. Some weight will be given, below, to the evidence selected for publication by the *U.S. News & World Report*. It is therefore worth noting that this weekly publication had its origin in the 1920s, has a circulation of two million, and 'is in no way connected with the U.S. government'. Ben F. Phlegar, Executive Editor, to RJ-J, 5 May 1982.

9. A. M. Schlesinger, Jr., *The Imperial Presidency* (New York, 1974), pp. 303–306.

10. '1984' is the title of the eleventh chapter in David Wise, *The American Police State: The Government against the People* (New York, 1976), pp. 352–366.

11. Martin Schram, *Running for President: A Journal of the Carter Campaign* (New York, 1977), p. 350.

12. Quoted in *ibid.*, p. 374.

13. 'Government Intervention', *Business Week*, 4 April 1977, p. 42.

14. Lewis J. Lord (Associate Editor), 'Battle Report in Carter's War on Big Government', *U.S. News & World Report*, 13 March 1978, p. 21.

15. Quoted in Charles D. Hobbs, *Ronald Reagan's Call to Action* (Nashville, 1976), p. 155.

16. *Financial Times*, 28 Jan. 1982; *Daily Telegraph*, 28 Jan. 1982.

17. Barnett in 'Time to Rein In' and the *Business Week* staff team in 'Government Intervention' both gave prominence to historical assumptions. The former gave equal weight to the expansion of the 1930s and 1960s (p. 49), but the latter placed heavy emphasis on developments since 1960 (p. 47). Peace Corps director R. Sargent Shriver had to insist that his agency was not an instrument of the Cold War: Gerard T. Rice, 'Kennedy's Children: The Peace Corps 1961–3' (Unpublished Ph.D. thesis, Univ. of Glasgow, 1980), p. 424.

18. John D. Lees, *The President and the Supreme Court: New Deal to Watergate* (Durham: British Association for American Studies Pamphlet in American Studies no. 3, 1980), p. 5.

19. My own italics.

20. Elizabeth Huckaby, *Crisis at Central High: Little Rock 1957–8* (Baton Rouge, 1980), pp. 3–5, 12–18.

21. According to his own account, President Eisenhower tried hard to find a way of avoiding a political and constitutional clash with Governor Faubus: Dwight D. Eisenhower, *Waging Peace 1956–1961* (London, 1965), pp. 165–6, 170. See pp. 168–9 for Eisenhower's constitutional justification for using federal force.

22. Richard H. Kohn, *Eagle and Sword: The Beginnings of the Military Establishment in America, 1783–1802* (New York, 1975), p. 158; Luke Grant, 'Violence in Labor Disputes and Methods of Policing Industry' (a report for the Research Division, U.S. Commission on Industrial Relations, c. 1914: National Archives, Washington, D.C.), p. 48.

23. See Harvey Wish, 'The Pullman Strike: A Study in Industrial Warfare', *Journal of the Illinois State Historical Society*, 32 (1939), pp. 288–312. Frank M. Kleiler, 'White House

Intervention in Labor Disputes', *Political Science Quarterly*, 68 (June 1953), 227–40 and Harold M. Hyman, 'Johnson, Stanton and Grant: A Reconsideration of the Army's Role in the Events Leading to Impeachment', *American Historical Review*, 66 (1960), 85–100.

24. 'If the day comes when we can obey the orders of our courts only *when we personally approve of them,* the end of the American system, as we know it, will not be far off': letter to an unspecified friend, quoted in Eisenhower, *Waging Peace*, p. 175.

25. Poll taken on 4 Oct. 1957: George H. Gallup, *The Gallup Poll: Public Opinion 1935–1971* (New York, 1972), p. 1517. Even in the South, Eisenhower managed to secure the cooperation of the committee of the Southern Governors' Conference: Eisenhower, *Waging Peace*, p. 173.

26. Fred P. Graham, 'A Contemporary History of American Crime', in H. D. Graham and T. R. Gurr (eds.), *The History of Violence in America* (New York, 1969), p. 495.

27. *Report of the National Advisory Commission on Civil Disorders* (New York, 1968), p. 100.

28. Poll taken on 18 Aug. 1968: Gallup, *The Gallup Poll*, p. 2154.

29. Hanson W. Baldwin, 'Intelligence Arm Vital: Congressional Obstacles for U.S. Agency Thought to Ignore a Big Lesson of War', *New York Times*, 24 April 1946: Baldwin, 'Intelligence – I [first of a series of five articles]', *New York Times*, 20 July 1948; Baldwin, 'Annex A: Outline of Testimony' (in closed hearings to a Senate committee, c. 1955–56), p. 1, in Baldwin papers, Yale Univ. Library, New Haven.

30. David Wise and Thomas B. Ross, *The Invisible Government* (1964; rept. New York, 1974), pp. 352–6.

31. *Ibid.*, 'Introduction' to 1974 reprint, p. vii.

32. Schlesinger, *Imperial Presidency*, pp. 167, 172.

33. Ray S. Cline, *The CIA Under Reagan Bush & Casey: The Evolution of the Agency from Roosevelt to Reagan* (Washington, D.C., 1981), p. 252; Harry Rositzke, *The CIA's Secret Operations: Espionage, Counterespionage, and Covert Action* (New York, 1977), p. 227.

34. Allegations in *L'Humanité* summarised in the London *Times*, 17 Feb. 1976; Wise, *Police State*, p. 222.

35. U.S. Senate, *Final Report of the Select Committee to Study Governmental Operations with Respect to Intelligence Agencies. Book 1. Foreign and Military Intelligence.* 94th Cong. 2nd sess. 26 April 1976, pp. 31 ff.

36. *Ibid.*, p. 38.

37. *Ibid.*, pp. 131–5.

38. Wise and Ross, *Invisible Government*, pp. 354–55. For a wide selection of press excerpts on covert operations, see Judith F. Buncher (ed.), *The CIA and the Security Debate, 1971–1975* (New York, 1976), pp. 113–30.

39. William Colby, *Honorable Men: My Life in the CIA* (London, 1978), p. 137. Colby was director of the C.I.A., 1973–75.

40. H. M. Wriston, 'Executive Agents in American Foreign Relations' (Unpublished Ph.D. thesis, Harvard Univ., 1922), pp. 326–60.

41. Schlesinger, *Imperial Presidency*, p. 244.

42. John D. Lees, 'Open Government in the USA: Some Recent Statutory Developments', *Public Administration* (Autumn 1979), 340–41.

43. See 'Spooks on Ice: Unleashing the CIA', *Time*, 9 Nov. 1981.

44. Schlesinger, *Coming*, p. 460.

45. Douglass C. North, *Growth and Welfare in the American Past: A New Economic History* (Englewood Cliffs, N.J., 1966), pp. 172–3, 176.

46. Estimate by Murray L. Weidenbaum, director of Washington University's Center for the Study of American Business, reported in 'Government Intervention', p. 47. For a detailed analysis of the problem, see Weidenbaum, *Business, Government, and the Public*, 2nd edn (Englewood Cliffs, N.J., 1981), pp. 197–307.

47. 'Government Intervention', p. 48.

48. Reagan's views on federal spending and inflation in Hobbs, *Call to Action*, p. 54. See also Mark I. Gelfland, 'The War on Poverty' in Robert A. Divine (ed.), *Exploring the Johnson Years* (Austin, 1981), pp. 134–5.

49. See Helmuth C. Engelbrecht, *Merchants of Death: A Study of the International Armaments Industry* (New York, 1934).

50. Dwight D. Eisenhower, 'Farewell Radio and Television Address to the American People', 17 Jan. 1961, in Russell F. Weigley (ed.), *The American Military: Readings in the History of the Military in American Society* (Reading, Mass., 1969), p. 156. See also Sidney Lens, *The*

*Military-Industrial Complex* (London, 1971).

51. Michael Ferber, 'A Time to Say No' (statement in 1967, in connection with the trial of Ferber, Dr. Benjamin Spock, and others, for organising resistance to the draft), in David R. Weber (ed.), *Civil Disobedience in America: A Documentary History* (Ithaca, 1978), pp. 273–4.

52. During the Vietnam War, the Committee for Nonviolent Action issued 'Thoreau Money' in New York City, New England and California, to be used 'to pay that 60% of your Federal taxes that goes for war': CNVA, *War Tax Protest* (n.d.), in the Applegarth Collection, Hoover Institution Library, Stanford, California.

53. J. K. Galbraith, *American Capitalism: The Concept of Countervailing Power* (London: 1952), p. 144 and *passim;* North, *Growth and Welfare*, pp. 99, 174, 176; *Structure and Change in Economic History* (New York, 1981), pp. 197, 201–202.

54. James M. Buchanan, 'Why Does Government Grow?' in Thomas E. Borcherding (ed.), *Budgets and Bureaucrats: The Sources of Government Growth* (Durham, N.C., 1977), p. 4.

55. Thomas E. Borcherding, 'One Hundred Years of Public Spending, 1870–1970', in Borcherding (ed.), *Budgets* pp. 26, 27.

56. See David Halberstam, *The Best and the Brightest* (New York, 1973).

57. See, however, Thomas C. Cochran, 'Did the Civil War Retard Industrialisation?' *Mississippi Valley Historical Review*, 48 (Sept. 1961), 197–210. According to a Brookings Institution report, 'the impact of alternative defense budgets on domestic output and employment' is 'a question that consistently arises in the consideration of defense spending': *Setting National Priorities: The 1973 Budget* (Washington, D.C., 1972), p. 165. This may well be true, but responsible public debate has skirted the issue of military *as opposed to* civilian spending.

58. Borcherding in Borcherding, *Budgets*, pp. 27, 30.

59. Borcherding in Borcherding, *ibid.*, p. 31.

60. Jacques S. Gansler, *The Defense Industry* (Cambridge, Mass., 1980), p. 19.

61. *Ibid.*, p. 19, and see *The Military Balance*, below.

62. One should bear in mind possible differences in the scope of the government sector in the two countries, but the contrast is still a striking one: *The Military Balance 1981–1982* (London: International Institute for Strategic Studies, 1981), pp. 12–13. President Reagan and his ambassador to the United Nations, Mrs. Jeane Kirkpatrick, called for a greater contribution from America's European allies: Reagan in Hobbs, *Call to Action*, pp. 49–50; Henry Brandon, 'Why America Fears Backlash over Europe', London *Sunday Times*, 13 Dec. 1981.

63. For an explanation, see Rhodri Jeffreys-Jones, *American Espionage: From Secret Service to CIA* (New York; 1977), pp. 19–20.

64. The anti-statist President Reagan explicitly endorsed the Peace Corps, if in measured and cautious language: Gerard T. Rice, *Twenty Years of Peace Corps* (Washington, D.C., 1981), pp. v, 87, 107.

65. See Frank A. Ninkovich, *The Diplomacy of Ideas: U.S. Foreign Policy and Cultural Relations 1938–1950* (Cambridge, 1981), pp. 22–3.

66. Perhaps memories lingered of a disastrous attempt to hem in the TVA in the 1950s: see William E. Leuchtenburg, *A Troubled Feast: American Society Since 1945* (Boston, 1973), p. 89.

## CHAPTER 11

1. For an historical overview of American overseas assistance and the impulses behind it, see Merle Curti, *American Philanthropy Abroad* (New Brunswick, N.J., 1963), p. 3.

2. Theodore C. Sorensen, 'The Election of 1960' in A. M. Schlesinger Jr., Fred L. Israel and William P. Hansen (eds.), *The History of American Presidential Elections, Vol. IV,* (London, 1971), pp. 34–64.

3. As Arthur M. Schlesinger Jr. noted in *A Thousand Days: John F. Kennedy In The White House* (Boston, 1965), p. 557, many Americans fondly remembered Franklin D. Roosevelt's Civilian Conservation Corps – unemployed young men who were paid by the federal government to perform public services during the Great Depression – and they longed to see the concept tried out overseas. In its origins at least, Schlesinger felt that the Peace Corps was 'undoubtedly suggested by Roosevelt's C.C.C.'

4. Hubert Humphrey was Kennedy's opponent in the Democratic presidential primary elections in West Virginia and Wisconsin in 1960. Humphrey certainly raised the issue of the Peace Corps during that campaign and he later claimed that Kennedy had picked up the idea from him. See, Hubert H. Humphrey, *The Education of a Public Man: My Life and Politics* (London, 1977).

5. The most memorable (and most often quoted) line from John F. Kennedy's presidential inaugural address on 20 January 1961.

6. John F. Kennedy, 'Staffing a Foreign Policy for Peace', 2 November 1960 in U.S. Senate, Freedom of Communications, *The Speeches of Senator John F. Kennedy, The Presidential Campaign of 1960* (Washington, D.C., 1961), pp. 1237–41. For a revisionist analysis of Kennedy's foreign policy stance see Richard J. Walton, *Cold War and Counterrevolution: The Foreign Policy of John F. Kennedy* (Baltimore, 1973).

7. For a description of the atmosphere in the United States in the late 1950s, see William L. O'Neill, *Coming Apart: An Informal History of America in the 1960's* (Chicago, 1971). Regarding the United States' destabilisation of foreign governments, it might be noted that the C.I.A. overthrew 'pro-Communist' governments in Iran in 1953 and Guatemala in 1954 and that it attempted to do so in Indonesia in 1958. It also helped install what its leaders hoped would be pro-western governments in Egypt in 1954 and in Laos in 1959. By 1960, according to some sources, the C.I.A. had also begun to plan the overthrow and murder of Fidel Castro in Cuba. See, Arthur M. Schlesinger Jr., *Robert Kennedy And His Times*, (Boston, 1978).

8. Eugene Burdick and William J. Lederer, *The Ugly American* (New York, 1960).

9. For this quotation, a description and analysis of the Kennedy years, and the Peace Corps' origins and activities see Harris Wofford, *Of Kennedys and Kings* (New York, 1980).

10. Sargent Shriver memorandum to Dean Rusk, 26 May 1961.

11. R. B. Texter (ed.), *Cultural Frontiers of The Peace Corps* (Cambridge, Mass. 1966), p. 323.

12. 'The Peace Corps' Daring New Look', *New Republic*, 19 February 1966, p. 15.

13. In fact, the Peace Corps was the only programme of the Kennedy era to be allowed the distinctive status of an 'emergency agency'.

14. Sargent Shriver, 'Two Years Of The Peace Corps', *Foreign Affairs*, (July 1963).

15. Harlan Cleveland, *The Future of The Peace Corps* (Aspen, Colo., 1977), p. 2.

16. Chuck Guminer (Volunteer in Senegal) in a letter to Peace Corps headquarters in Washington, D.C., 20 March 1963, The John F. Kennedy Memorial Library, Boston, Mass. (henceforth "JFK Library").

17. Sargent Shriver, 'Two Years Of The Peace Corps', *Foreign Affairs*, (July 1963).

18. Sargent Shriver memorandum to all Peace Corps Representatives, 8 August 1963, JFK Library.

19. Peace Corps' 'Evaluation Report' on Niger, 1963, Peace Corps Library, Washington, D.C.

20. For a revisionist interpretation of the Peace Corps as an arm of U.S. cultural and political imperialism, see Marshall Windmiller, *The Peace Corps and Pax Americana* (Washington, D.C., 1970).

21. Sargent Shriver memorandum on 'Policies and Criteria for Selection of Peace Corps Projects', 19 July 1962, JFK Library.

22. Thomas Quimby (former Peace Corps Director in Liberia), oral history interview conducted by the John F. Kennedy Memorial Library.

23. David Wise and Thomas B. Ross, *The Invisible Government* (New York, 1974), pp. 277–8.

24. Stanley J. Grogan (Assistant Director, C.I.A.) memorandum to Pierre Salinger, 28 February 1962. The understanding between Kennedy and the C.I.A. regarding the Peace Corps was referred to in Peace Corps circles as 'The Treaty', JFK Library.

25. Incident cited by Charles Peters in personal interview with Gerard T. Rice in Washington, D.C., 18 December 1978.

26. John F. Kennedy, 'Remarks to Peace Corps Headquarters Staff', 14 June 1962, *Public Papers of the President (1962)*, vol. 2, p. 482.

27. Dean Rusk, 'Remarks to the Peace Corps National Advisory Council', 22 May 1961, JFK Library.

28. The smaller numbers of Volunteers in the 1970s need not be equated with a decline in the Peace Corps' overall effectiveness. After its first five years of tremendous growth, the Peace Corps preferred to concentrate on the quality of Volunteers sent overseas rather than the quantity. Indeed, one of the major criticisms of the Peace Corps in the 1960s was that there was an over-concentration on numbers *per se*.

29. A group known as the Committee of Returned Peace Corps Volunteers used this phrase. Small, radical, and formed in 1964, it was not officially associated with the Peace Corps. It vehemently protested against the American military presence in Vietnam.

30. ACTION, not an acronym, was the federal organisation established by President Nixon in July 1971 to house American official volunteer efforts, both at home and abroad. Included in ACTION, therefore, were the Peace Corps, Volunteers in Service in America, the Foster Grandparent Program and a number of other voluntary service programmes.

31. Roger L. Landrum, *The Role of the Peace Corps in Education in Developing Countries: A Sector Study* (Washington, D.C., 1981), pp. 7 and 16.

32. Robert Kennedy in *The Volunteer* magazine (November 1966); Thanat Khoman quoted in an oral history interview conducted by the John F. Kennedy Memorial Library, c. 1965.

33. Doug Bennett, 'Remarks to Peace Corps headquarters staff', 10 September 1980, quoted in *ACTION Update* (November 1980).

34. U.S. ACTION (Evaluation Division), *A Survey of Former Peace Corps Volunteers and VISTA Volunteers, Volume I – The Past Peace Corps Experience* (Washington, D.C., 1979).

35. *Ibid.* Also, for an interesting interpretation of the 'new generation' assuming power and leadership in the United States, see David S. Broder, *Changing Of the Guard* (New York, 1981). See pp. 58–62, in particular.

CHAPTER 12

1. I adapt the title from Robert F. Nagel's 'Federalism as a Fundamental Value: National League of Cities [v. Usery] in Perspective', *Supreme Court Review* (1982), 81. Jessie H. Choper, 'The Scope of National Power Vis-à-Vis the States: The Dispensability of Judicial Review', *Yale Law Journal*, 86 (1977), 1552. Both Nagel and Choper analysed the Supreme Court's controversial decision in *National League of Cities* v. *Usery*, 426 U.S. 833 (1976), in which the court held that extension of the Fair Labor Standards Act to most state employees violated the principle of federalism. Noteworthily, these law academics, the Supreme Court Justices in *Usery*, and many other constitutional specialist-lawyers reacted to *Usery* in terms of federalism's enduring values and existence. In March 1983, even as this essay went into proof form, the Supreme Court reversed its own *Usery* ruling, again by 5–4, and again stressed the enduring values of federalism, though with differing judgements compared to *Usery*. *E.E.O.C.* v. *Wyoming*, No. 81-554 (51 *Law Week*, p. 4219 (1983)).

2. William R. Brock, *Parties and Political Conscience, American Dilemmas, 1840–1850* (Millwood, N.Y: 1979), pp. xiv–xvi.

3. See, for the best statements to this effect, as well as the most complete bibliography for a very large literature, Harry N. Scheiber, 'American Federalism and the Diffusion of Power: Historical and Contemporary Perspectives', *University of Toledo Law Review*, 9 (1978), 619; 'Federalism and Legal Process; Historical and Contemporary Analysis of the American System', *Law and Society Review*, 14 (1980), 663; 'American Constitutional History and the New Legal History: Complementary Themes in Two Modes', *Journal of American History*, 68 (1981), 337.

4. K. Hall, H. M. Hyman and L. Sigal (eds.), *The Constitutional Convention as an Amending Device* (Washington, D.C., 1981); Geoffrey Bruun, 'The Constitutional Cult in the Early Nineteenth Century'; in Conyers Read (ed.), *The Constitution Reconsidered* (New York, 1938), pp. 261–269 and *passim*.

5. Brock, *Parties*, pp. xiv–xvi. Arthur Bestor, 'The American Civil War as a Constitutional Crisis', *American Historical Review*, 59 (1964), 329, wrote: 'The configurative role that constitutional issues played is the point of crucial importance'. Constitutional theorising became welded to politics as well as to jurisprudence, and made state secessions an ultimate recourse of any militant minority.

6. Brock, *Parties*, pp. xiv–xvi; H. M. Hyman, *A More Perfect Union: The Impact of the Civil War and Reconstruction on the Constitution* (New York, 1973), chs. 1, 2, 5, and pp. 68–9.

7. In 1860, John Bouvier's *Law Dictionary* (9th ed.), had no entry for federalism. Instead this useful standard professional tool contented itself, as does the 1977 English law dictionary cited below, with defining, in cursory manner, federal government: 'This term is commonly used to express a league or compact between two or more states. In the United States the central government of the Union is federal. The constitution was adopted "to

form a more perfect union among the states, for the purpose of self-protection and for the promotion of their mutual happiness'''. Cf. John B. Saunders (comp.), *Mozley & Whiteley's Law Dictionary* (9th edn, London, 1977): 'A government formed by the aggregation of several states, previously independent, in such manner that the sovereignty over each of the states resides thenceforth in the aggregate of the whole, while each of the states, though losing its individual sovereignty, retains nevertheless important political powers within its own territory, and shares the sovereignty of the entire federation with the other states, and (in general) with a new legislative or executive body having a limited jurisdiction over the entire area of the federation, and called "the general government"'. A view of federalism popular in the mid twentieth century is in William T. Hutchinson, 'Unite to Divide; Divide to Unite: The Shaping of American Federalism', *Mississippi Valley Historical Review*, 46 (1959), 3–18. Scheiber's several articles, cited in no 1 above, offer both definitions and bibliography.

8. Morton Grodzins (edited by Daniel J. Elazar), *The American System: A New View of Government in the United States* (Chicago, 1966), pp. 4, 8; Daniel Elazar, *The American Partnership: Intergovernmental Cooperation in the Nineteenth Century* (Chicago, 1962). 'There has never been a time', Grodzins wrote in R. Goldwin (ed.), *A Nation of States*, (Chicago, 1963), p. 7, 'when federal, state, and local functions were separate and distinct. Government does more things in 1963 [as Grodzins was writing] than it did in 1790 or 1861; but in terms of what government did, there was as much sharing than as today'. See also Scheiber, 'American Federalism and the Diffusion of Power', 622.

9. James McIntosh *et al* (eds.), *The Papers of Jefferson Davis* (Baton Rouge, 1981), vol. III, pp. 342–3.

10. Quoted in Scheiber, 'Federalism and Legal Process', 673.

11. H. M. Hyman and William Wiecek, *Equal Justice Under Law: American Constitutional Development, 1835–1875* (New York, 1982), chs. 8–14; Michael Les Benedict, 'Preserving Federalism: Reconstruction and the Waite Court', *Supreme Court Review* (1979), 39–79; Phillip S. Paludan, 'The American Civil War Considered as a Crisis in Law and Order', *American Historical Review*, 77 (1972), 1013–1034, 'John Norton Pomeroy, State Rights Nationalist', *American Journal of Legal History*, 12 (1968), 275–293. Important contemporary insights are in George T. Curtis, *Constitutional History of the United States* (2 vols., New York, 1896) vol. II, pp. 547–548; 'Law Address of Ex-Senator James R. Doolittle, Delivered before the Union College of Law at Chicago, June 6, 1879', ed. Duane Mowry, in *Journal of the Illinois Historical Society*, 19 (1926), 77–93; D. D. Field, 'Centralisation in The Federal Government', *North American Review* (1881), 407–426; (1926), 77–93; T. D. Woolsey, 'Nature and Sphere of Police Power', *Journal of Social Science*, 3 (1871), 97–114; G. F. Edmunds, 'The State and the Nation', *North American Review* (1881), 338–352.

12. Hyman and Wiecek, *Equal Justice*, ch. 13.

13. H. M. Hyman (ed.), *The Radical Republicans and Reconstruction, 1861–1870* (New York, 1967), intro, pp. xvii–lxviii; W. Rumble, *American Legal Realism; Skepticism, Reform, and the Judicial Process* (Ithaca, N.Y., 1968).

14. Don E. Fehrenbacher, 'Disunion and Reunion', in John Higham (ed.), *The Reconstruction of American History* (New York, 1962), pp. 111–12 and *passim;* R. N. Stromberg, *Redemption By War: The Intellectuals and 1914* (Lawrence, Ka., 1982); Hyman, *Radical Republicans*, pp. xxxvi–xxxix.

15. John Higham, 'Beyond Consensus; The Historian as Moral Critic', *American Historical Review*, 47 (1962), 193–216; Scheiber, 'Federalism and Legal Process', 664.

16. In Thomas J. Pressly, *Americans Interpret Their Civil War* (New York, 1962), p. 302.

17. Theodore C. Sorensen, *Kennedy* (New York, 1965), p. 4.

18. Thurgood Marshall quoted in A. M. Schlesinger, Jr., *Robert F. Kennedy and His Times* (New York, 1978), p. 305; and see L. H. Gudel-Rosenthal and H. J. Eschler, 'Community Resistance to School Desegregation: Enjoining the Undefinable Class', *University of Chicago Law Review*, 54 (1977), 111–165.

19. See the bibliography in James M. McPherson, *Ordeal By Fire: The Civil War and Reconstruction* (New York, 1982), pp. 657–694; and Higham, *Reconstruction of American History, passim;* J. Higham, L. Krieger and F. Gilbert, *History* (Englewood Cliffs, N.J., 1965), part III.

20. See, as example, Forrest McDonald, *A Constitutional History of the United States* (New York, 1982); Raoul Berger, *Government By Judiciary: The Transformation of the Fourteenth Amendment* (Cambridge, Mass., 1977). Additionally, note that in textbooks on the American Civil

War and Reconstruction, books in which the impact of that war and its aftermath on
federalism is always a central theme, the question of the authors' attitudes towards the
wars of his own generation colour the treatments each book presents of the Civil War. See
Frances Fitzgerald, *America Revised: History Schoolbooks in the Twentieth Century* (Boston,
1979), esp. pp. 8–9, 85–7, 157; James G. Randall, *The Civil War and Reconstruction* (1937;
rev. ed., with David Herbert Donald, Boston, 1962); Peter J. Parish, *The American Civil War*
(New York, 1975), and McPherson, *Ordeal by Fire.*

21. Brock, *Parties*, p. xv; Scheiber, 'Federalism and Legal Process', 668.
22. Michael Reagan, *The New Federalism* (New York, 1972), p. 3. See also Edward S. Corwin,
    'The Passing of Dual Federalism', *Virginia Law Review*, 36 (1950), 1–24.
23. Morton Keller, *Affairs of State: Public Life in Late Nineteenth Century America* (Cambridge,
    Mass., 1977); Thomas K. McGraw (ed.), *Regulation in Perspective: Historical Essays*,
    (Cambridge, Mass., 1981), *passim;* William E. Nelson, *The Birth of Bureaucracy and the
    Institutionalisation of Pluralism in Nineteenth Century America* (Cambridge, Mass., 1982),
    Patricia M. L. Allan-Lucie, 'Freedom and Federalism, Congress and Courts, 1861–1866',
    (Unpublished Ph.D. thesis, University of Glasgow, 1972).
24. Diel Wright, *Understanding Intergovernmental Relations* (Boston, 1978), p. 19, offers this list:
    Dual, orthodox, classic, polis, traditional, cooperative, bargaining, integrated, interdepen-
    dent, creative, new, permissive, functional, pragmatic, morganic, pluralistic, monarchic,
    perfect, imperfect, direct, private, picket fence, coercive, competitive, centralised,
    decentralist, peripheralised, fused, corporate, national, social, oligarchic, unitary,
    constitutional, international, military, political, monistic, polar, total, partial, contract,
    feudal-functional, incipient.
25. Scheiber, 'Federalism and Legal Process', 664.
26. Quoted in *ibid.*
27. Sanford V. Levinson,'New Perspectives on the Reconstruction Court', *Stanford Law Review*,
    26 (1974), 461–480; Nathan Dane, *General Abridgement and Digest of American Law* (9 vols.,
    Boston, 1829), vol. IX, App., 32–3; see also Hyman, *A More Perfect Union*, ch. 1.
28. H. M. Hyman, foreword to G. Edward White, *Patterns of American Legal Thought*
    (Charlottesville, Va., 1978), pp. vii–xiv.
29. K. C. Wheare, *Federal Government* (4th ed., London, 1963), p. 156.
30. Scheiber, 'Federalism and Legal Process', 668.
31. *Ibid.*, on Vietnam; Scheiber, 'American Constitutional History',.338, on radical orientation;
    'American Federalism', 619, on Madison; and see, generally, Irwin Unger, '"The New'
    Left" and American History', *American Historical Review*, 76 (1967), 1253–60; Herman Belz,
    'New Left Reverberations in the Academy: The Antipluralist Critique of the Constitu-
    tionalism', *Review of Politics*, 36 (1974), 265–283.
32. William Riker, in *Comparative Politics*, 2 (1969), 135 and 145. See too his *Federalism: Origin,
    Operation, Significance* (Boston, 1964).


A SUMMING UP


1. Professor Hyman's paraphrase in Chapter 12.
2. H. M. Wriston, 'Executive Agents in American Foreign Relations' (Unpublished Ph.D.
   thesis, Harvard University, 1922), pp. 131–2.
3. See the 'Authors' Preface' and Chapter 10.
4. Wiebe's phrase 'to social control and to social release', is quoted in Chapter 7. See
   reference (no 45) in Chapter 10 to Douglass C. North's thesis in *Structure and Change in
   Economic History* (New York, 1981).
5. E. H. Carr, *What is History?* (London, 1961), p. 126.
6. See, for example, Fry's finding that public expenditure accounted for 13 per cent of G.N.P.
   before 1910, 23 per cent after 1920, and 36 per cent after 1946: Geoffrey K. Fry, *The
   Growth of Government: The Development of Ideas about the Role of The State and the Machinery and
   Functions of Government in Britain since 1780* (London, 1979), p. 2. Fry, like his American
   counterparts, decided to concentrate on government's 'economic and social provision', but
   noted that the 'traditional' functions of government in Britain were 'law and order,
   defense, conduct of foreign policy', and – perhaps a significant point of departure from any
   comparable American list – 'imperial management' (p. 4).

7. The assumption that it was wrong to be different was implicit in the Samuel Plimsoll-sponsored enquiry into the treatment of American history in British secondary school textbooks in the late nineteenth century, and in the textbooks themselves: 'English Methods of Teaching American History', in *Report of the Commissioner of Education for the Year 1894–95* (Washington, D.C., 1896), in Robert D. Barendsen (comp.), *The American Revolution: Selections from Secondary School History Books of Other Nations* (Washington, D.C., 1976), p. 89. Cf. the following publication, sponsored by the American Historical Association and the Historical Association with the cooperation of the British Association for American Studies; Ray Allen Billington *et al.*, *The Historian's Contribution to Anglo-American misunderstanding: Report of a Committee on National Bias in Anglo-American History Textbooks* (London, 1966).

8. See Sigmund Skard, *American Studies in Europe: Their History and Present Organisation* (2 vols. (Philadelphia, 1958), vol. I, pp. 48–49.

9. One might speculate that the Scots have shown a facility for understanding the federal system of government in America because they invented it. On the influence in America of Scottish Enlightenment figures, see Douglass Adair, 'Politics Reduced to Science: Hume, Madison, and the Tenth *Federalist*', *Huntingdon Library Quarterly*, 20 (1957), pp. 343–360, Garry Wills, *Inventing America: Jefferson's Declaration of Independence* (Garden City, N.Y., 1978), p. 289 and *passim*. Adair and Wills describe the remarkable affinity between the outlook of certain Scots and Americans in the late eighteenth century without, perhaps, proving beyond doubt that there was a major direct influence.

10. Hugh Brogan, 'Tocqueville and the American Presidency', *Journal of American Studies*, 15 (December 1981), p. 365.

11. Perhaps only the Germans rivalled them. See Skard, *American Studies in Europe*, vol. I, pp. 212, 350 no 2.

12. The Scotsman F. S. Oliver, whose ideas are held to have influenced the Union of South Africa (1910), as well as the widely received cooperative ideas of Lord Lothian (British ambassador to the United States, 1939–1940), remarked of his proposed British imperial union: 'Its aim is the security of a great inheritance, and while it will augment the resources and the power of every member of the union, it will also touch each separate state and private citizen with a finer courage and a finer dignity' (*Alexander Hamilton: An Essay on American Union*, London and Edinburgh, 1906), p. 459. Oliver professed ignorance about modern America (p. 416), and it is no slight on his considerable reputation to say that he wrote eighteenth-century American history as propaganda for twentieth-century British Empire politics.

   On the link between the ideas of British Commonwealth and world peace, see John E. Kendle, *The Round Table Movement and Imperial Union* (Toronto, 1975) p. 174.

13. One of the more provocative writers on this subject is the current Librarian of Congress, the sociologist and historian Daniel J. Boorstin. See, for example, his *The Americans: The Colonial Experience* (Harmondsworth, 1958), pp. 13, 395.

14. Pieter Geyl, *Use and Abuse of History* (New Haven, 1955), pp. 77, 89.

# Some Suggestions for Further Reading

Little has been published by way of general analysis of the growth of federal power in American history. There are vast numbers of books on individual presidents and on the presidency; and the American political *process* – in the past as well as in the present – has received very extensive study. Congress has been subjected to relatively limited systematic historical scrutiny, although specific congressional crises have been thoroughly examined. Much more attention has been given to the history of the Supreme Court; one helpful introduction to the constitutional history of federal power is Robert G. McCloskey's *The American Supreme Court* (Chicago: Chicago University Press, 1960). And Raoul Berger's *Government by Judiciary: The Transformation of the Fourteenth Amendment* (Cambridge, Mass. and London: Harvard University Press, 1977) offers one controversial example of the way in which legal and constitutional scholars discuss the extension of federal powers and the allocation of those expanding powers between *branches* of the federal government. The economic history of federal activity is treated in Jonathan R. T. Hughes, *The Governmental Habit: Economic Controls from Colonial Times to the Present* (New York: Basic Books, 1977). Morton Keller's *Affairs of State: Public Life in Late Nineteenth Century America* (Cambridge, Mass.: Belknap Press, 1977) illuminates the nature of governmental activity on a variety of fronts in a particular period. An exhaustive history of the growth of the federal government's administrative apparatus is provided by Leonard D. White: *The Federalists: A Study in Administrative History, 1789–1801* (New York: Macmillan, 1948); *The Jeffersonians: A Study in Administrative History, 1801–1829* (New York: Macmillan, 1951); *The Jacksonians: A Study in Administrative History, 1829–1861* (New York: Macmillan, 1954); *The Republican Era: A Study in Administrative History* (New York: Macmillan, 1958). Some general histories of the U.S.A. are also, implicitly, accounts of the expansion of federal power; such, for example, is William R. Brock's *The Evolution of American Democracy* (New York: Dial Press, 1970). And J. R. Pole's *The Pursuit of Equality in American History* (Berkeley: University of California Press, 1978) tells us a great deal about one important facet of the extension of federal activity.

The specialist literature on federal power in various periods of American history is a little uneven in chronological spread and in quality, but is more abundant than the general literature. What follows is a guide to further reading on the themes of the particular chapters, based on the recommendations and observations of the authors of those chapters.

*Introductory.* On the growth of federal spending, a good summary is Charles L. Schultze, 'Federal Spending: Past, Present, and Future' in Henry Owen and Charles L. Schultze (eds.), *Setting National Priorities. The Next Ten Years* (Washington, D.C.: the Brookings Institution, 1976), pp. 323–69. Intergovernmental financial relations are examined in George F. Break, *Financing Government in a Federal System* (Washington, D.C.: the Brookings Institution, 1980). Federal planning in general is very well analysed in Otis L. Graham, Jr., *Toward A Planned Society: From Roosevelt to Nixon* (New York and London: Oxford University Press, 1976). Paul L. Murphy, *The Constitution in Crisis Times, 1918–1969* (New York: Harper and Row, 1972) provides an excellent introduction to the constitutional issues raised by the recent growth of federal power. A subtle analysis of the arguments proposed by contemporary critics of the American Leviathan is offered by Peter Steinfels, *The Neoconservatives: The men who are changing America's politics* (New York: Simon and Schuster, 1979).

*Chapter 1.* For a direct amplification of the points made in this chapter, see J. R. Pole, *The Gift of Government: an Essay on Political Responsibility from the English Restoration to American Independence* (Athens, Ga.: University of Georgia Press, 1983) and, for further reading: Hans Kohn, *American Nationalism* (New York: Macmillan, 1957); Russell B. Nye, *The Cultural Life of the New Nation, 1776–1830* (London: Harper and Row, 1960); Merle C. Curti, *The Growth of American Thought* (New York: Harper, 1943); Paul C. Nagel, *One Nation Indivisible: the Union in American Thought, 1776–1861* (New York: Oxford University Press, 1964); Kenneth M. Stampp, 'The Concept of a Perpetual Union' in his *The Imperiled Union: Essays on the Background of the Civil War* (New York: Oxford University Press, 1980); Jack N. Rakove, *The Beginnings of National Politics: an Interpretive History of the Continental Congress* (New York: Alfred A. Knopf, 1979); and Alan Heimert, *Religion and the American Mind from the Great Awakening to the Revolution* (Cambridge, Mass.: Harvard University Press, 1966).

*Chapter 2.* The principal authorities on the slavery and sectional issues are Glover Moore, *The Missouri Controversy, 1819–1821* (Lexington, Ky.: University of Kentucky Press, 1953); David Brion Davis, *The Problem of Slavery in the Age of Revolution, 1770–1823* (Ithaca: Cornell University Press, 1975); and Duncan J. MacLeod, *Slavery, Race and the American Revolution* (Cambridge: Cambridge University Press, 1974). Moore treats his subject matter largely in terms of party and sectional power struggles; Davis is full of insights about early anti-slavery but hardly touches upon the events of 1819 – moreover, although he is quick to suggest a close relationship between anti-slavery and capitalism he does not suggest the reverse, namely, a close relationship between pro-slavery and anti-capitalism; Dr MacLeod's chapter is an extension of aspects of his book, above, dealing more fully with the situation in 1819 and broadening the context of the republican ideas he discussed earlier. The economic philosophies of republicanism are best treated in Drew McCoy, *The Elusive Republic: Political Economy in Jeffersonian America* (Chapel Hill: University of North Carolina Press, 1980) although the nature and significance of early American capitalism is now a subject of considerable controversy – witness the article by Joyce Appleby cited in note 4. A suggestive treatment of the persistence of republican thinking is contained in an article by Robert E. Shalhope, 'Thomas Jefferson's Republicanism and Ante-bellum Southern Thought', *Journal of Southern History*, 42 (1976), 529–56.

*Chapter 3.* Two books that discuss the relationship between antislavery and concepts of federal government are Lewis Perry, *Radical Abolitionism: Anarchy and the Government of God in Antislavery Thought* (Ithaca and London: Cornell University Press, 1973) and William M. Wiecek, *The Sources of Antislavery Constitutionalism in America, 1760–1848* (Ithaca and London: Cornell University Press, 1977). See, also, John Mayfield, *Rehearsal for Republicanism: Free Soil and the Politics of Antislavery* (Port Washington, N.Y. and London: National University Publications, Kennikat Press, 1980); Eric Foner, *Free Soil, Free Labor, Free Men: The Ideology of the Republican Party before the Civil War* (New York: Oxford University Press, 1970); Ronald G. Walters, *The Antislavery Appeal: American Abolitionism after 1830* (Baltimore and London: Johns Hopkins University Press, 1976); and John L. Thomas, *The Liberator: William Lloyd Garrison, A Biography* (Boston and Toronto: Little, Brown and Co., 1963).

*Chapter 4.* The best general work on the early political economists is Paul K. Conkin, *Prophets of Prosperity: America's First Political Economists* (Bloomington, Ind.: University of Indiana Press, 1980). Chapters X and XI are devoted to Carey as a theorist. A good account of Carey's political activities is Arthur M. Lee, 'Henry C. Carey and the Republican Tariff', *Pennsylvania Magazine of History and Biography*, 81 (1957), 280–302. These two contributions complement Dr Collins's analysis. Daniel W. Howe, *The Political Culture of the American Whigs* (Chicago: University of Chicago Press, 1979) has much to say about Whigs' attitudes to 'active' federal government; pp. 108–22 discuss Carey. For various technical writings on Carey's work, see: A. D. H. Kaplan, *Henry Charles Carey: A Study in American Economic Thought* (Baltimore: Johns Hopkins University Studies in Historical and Political Science, 1931); Arnold W. Green, *Henry Charles Carey, Nineteenth Century Sociologist* (Philadelphia: University of Pennsylvania Press, 1951); and Rodney J. Morrison, 'Henry C. Carey and American Economic Development', *Explorations in Entrepreneurial History*, 2nd Series, 5 (1967–8), 132–144.

*Chapter 5.* William Wiecek's *Sources of Antislavery Constitutionalism* and Morton Keller's *Affairs of State*, already cited above, are also useful ancillary reading for this chapter. Of further utility are Jacobus ten Broek, *Equal Under Law*, (new edn. rev., New York: Macmillan, Collier Books, 1965) James H. Kettner, *The Development of American Citizenship, 1608–1870* (Chapel Hill: University of North Carolina Press, 1978); Michael Les Benedict, *A Compromise of Principle: Congressional Republicans and Reconstruction 1863–1869* (New York: Norton, 1974) and Harold M. Hyman, *A More Perfect Union: The Impact of the Civil War and Reconstruction on the Constitution* (Boston: Houghton Mifflin, 1973).

*Chapter 6.* Any consideration of late nineteenth-century politics must now begin with Morton Keller's *Affairs of State,* already cited, which is both compendious and full of rewarding insights. Most interpretations of politics and society in this period have been strongly influenced by the work of Samuel P. Hays and Robert H. Wiebe, both of whom present versions of what Louis Galambos calls the 'organisational thesis'. See Wiebe's *The Search for Order, 1877–1920* (New York and London: Macmillan, 1967) and the essays by Hays helpfully collected in *American Political History as Social Analysis* (Knoxville, Tenn.: University of Tennessee Press, 1980). H. Wayne Morgan, *From Hayes to McKinley: National Party Politics, 1877–1896* (Syracuse, N.Y.: Syracuse University Press, 1969) is almost obsessively anecdotal, but it is a typical example of recent attempts to redeem the reputation of Gilded Age politics. However, more understanding of political behaviour and institutions may be derived from reading more specialised studies, such as David J. Rothman, *Politics and Power: The United States Senate, 1869–1901* (Cambridge, Mass.: Harvard University Press, 1966); and Robert D. Marcus, *Grand Old Party: Political Structure in the Gilded Age* (New York: Oxford University Press, 1971).

*Chapter 7.* Before coming to grips with Robert Wiebe's stimulating if controversial book *The Search for Order*, which is as relevant to this chapter as it was to the last, readers may wish to consult a selection of the following: Jerry Israel (ed.), *Building the Organizational Society* (London: Collier–Macmillan and New York: Free Press, 1972); Otis L. Graham, Jr., *The Great Campaigns: Reform and War in America, 1900–1928* (Englewood Cliffs: Prentice-Hall, 1971); Otis L. Graham, Jr., *An Encore for Reform: The Old Progressives and the New Deal* (New York: Oxford University Press, 1967); David Kennedy, *Over Here: The First World War and American Society* (New York: Oxford University Press, 1980); and Robert D. Cuff, *The War Industries Board: Business–Government Relations during World War I* (Baltimore and London: Johns Hopkins Press, 1973).

*Chapter 8.* Students seeking the spirit of the period will find it conveyed in Katherine Anne Porter's novella, *Pale Horse, Pale Rider* (1939). The perspectives supplied in Dr Cook's chapter depart from those supplied in earlier studies: Robert K. Murray, *Red Scare: A Study in National Hysteria,*

*1919–1920* (Minneapolis: University of Minnesota Press, 1955); Stanley Coben, *A. Mitchell Palmer, Politician* (New York: Columbia University Press, 1963); Burl Noggle, *Into the Twenties: The United States from Armistice to Normalcy* (Urbana: University of Illinois Press, 1974); and Constance McLaughlin Green, *Washington: Capital City, 1879–1950* (Princeton, N.J.: Princeton University Press, 1963). On the problems occasioned by joint local, state and federal responsibility for law enforcement during labour and race disorders, see Rhodri Jeffreys-Jones, *Violence and Reform in American History* (New York: New Viewpoints, 1978), Chapter IX, 'Government and Order'.

*Chapter 9.* James T. Patterson's *The New Deal and the States: Federalism in Transition* (Princeton, N.J.: Princeton University Press, 1969) is the obvious starting-point for reading in the burgeoning field of federal–state relations in the 1930s. The literature considered in Dr Badger's chapter is vast, but it would be sensible to start with the following: John Braeman, Robert H. Bremner, and David Brody (eds.), *The New Deal*, 2 vols., Vol 2, *The State and Local Levels* (Columbus: Ohio State University Press, 1975); David Brody, *Workers in Industrial America: Essays on the Twentieth-Century Struggle* (New York, Oxford: Oxford University Press, 1980); Michael S. Holmes, *The New Deal in Georgia: An Administrative History* (Westport, Conn., London: Greenwood Press, 1975); Charles H. Trout, *Boston, The Great Depression and the New Deal* (New York: Oxford University Press, 1977); John M. Allswang, *The New Deal and American Politics: A Study in Political Change* (New York: Wiley, 1978); and Barbara Blumberg, *The New Deal and the Unemployed: The View from New York City* (Lewisburg: Bucknell University Press, 1979).

*Chapter 10.* There are some stimulating and informative economic essays on the post-1945 period: Murray L. Weidenbaum (ed.), *Business, Government, and the Public*, 2nd edn (Englewood Cliffs, N.J.: Prentice-Hall, 1981); Thomas E. Borcherding (ed.), *Budgets and Bureaucrats: The Sources of Government Growth* (Durham, N.C.: Duke University Press, 1977); and Hugh Rockoff, 'Price and Wage Controls in Four Wartime Periods', *The Journal of Economic History*, 41 (1981), 381–401. The literature is otherwise thin, but the following would suggest some ideas: Alonzo L. Hamby, *Beyond the New Deal: Harry S. Truman and American Liberalism* (New York: Columbia University Press, 1973); Barry Goldwater, *The Conscience of a Conservative* (New York: Hillman Books, 1960); and Arthur M. Schlesinger, Jr., *The Imperial Presidency* (New York: Popular Library, 1974).

*Chapter 11.* For descriptions, brief histories and bibliographies pertaining to over a hundred federal agencies, ranging from the Freedmen's Bureau to Amtrack, see Donald R. Whitnah (ed.), *Government Agencies, The Greenwood Encyclopedia of American Institutions* (Westport, Conn.: Greenwood Press,

1983). On the early years of the Peace Corps itself, we await the publication by the University of Notre Dame Press of Dr Rice's own book, *Kennedy's Children: The Peace Corps, 1961–3*. For further reading on the Peace Corps, see Brent K. Ashabranner, *A Moment in History: The First Ten Years of the Peace Corps* (Garden City, New York: Doubleday & Co., 1971); Kevin Lowther and C. Payne Lucas, *Keeping Kennedy's Promise: The Unmet Hope of the New Frontier* (Boulder, Colorado: Westview Press, 1977); J. Norman Parmer (ed.), 'The Peace Corps' in *The Annals of the American Academy of Political and Social Science* (Philadelphia, May 1966); Gerard T. Rice, *Twenty Years of Peace Corps* (Washington, D.C.: U.S. Government Printing Office, 1981); Sargent Shriver, *Point of the Lance* (New York: Harper and Row, 1966); and Harris Wofford, *Of Kennedys and Kings* (New York: Farrar, Straus and Giroux, 1980).

*Chapter 12.* Professor Hyman's chapter is itself a rich repository of references to scholars' views on American federalism. It is especially and unusually helpful as a guide to recent and forthcoming publications. A further guide to publications on federalism's history, problems, and prospects is in Harry N. Scheiber, 'Federalism and Legal Process: Historical and Contemporary Analysis of the American System', *Law and Society Review*, 14 (1980), 713–722. Carl L. Becker's *The Declaration of Independence* (New York: Alfred A. Knopf, 1956) and Andrew McLaughlin's *The Foundations of American Constitutionalism* (New York: New York University Press, 1932) provide settings for the varied and complex manifestations of federalism analysed in Professor Hyman's chapter.

# Index